Psychotherapeutic Change through the Group Process

Psychotherapeutic Change through the Group Process

Dorothy Stock Whitaker
& Morton A. Lieberman

Routledge
Taylor & Francis Group
LONDON AND NEW YORK

First published 1964 by Transaction Publishers

Published 2017 by Routledge
2 Park Square, Milton Park, Abingdon, Oxon OX14 4RN
711 Third Avenue, New York, NY 10017, USA

First issued in hardback 2017

Routledge is an imprint of the Taylor & Francis Group, an informa business

Library of Congress Catalog Number: 2008002624

Library of Congress Cataloging-in-Publication Data

Whitaker, Dorothy Stock, 1925-
[Psychotherapy through the group process]
Psychotherapeutic change through the group process / Dorothy Stock Whitaker and Morton A. Lieberman.
p. ; cm.
Originally published: Psychotherapy through the group process. New York : Atherton, c1964, in series: Atherton Press behavioral science series.
Includes bibliographical references and index.
ISBN 978-0-202-36231-1 (alk. paper)
1. Group psychotherapy. I. Lieberman, Morton A., 1931- II. Title.
[DNLM: 1. Psychotherapy, Group. WM 430 W577p 1964a]

RC488.W46 2008
616.89'152—dc22 2008002624

ISBN 13: 978-1-138-53112-3 (hbk)
ISBN 13: 978-0-202-36231-1 (pbk)

Preface

This book presents a theory about the relation between the properties of groups and therapeutic change. Our purpose is to develop a view of groups which accounts for the diversity, complexity, and fluidity of the group situation—a view which examines the group in depth, attending not only to overt events, but also to covert aspects of the situation; not only to manifest behaviors, but to underlying motivations; not only to the cognitive, rational aspects of the group, but to the intense affect which may be generated under conditions of group interaction; not merely to the group or merely to the individual, but to the individual *in* the group and to the group as the context for personal experience and change. We address ourselves to both the theoretician and the practitioner. To the theoretician we suggest a way of looking at groups which, although developed with reference to therapy groups, has relevance for other types of groups. To the practicing group therapist we suggest that the group forces are a potent element in determining the nature of the patient's therapeutic experience, that the group can work for good or ill, and that the therapist who is in touch with group forces is in an optimal position to utilize the group situation for maximum therapeutic benefit.

We shall proceed by presenting and discussing a series of propositions about the functioning of the group and its meaning for the therapeutic process and the therapist's role. Clinical examples have been selected which most adequately and succinctly clarify successive propositions.

Though this book is not a report of research, much of the thinking presented here was initially explored in research studies. Separate investigations considered the ways in which patients and therapists viewed group events, the nature of deviation, and the development of group standards; factors associated with therapeutic improvement and therapeutic failure; and characteristic concerns of early sessions. These, plus several discussions of theory and methodology, have been published separately.

Our working procedure has been to study intensively a relatively small number of groups, depending upon careful observation of natural groups rather than upon laboratory experimentation. That is, we have chosen to undertake detailed, microscopic analyses rather than large-scale data collection; we have studied natural groups which existed for a relatively long time rather than short-term groups especially set up under laboratory conditions. Our over-all attempt has been to understand the processes of therapy groups in all their clinical richness and intricacy and yet to impose a scientific discipline and control on our analyses. This has meant a continuing attempt to develop appropriate analytic procedures so that clinical analyses can be as firmly rooted as possible in concrete data and reproducible methods.

Our investigations of therapy groups have been conducted in two settings: the Veterans Administration Research Hospital in Chicago and the Department of Psychiatry at The University of Chicago. From 1955 to 1957, while at the Veterans Administration Hospital, we concentrated on short-term groups of hospitalized veterans. Most typically, these patients were suffering from acute states of anxiety or crippling character problems. A certain number were recovering from schizophrenic episodes, but only a few were frankly psychotic. With the move to The University of Chicago in 1957, it became possible to study both adolescent and adult long-term outpatient groups. One of these, a group of late-adolescent patients, was studied intensively throughout its eighty-seven–session life. Excluded from our study are groups composed of patients with specialized problems such as alcoholism, narcotics addiction, or delinquency. In addition to the groups which we conducted, we had the opportunity to observe or study a number of groups conducted by colleagues. This has made it possible for us to become familiar with a broad range of therapeutic styles and theoretical positions.

Prior to the studies on therapy groups, which began in 1955, we both participated in a series of investigations on non-therapy (task and training) groups, under the general direction of Herbert A. Thelen. A continuing association with the National Training Laboratories has provided invaluable experience with non-therapeutic groups. Such experiences have helped us to place our work in context and to test the applicability of our thinking about therapy groups to other types of groups.

The work of W. R. Bion and the work of Thomas French have been most important in influencing our thinking about groups. Bion's series of papers, "Experiences in Groups," suggested ways of conceptualizing group events in terms of shared covert needs and motivations and emphasized the importance of both cognitive and emotional aspects of group functioning.[1] French's concept of the "focal conflict," developed for application to individual psychoanalytic sessions and dreams, suggested a theoretical approach to groups which could do justice to the varied aspects of the situation and yet organize and conceptualize group events in concise terms.[2] The approach originally inspired by French has been extended and developed in some detail and now forms the core of our view of the group psychological process.

Among those who have personally participated in and contributed to this work, we wish to mention first Prof. Herbert A. Thelen, who introduced us to the study of small-group interaction. It was in his laboratory that we participated in a number of studies of small task and training groups, struggling with problems of research design and methodology and attempting to understand the individual in terms of the group and the group in terms of the individual. Dr. Roy M. Whitman played a major role by introducing us to therapeutic groups and by participating in exploratory studies in applying focal-conflict theory to group interaction. Drs. Thomas French and Philip F. D. Seitz participated in a series of seminars in which group-therapy protocols were studied in an attempt to test the feasibility of conceptualizing group events in focal-conflict terms. Since 1957, we have benefited from the help of a number of research assistants and colleagues: Charles Van Buskirk, Joanne Holden, Margaret Nuttall, Robert Williams, and June

[1] *Experiences in Groups, and Other Papers* (New York and London: Basic Books, Inc., and Tavistock Publications, 1961).

[2] *The Integration of Behavior,* I, II (Chicago: University of Chicago Press, 1952).

Strain. We have observed or studied groups conducted by Drs. Robert S. Daniels, Robert Drye, Marie Duncan, Martin Lakin, Herbert Lessow, Robert F. McFarland, George G. Meyer, Valerie Raulinitis, Roy M. Whitman, and Mary Wicks; Joanne Holden; and Anthony Vattano. Several persons read all or portions of the first draft of this manuscript and provided truly invaluable help in sharpening, condensing, and organizing the material in the book. We are most grateful to Jerome D. Frank, William E. Henry, Joanne Holden, Irving L. Janis, and Philip F. D. Seitz. Ann Welch, Carol Ramey, Sharon Forrest, and Linda Putnam worked intrepidly in typing and preparing the manuscript.

Finally, we are most grateful to the National Institute of Mental Health, which has provided financial support for our research efforts from 1955 to the present.[3] It has been this support which has enabled us to explore, to test, and finally to summarize in this book our thinking about the group-therapeutic processes.

Dorothy Stock Whitaker
Morton A. Lieberman

[3] Research activity was supported in part by two successive grants from the National Institute of Mental Health (M-1048 and MH 06027) and by a Public Health Service research career program award (K3-14, 931) from the National Institute of Mental Health.

Table of Contents

PREFACE *vii*

PART I: THE GROUP PROCESSES: THE CONTEXT OF THERAPY *1*

1. Problem and Purposes *3*
2. A Focal-Conflict Model *14*
3. Equilibrium and Change *41*
4. Group Themes *63*
5. Group Culture *95*
6. Development of the Group *116*

PART II: THE INDIVIDUAL'S THERAPEUTIC EXPERIENCE *141*

7. The Patient's Experience *143*
8. The Therapeutic Process *161*

PART III: THE THERAPIST'S CONTRIBUTION *187*

9. Strategy, Position, and Power *189*
10. General Policy *204*
11. Influence through Participation *216*

PERSPECTIVE *239*

12. Other Theories *241*
13. The Threat and Promise of the Group *285*

BIBLIOGRAPHY *294*

INDEX *301*

I

The Group Processes: The Context of Therapy

Arguments about "existence" may seem metaphysical in nature and may therefore not be expected to be brought up in empirical sciences. Actually, opinions about existence or nonexistence are quite common in the empirical sciences and have greatly influenced scientific development in a positive and a negative way. Labeling something as "nonexisting" is equivalent to declaring it "out of bounds" for the scientist. Attributing "existence" to an item automatically makes it a duty of the scientist to consider this item as an object of research; it includes the necessity of considering its properties as "facts" which cannot be neglected in a total system of theories; finally, it implies that the terms with which one refers to the items are acceptable as scientific "concepts" (rather than as "mere words").

—Kurt Lewin

1

Problem and Purposes

Processes characteristic of the group as a whole are an intrinsic and inevitable aspect of all groups no matter what their size or function. In a therapy group, group processes not only "exist," but are a major factor influencing the nature of each patient's therapeutic experience. The manner in which each patient contributes to, participates in, and is affected by the group processes determines to a considerable degree whether he will profit from his group therapy experience, be untouched by it, or be harmed by it. The therapist can influence the character and development of the group and thereby influence the individual's therapeutic experience. It is, therefore, important that the therapist have some understanding of the group processes and their meaning for the therapeutic process.

As this over-all statement of our position suggests, we regard the group processes which emerge in therapy groups as worthy of serious and careful investigation. To paraphrase Kurt Lewin, we shall attribute "existence" to these group processes and shall systematically discuss their character, their relevance to the therapeutic experience, and their implications for the therapist's role.

Two questions may be asked about group processes in therapy groups. The first is whether such processes can be observed; the second is whether and in what manner group processes are relevant to the therapeutic progress of individual patients. In our view, the first question is no longer an issue, but the second is both crucial and unresolved.

Although it is now generally accepted that any small face-to-face group, including a therapy group, can be described in terms of its characteristics as a social system, this was not always so. During the 1920's, concepts such as "group mind" or "group unconscious" were matters of controversy in social psychology. Such terms are no longer in general use, not because they have no meaningful elements, but because the phenomena to which they refer are now better understood and no longer need to be discussed in such mystical terms. Although social psychologists no longer talk about the group mind, they do talk about group goals, atmosphere, sociometric structure, or communication pattern. These are characteristics or properties of the group as a whole. They derive from the interaction of the members in lawful ways, yet constitute attributes of the group as a system.

Historically, the factor which probably contributed more than any other to the resolution of these early issues was the development of relevant methodology. Until appropriate techniques were available, there were no means for exploring group phenomena. Pioneer work by Lewin, S. E. Asch, and others paved the way for the controlled observation of groups and the experimental manipulation and examination of group variables.[1] Evidence accumulated to show that small face-to-face groups can be described in terms of properties belonging to the group as a whole. That is, many diverse phenomena can be understood if the group is conceptualized as a social system comprised of elements which have a lawful relation to one another. Such elements can be shown to operate in a variety of groups independently of the specific membership of the group. Furthermore, such total group characteristics have been shown to have an important impact on the behavior of individual members.

The crucial question for group therapists is no longer whether the therapy group can be described in terms of such variables as atmosphere, cohesion, communication patterns, roles, standards, and the like. Rather, the issue is whether regarding the group in these terms is of any use to the therapist in the light of his primary goal, contributing to the personal growth of the patient. To state this more formally, the real question is whether and in what manner characteristics of the therapy group as a social system are relevant to the therapeutic process.

In the literature on group therapy, one finds a range of positions on this issue. Group processes are variously regarded as factors to be utilized, overcome, or ignored. One position is that, although therapy groups may be described in terms of the "dynamics of the group," group dynamics are detrimental to the therapeutic aim. Perhaps the most articulate proponent of this point of view is S. R. Slavson:

> Thus, even the most common group dynamics described are not permitted to operate, for it is the task of the therapist . . . to uncover the underlying, most often the hostile feelings, from which reactions flow. Thus, dynamics in therapy groups are "nipped in the bud" as it were, for just as soon as responses are analyzed and related to their emotional sources, they no longer operate. . . . Thus, *the therapeutic aim in its very nature is antagonistic to group formation and group dynamics.*[2]

Wolf and Schwartz are even more strongly convinced that attention to group-level processes in therapy groups is likely to defeat the therapeutic goal; they regard group processes as inherently destructive to the individual.[3] Nathan Locke suggests that the characteristics of the group are a side issue; a similar position is advanced by Helen Durkin, who suggests that, although forces exist which may be described as belonging to the group as a whole, they tend to be irrelevant to the therapeutic work of the group.[4]

In sharp contrast to these positions are the views put forth by such group therapists as S. H. Foulkes, W. R. Bion, George Bach, Henry Ezriel, and Jerome D. Frank.[5] Although they differ in many respects, these writers share the view that group processes are central to the therapeutic process.

Bion views the group as the vital instrument of therapy which must be properly utilized and exploited by the therapist: ". . . [W]e are not concerned to give individual treatment in public, but to draw attention to the actual experiences of the group, and . . . the way in which the group and individual deal with the individual." And, later:

> This point is critical; if the psychiatrist can manage boldly to use the group instead of spending his time more or less unconsciously apologizing for its presence, he will find that the immediate difficulties produced are more than neutralized by the advantages of a proper use of his medium.[6]

The stand which one takes on this general issue may depend in part on underlying assumptions about the character of therapy and the nature of emotional illness. Most group therapists recognize important differences between therapy conducted in a group and therapy conducted in a two-person situation. However, the curative model—assumptions about what it is in the treatment situation that helps the patient—is usually translated rather directly from individual to group psychotherapy. For example, the exploration of transference relationships and interpretations of resistance by means similar to those used in individual therapy may be seen as the heart of the treatment. Given such a position, it might seem to follow that attention to total group processes is foreign, useless, or even harmful to these essential therapeutic maneuvers. The way in which the therapist defines emotional illness is also a factor. Slavson's model is essentially an intrapersonal one in which psychotherapy is aimed at freeing the patient from his neurotic inhibitions and problems. Foulkes, on the other hand, is inclined to see emotional illness as rooted in disturbed interpersonal relationships:

> We conceive all illness as occurring and originating within a complex of interpersonal relationships. Group psychotherapy is an attempt to treat the total network of disturbance either at the point of origin in the root—or primary—group, or, through placing the disturbed individual under conditions of transference, in a group of strangers or proxy group.[7]

In our view, the eventual resolution of these issues will not require a choice between irreconcilable alternatives—either the psychoanalytic or the group dynamic explanation. Rather, what is required is an understanding of the manner in which group processes, individual processes, and therapeutic processes exist in complex relationships. We do not see group processes as either consistently constructive or consistently destructive to therapeutic goals. Rather, our position is that they have no such universal and unilateral impact. Depending on their character, group processes may sometimes facilitate therapy. Sometimes they may interfere. The real questions are how and when the therapist can use them to produce useful therapeutic experiences. In order to answer these questions, it is necessary to examine group-level aspects of therapy groups in some detail to determine their impact on the individual and the therapeutic process.

One might wonder why it is that group therapists have not turned to social psychology for an understanding of group processes in therapy groups.[8] We believe it is not because the concepts developed by social psychologists cannot be applied to therapy groups, but because many of the concepts seem irrelevant to the therapeutic process or of only academic interest because they deal with variables which the therapist cannot influence. The social psychologist who studies groups usually does so in order to understand certain properties of the group or relationships among certain properties. He may be interested in the problem-solving process, the decision-making process, the distribution of power in the group, or the communication pattern. Although such phenomena can be observed in therapy groups, they are likely to be of little interest to the group therapist because they seem so removed from his primary interest—therapeutic change in the individual. Even when the social psychologist focuses on the impact of group variables on the individual, he is likely to be interested in such variables as sense of achievement, changes in attitude or judgment, and so on. Although these are attributes of the individual, they are related only indirectly to the kind of change in which the group therapist is interested.

The group therapist may also feel that the work of the social psychologist has little practical importance because many of the variables cannot be manipulated in the group therapeutic setting. For purposes of experimentation and study, the social psychologist may, for example, open or close certain channels of communication or distribute relevant information unevenly among the group members. Such manipulations are outside the tradition of group therapy and, in general, are inconsistent with his goals.

What is required is a theory of group processes relevant to the task and goals of psychotherapy. To be useful to the group therapist, a theory of group functioning must focus on factors which bear on the therapeutic process and which are subject to the influence of the practicing therapist. We assume that the therapeutic process—that which must occur within the individual if positive personal change is to take place—is essentially the same no matter what the therapeutic setting. The corrective emotional experience, sometimes accompanied by insight, is regarded as fundamental to therapeutic change. A useful theory of group therapy must, then, examine the manner in which this therapeutic process occurs in the special milieu of the group. The group processes form the context of therapy. The group situation is in constant flux, and the individual in a continuously shifting position with relation to group forces. Under certain group conditions, potentially useful experiences may occur. Under others, anti-therapeutic experiences take place. Thus, it becomes important to identify the character of the group context in order to understand its impact on the individual.

The list of variables which the group therapist can influence is a brief one: the size and composition of the group, the physical setting and the frequency of the sessions, the kind of outside individual contacts (if any) he provides for each of the patients, and his own participation during the group sessions. A useful theory of group therapy should aid the therapist in selecting the techniques and situations which are most likely to help the patients. Of the variables which the therapist can control, his own participation—what he says and when he says it—seems the most crucial. And in order to study the impact of the therapist's participation, it is necessary to understand the character and impact of his interventions in the context of the fluctuating group situation.

For several reasons, then, a theory about group therapy must establish a way of conceptualizing the changing group situation. This situation is important because it is the background against which to examine the therapist's participation, the patients' participation, and the shifting meaning of the group experience for each patient. The following appear to be significant questions:

1. What kinds of emotional issues emerge in therapy groups; how are these expressed and handled?

2. How can one conceptualize the diverse and shifting events of a single therapy session?

3. What are the long-term developmental characteristics of a therapy group?

4. In what ways does the past history of a therapy group affect its current operation?

5. What are the relationships among personality, individual behavior, and the character of the group?

6. What is the impact of the group on the patient's experience: which group conditions contribute to personal growth and which interfere?

7. How does the group therapist contribute to the patient's therapeutic experience?

We shall present a series of propositions which attempt to deal in detail with these and related questions. Part I deals primarily with the character of the group process and is directed to questions 1, 2, 3, and 4; it defines the character of the group therapeutic milieu. Because the group's only constant feature is change, our efforts are directed to understanding the pattern of diversity and the order in change. In Chapter 2, we suggest a view of group events which perceives the diverse elements of the group situation in relation to shared, covert, affective issues. Crucial affective issues and shared conflicts develop to which the patients direct coping efforts. Chapters 3 and 4 are devoted to understanding continuity and change in the group process—first in a single group session and then in a series of sessions linked by the same theme or shared emotional concern. Chapter 5 considers the issue of the group's culture—the unique and usually implicit standards, practices, and values which develop in each group and which, in our view, can have both limiting and enabling effects on the therapeutic experience. Chapter 6 returns to the problem of change, taking a long-range view and considering the over-all developmental characteristics of the group. Both theme (Chapter 4) and culture (Chapter 5) are basic to our view of group development, for we emphasize the recurrence of basic affective issues and themes under broadening cultural conditions. Part I, then, attempts to formulate the character of the group processes in ways which we think are important for understanding the context of therapy. Although we do not consider, except by implication, the relevance of the group processes for the therapeutic process or the therapist's role, this part of the book lays the essential groundwork for the discussion which follows.

Part II considers the individual's experience in the group, particularly the impact of the group processes on the therapeutic experience. This section is directed to questions 5 and 6. In it, we discuss the individual's neurotic dilemma on entering the group, the manner in which he experiences the group situation, and the motives which underlie his behavior in the specific setting (Chapter 7). In Chapter 8, there is a more specific discussion of the therapeutic process—the kinds of experiences which the patient must undergo if positive therapeutic change is to take place and the various ways in which the group processes may affect the individual. In this chapter, we consider the specifics of the therapeutic experience, attempting to delineate the various positions in which the patient may find himself with regard to group forces and to define the group conditions under which positive therapeutic, as opposed to damaging, experiences are likely to occur.

Part III focuses on the manner in which the therapist can contribute to the therapeutic process. The previous sections have defined the character of the group processes and their impact on the individual's therapeutic experience; this section takes up the issue of what the therapist can do to direct the group situation in order to maximize its therapeutic potential. We begin, in Chapter 9, with a consideration of the therapist's strategy, position, and power in the group. Here we attempt to differentiate and compare the therapist's position and influence with that of the patients and the group therapist's position and influence with that of the therapist in a two-person relationship. We also describe a general strategy by which the therapist concentrates on group processes and on the individual in the context of group processes. This strategy, which we endorse, is contrasted with another which focuses more exclusively on the individual patient and tends to disregard group forces. Chapters 10 and 11 deal more specifically with the therapist's role. Chapter 10 discusses decisions about composition and over-all policy, considered in the light of the character of group processes and the potential impact of the group on each patient. Chapter 11 considers the therapist's participation during the group sessions and concentrates on the ways in which the therapist can work toward establishing potentially beneficial group conditions and can forestall or minimize the establishment of destructive group conditions.

This presentation is directed primarily to group therapists, and all of the illustrative material is drawn from therapy groups. Yet we believe that the view of group functioning which is presented here is relevant to other kinds of groups as well. Part I, particularly, can be read as a general theory of group processes. Certain sections of Part II are also relevant to non-therapeutic groups—for example, the discussions about covert motivational factors which mediate personality, behavior, and social context and about the group conditions under which the individual experiences comfort or threat. In Part III, the material on the therapist's position and power in the group applies, with some modifications, to the position and the power of any group leader. Our discussion of the therapist's strategy, decisions, and tactics is specifically directed toward the goals of the group therapist, which are different from the goals of the leader of a problem-solving group or the head of an organization. But the fundamental point—that a leader operates within the context of group forces and utilizes them in ways which are consistent with certain goals—holds not only for therapy groups, but for other face-to-face problem-solving groups and larger organizations. In this volume, we do not spell out these additional applications systematically, although we occasionally point to other groups for purposes of contrast.

Parts I, II, and III are a statement and elaboration of theory. We have added a final section—"Perspective"—which attempts to place our work in the context of other theoretical views and considers some general issues of theory development. Chapter 12 reviews a series of theoretical questions to which group therapists have addressed themselves and attempts to contrast our thinking with that of others. Chaper 13 reviews the power and potential of the group. Here, we acknowledge the potency of emotional forces which may be released under group conditions and attempt to examine the threat of group forces to the integrity of the individual personality and the promise which the group holds for personal growth and change.

Notes

[1] Kurt Lewin, "Frontiers in Group Dynamics: Concept, Method, and Reality in Social Science: Social Equilibria and Social Change," *Human Relations,* I (1947), 5–41; *idem, Field Theory in Social Science* (New York: Harper & Brothers, 1951); S. E. Asch, "Effects of Group Pressure upon the Modification and Distortion of Judgments," in *Groups, Leadership and Men: Research in Human Relations,* ed. H. Guetzkow (Pittsburgh: Carnegie Press, 1951).

[2] S. R. Slavson, "Are There 'Group Dynamics' in Therapy Groups?" *International Journal of Group Psychotherapy,* VII (1957), 144–145.

[3] Alexander Wolf and Emanuel K. Schwartz, *Psychoanalysis in Groups* (New York: Grune and Stratton, 1962).

[4] Norman Locke, *Group Psychoanalysis: Theory and Technique* (New York: New York University Press, 1961); Helen Durkin, "Toward a Common Basis for Group Dynamics: Group and Therapeutic Processes in Group Psychotherapy," *International Journal of Group Psychotherapy,* VII (1957), 115–130.

[5] S. H. Foulkes, "Group Analytic Dynamics with Specific Reference to Psychoanalytic Concepts," *International Journal of Group Psychotherapy,* VII (1957), 40–52; *idem,* "Group Process and the Individual in the Therapeutic Group," *British Journal of Medical Psychology,* 34 (1961), 23–31; *idem, Introduction to Group-Analytic Psychotherapy* (New York: Grune and Stratton, 1949); *idem,* "Psychotherapy 1961," *British Journal of Medical Psychology,* 34 (1961), 91–102; *idem,* "The Application of Group Concepts to the Treatment of the Individual in the

Group," in Bertrand Stokvis (ed.), *Sources of Conflict in Contemporary Group Psychotherapy* ("Topical Problems of Psychotherapy," Vol. II [New York and Basel: S. Karger, 1960]), pp. 1–15; S. H. Foulkes and E. J. Anthony, *Group Psychotherapy: The Psychoanalytic Approach* (Baltimore: Penguin Books, 1957); W. R. Bion, *Experiences in Groups, and Other Papers* (New York and London: Basic Books, Inc., and Tavistock Publications, 1961); *idem,* "Group Dynamics: A Re-View," *International Journal of Psychoanalysis,* 33 (1952), 235–247; George Bach, *Intensive Group Psychotherapy* (New York: Ronald Press, 1954); Henry Ezriel, "A Psychoanalytic Approach to Group Treatment," *British Journal of Medical Psychology,* 23 (1950), 59–64; *idem,* "A Psychoanalytic Approach to the Treatment of Patients in Groups," *Journal of Mental Science,* XCVI (1950), 774–779; *idem,* "Experimentation Within the Psychoanalytic Session," *British Journal for the Philosophy of Science,* 7 (1956), 29–48; *idem,* "Reply to Mr. Spilsbury," *British Journal for the Philosophy of Science,* 7 (1956), 342–347; *idem,* "The Role of Transference in Psycho-Analytic and Other Approaches to Group Treatment," *Acta Psychotherapeutica,* 7 (1959) Supplement, 101–116; J. D. Frank, "Some Aspects of Cohesiveness and Conflict in Psychiatric Out-Patient Groups," *Johns Hopkins Hospital Bulletin,* 101 (1957), 224–231; *idem,* "Some Values of Conflict in Therapeutic Groups," *Group Psychotherapy,* 8 (1955), 142–151; J. D. Frank and Eduard Ascher, "Corrective Emotional Experiences in Group Therapy," *American Journal of Psychiatry,* 108 (1951), 126–131; J. D. Frank, Eduard Ascher, Joseph B. Margolin, Helen Nash, Anthony R. Stone, and Edith J. Varon, "Behavioral Patterns in Early Meetings of Therapeutic Groups," *American Journal of Psychiatry,* 108 (1952), 771–778; J. D. Frank, "Some Determinants, Manifestations, and Effects of Cohesiveness in the Therapy Groups," *International Journal of Group Psychotherapy,* 7 (1957), 53–63; J. D. Frank, Joseph B. Margolin, Helen Nash, Anthony R. Stone, Edith J. Varon, and Eduard Ascher, "Two Behavior Patterns in Therapeutic Groups and Their Apparent Motivation," *Human Relations,* III (1952), 289–317; Florence Powdermaker and J. D. Frank, *Group Psychotherapy* (Cambridge: Harvard University Press, 1953).

[6] W. R. Bion, *Experiences in Groups, and Other Papers,* pp. 80–81.

[7] S. H. Foulkes, "Group Analytic Dynamics with Specific Reference to Psychoanalytic Concepts," p. 42.

[8] George Bach has undertaken the only systematic review of the relevance of social psychological research and concepts to group therapy in his book, *Intensive Group Psychotherapy.*

2

A Focal-Conflict Model

In any therapy group in which the therapist does not control the content or the procedure, a session is likely to take the following form. As the patients gather, there is a period of unofficial talk—perhaps about some event from the preceding session, perhaps about an experience that someone has had since the last meeting, or perhaps about some neutral outside happening. Several conversations may go on at once, with the patients talking in pairs or threes; one or two may be silent. The conversation may be general. The atmosphere might suggest depression, tension, distance, or casual friendliness. Then at some signal—perhaps the closing of a door, the arrival of the therapist, or simply the clock indicating that the starting time has arrived—the session "begins."

After a pause or a longer silence, an initial comment is made. It may reflect some personal concern, some reaction to the previous session, or some reference to the current situation. The speaker may direct his comment to the therapist, to another patient, or to the entire group. The initial comment is followed by another which may or may not appear related to the first one. If it seems related, it may be a response to the topic just introduced, or it may be stimulated by the emotion of the original statement and have little to do with the content. It may be a response to some relationship established earlier in the group's history. Comment follows comment, and a conversation develops. There is some coherence to this conversation, so that the group can be described as talking "about" something. Occasionally the conversation may become disjointed. There may be abrupt shifts in topic, lapses into silence, and illogical elements. The mood may shift, and the rhythm and pace of the discussion may vary. Some patients may talk a great deal, others very little. From time to time, the therapist may enter the discussion, directing his remarks to one person or to the group in general. He may comment about the mood of the group, the character of the interaction, or a problem of a patient.

Some comments get "lost" in the group, as if no one hears them; others are built upon and form the predominant topics and themes. The patients may express such emotions as anger, delight, suspicion, nervousness, or superiority. Some feelings and attitudes are expressed in words; others come through in non-verbal behavior. Certain patterns may emerge in terms of who dominates, who is silent, who talks to whom, and who expresses what feelings. After about an hour of complex interaction, the therapist will signal that the time is up, and the group will disperse. It will meet a few days later for another session.

What has happened? We assume that the diversity observed during a group-therapy session is apparent rather than real and that the many different elements of the session "hang together" in relation to some underlying issue. For example, the first session of an inpatient group was marked by long tense silences, brief staccato periods in which the patients compared notes about physical ills but seemed careful to avoid references to psychological worries, and an animated period in which the patients discussed the architecture of the hospital and wondered whether it was well designed and built on solid ground. On the surface these elements are diverse and unrelated, but they gain a certain coherence if one assumes that they all refer to some shared underlying uneasiness about having been placed in a group and a shared concern about the competence and strength of the therapist. As another example, a group of patients which had been meeting for some time were told that the sessions were to be interrupted for the therapist's vacation. They warmly wished him a good time, ignored him for the rest of the session, and turned to an older member for information about college admission procedures and policies about "dumping" students after the end of the first year. Again, these elements gain coherence if one assumes that they all refer to shared underlying feelings about the impending separation from the therapist.

In this view, the observable elements of the session constitute the manifest material. These elements include not only content, but also non-verbal behaviors, mood, pace, sequence, and participation pattern. Thus, an animated period in which everyone joins the discussion is an element of the session, as is a period of desultory conversation or a period of sober but ritualistic "work" on one patient's problems. A seating pattern in which the chairs on either side of the therapist are left vacant is an element of the session, as is a seating pattern in which male and female patients take chairs on opposite sides of the room. Non-verbal behaviors—looking only at the floor when speaking, directing oneself exclusively to the therapist, or directly engaging one another—are also important elements.

We assume that a subsurface level exists in all groups, but is hardest to detect in groups in which the manifest content is itself relatively coherent and internally consistent. When a group is talking about something, one might assume that this is all that is happening. In the brief illustrations just presented, one group was talking about architecture, and the other about college policies. Yet, even when the group situation consists of a conversation which is coherent in itself, we assume that another level of meaning also exists, for, even in such a group, breaks and shifts occur in the topic under discussion. There are reversals and non-verbal accompaniments, suggesting that to assume that only a conversation is going on is to miss an important aspect of the situation. In therapy groups, covert levels are most apparent in groups of sicker patients, where there is less capacity to maintain coherence on an overt, public level. However, even in non-therapeutic groups, one can observe the same phenomenon.[1]

The covert meaning of the manifest material is not likely to be within the patients' awareness. From the patients' point of view, the conversation *is* about architecture or college admission policies. But an observer is in a position to grasp the underlying issue. Once he "sees" the core issue, aspects of the session which might on the surface appear diverse, contradictory, or meaningless gain coherence and meaning.

This view assumes that the successive manifest elements of the session are linked associatively[2] and that they refer to feelings experienced in the here-and-now situation. Whatever is said in the group is seen as being elicited not only by the strictly internal concerns of the individual, but by the interpersonal situation in which he finds himself. Of all the personal issues, worries, impulses, and concerns which a patient *might* express during a group session, what he actually expresses is elicited by the character of the situation. Moreover, a comment is likely to include a number of elements and is responded to selectively by others. An individual may make a comment which includes a half-dozen elements. As the others listen to an individual's highly personal contribution, they will respond to certain aspects and ignore others. The aspects which are picked up and built upon are in some way relevant to the other patients and gradually become an emerging shared concern. As this suggests, the group-relevant aspect of an individual's comment is defined by the manner in which the other patients react to it. To cite an example, in an inpatient group a patient told a story about a man who had been misunderstood when he used the word "intimate." It was known that this was a personal concern of this patient, who was always apologizing for his sexual thoughts. However, the comments by other patients elaborated on the "misunderstood" aspect of his comment and ignored the "intimate" aspect. We therefore assume that being misunderstood was the shared concern and that the issue of intimacy was not a common concern.

We assume that the content of the session, no matter how seemingly remote, refers to here-and-now relationships and feelings in the group. The patients who worry about the competence of the architect and the strength of the building are really worrying about the competence and strength of the therapist. The patients who complain about college administrators who "dump" their students after the first year are really expressing resentment toward the therapist. The same is true for elements of the session other than the manifest content. Non-verbal behavior, such as a seating arrangement in which male and female patients sit on opposite sides of the room, might reflect concern about heterosexual contact in the group. A participation pattern in which one patient is allowed to dominate might mean that the others are using him to protect themselves from having to participate.

Our point of view is similar to that of Henry Ezriel, who uses the term "common group tension" to refer to the covert, shared aspect of the group process:

> The manifest content of discussions in groups may embrace practically any topic. They may talk about astronomy, philosophy, politics or even psychology; but it is one of the essential assumptions for psychoanalytic work with groups that, whatever the manifest content may be, there always develops rapidly an *underlying* common group problem, a *common group tension* of which the group is not aware but which determines its behaviour. . . . In the beginning of each session there is always some probing when some member of the group, who seems to feel a particular urge to speak, broaches one subject or another. Often a remark made by one member is not taken up by anybody, apparently because nobody can fit it into what is unconsciously at the back of his or her mind. If, on the other hand, it can be fitted

> in . . . if it "clicks" with the unconscious phantasy of another member, and then perhaps with that of a third, then gradually the subject catches on and becomes *the* unconsciously determined topic of the group. . . .[8]

The view of the group situation developed so far is summarized in Proposition 1.

Proposition 1	*Successive individual behaviors are linked associatively and refer to a common underlying concern about the here-and-now situation.*

We view the covert, shared aspects of the group in terms of forces and counterforces, particularly those involving the shared impulses, wishes, hopes, and fears of the patients. For example, in a session presented in detail later in this chapter, there emerged scattered clues that many of the patients in the group wished to be unique and to have a special, close relationship with the therapists. At the same time, there was awareness that the other patients would not permit this and then, more strongly, fear that the therapists would punish them or retaliate in some way. As the session went on, the patients seemed to search for things that they had in common, finally agreeing that they were all alike in some surface traits. Such a session can be understood in light of the force of the wish to have a uniquely gratifying relationship with the therapist and the counterforce of the fear of retaliation. The wish and the fear constitute opposing forces: the fear prevents the wish from being expressed directly or perhaps even recognized. The wish cannot be pursued actively or thoroughly satisfied. At the same time, the wish cannot quite be given up and keeps the fear in the foreground. This situation creates tension in the group. The patients are beset with strong, conflicting feelings and impulses which are, at best, only dimly perceived. Strong impulses are exerting pressure, yet the patients can neither express nor recognize them. Under such circumstances, the patients attempt to find some way of dealing with their conflicting wishes and fears. In the above illustration, the search for things in common and the final agreement that everyone is alike can be seen as an attempt to allay their fears. It is as if the patients were saying, "Don't punish me; I didn't ask the therapist for anything special." Of course, such a solution cannot really be satisfying, since it involves renouncing the wish. It might temporarily reduce anxiety, however.

In attempting to describe the covert, shared aspects of the group's life, we have adopted a theoretical language which utilizes the key terms "group focal conflict," "disturbing motive," "reactive motive," and "solution."[4] The events of a group-therapy session are conceptualized in terms of a slowly emerging, shared covert conflict consisting of two elements—a disturbing motive (a wish) and a reactive motive (a fear). These two elements constitute the group focal conflict. The term "group focal conflict" summarizes the key features of this view of groups, indicating that the disturbing and reactive motives conflict, pervade the group as a whole, and are core issues engaging the energies of the patients. Concomitant with the group focal conflict, one sees various attempts to find a solution. A group solution represents a compromise between the opposing forces; it is primarily directed to alleviating reactive fears but also attempts to maximize gratification of the disturbing motive. Thus the group session just described could be summarized in the following diagram. This form, which will appear throughout the book to summarize group situations in focal-conflict terms, uses the symbol "X" to indicate "opposed by" or "in conflict with."

disturbing motive		*reactive motive*
wish to be unique and singled out by the therapists for special gratification	X	fear of disapproval and retaliation by the therapists

solution
all be alike

This conceptualization of the character of the underlying shared concerns can be stated in the following two propositions.

Proposition 2	*The sequence of diverse events which occur in a group can be conceptualized as a common, covert conflict (the group focal conflict) which consists of an impulse or wish (the disturbing motive) opposed by an associated fear (the reactive motive). Both aspects of the group focal conflict refer to the current setting.*
Proposition 3	*When confronted with a group focal conflict, the patients direct efforts toward establishing a solution which will reduce anxiety by alleviating the reactive fears and, at the same time, satisfy to the maximum possible degree the disturbing impulse.*

No two group sessions are exactly alike in the group focal conflict which emerges. Even when similar feelings are involved, they are expressed in unique imagery. The solution may also vary in the manner in which it copes with the patients' fears and in the extent to which it satisfies and expresses the disturbing motive. The following examples illustrate some of the variations.

In an outpatient group of schizoid young men, there were a number of symbolically expressed indications of resentment toward the therapist because of his failure to provide direction. For example, the patients shared complaints about the local library: the filing system was chaotic, nothing was labeled, and the librarians were of no help. At the same time, the patients hinted at fears of abandonment and fears of possible angry reactions from the therapist. One patient reported an early memory in which he pitted his will against that of his mother, who threatened to leave if he did not comply with her wishes.

The patients also reported that, following the previous meeting, they had discussed matters and decided to talk and talk rather than to ask the therapist questions. In this way, they expressed thinly veiled anger toward the therapist, as well as compliance with the therapist's implied demand that they, not he, provide direction. This session was summarized as follows:

disturbing motive		*reactive motive*
resentment toward the therapist	X	fear of abandonment and of the therapist's angry reaction

solution

band together to express angry compliance

Focal conflicts in which the disturbing motive involves covert, shared resentment toward the therapist are, of course, not uncommon. Such feelings are expressed in many ways, depending on the character and composition of the group. For example, in an inpatient group of schizophrenic patients, the following occurred:

> Bill responded to Lester's account of his problem by saying, "I have a similar problem. When you have legal problems, you go to authorities, and they don't want to give you any help." He mentioned having "done wrong with" a girl, then told about a friend who had been given the electric chair for robbery. He corrected himself, "No, it must have been for something more serious than that." He again complained that whenever he went for help, "There's no satisfaction." Larry agreed: "He is right—you can't get protection."

In an outpatient neurotic group, similar feelings were expressed in different terms:

> There was some agreement that the trouble with officers in the Army was that they always expected their men to do things that they were frightened to do themselves. Jerry said that the officers "learned never to turn their backs on their men," and Tom said he actually knew of a case in which an officer had been killed by one of his own men during a battle. The man was never found out or punished because it was assumed the officer had been killed by the enemy.

In another group, composed of nonpsychotic patients, the members drew on shared hospital experiences in order to express anger toward the therapist over presumed deprivation:

> There were shared complaints about the patients' cafeteria, especially about having to stand in line for so long. Bert told of being too late for dessert because the cafeteria had run out, but George said, "It's not that they don't have it; they don't want to give it to you." Others said they got enough food, but it was always cold. Grover said that his "big gripe" was with the clothing room and told of an experience in which the clerk was so slow and disinterested that he had had to forego part of his week-end pass.

Sometimes a precipitating event which activates a particular focal conflict can be identified. For example, in an inpatient group of patients with psychosomatic complaints, one patient, with great difficulty and misgiving, confessed his long-time fear of being followed and attacked. Between this session and the next, one of the other patients in the group approached this patient from behind, tapped him on the shoulder, and "teased" him by saying, "Hey, somebody's following you." Clearly, this was the precipitating event for what happened in the next session. The victim of this "joke," after some false starts and prodding from the others, appealed to the therapist: "What do you think of a fellow who hurts another fellow with things that are said here? Don't you think that shouldn't be allowed?" He, as well as the others, was quite reluctant to mention names but persisted in pressuring the therapist to censure such behavior. The meeting was summarized in the following focal-conflict terms:

precipitating event

between sessions, a violation by one patient of an implicit group standard

disturbing motive		*reactive motive*
angry, destructive feelings toward one patient	X	fear of guilty feelings about tattling

solution

get the therapist to express and implement angry feelings

The impulses and fears involved in a group focal conflict exist outside the awareness of the patients. Although an outside observer can perceive and link the covert references to a shared concern, the individual who is in the focal conflict does not have this perspective. Under some circumstances, the patients may become aware or may be helped to become aware of these feelings. Ordinarily, however, and especially during the period in which the focal conflict is emerging, the patients are not in a position to recognize the character of the disturbing or reactive motives. A solution differs in character from either a disturbing or a reactive motive. It is usually expressed in more direct terms and is more readily observed. The patients may be aware of the content of the solution, although they are not likely to perceive its relevance to the underlying focal conflict.

A struggle about an emerging solution sometimes develops among the members. When this occurs, we refer to the group as being in a state of "solutional conflict"; one solution is acceptable to most of the patients, but one or two fight against it or offer a conflicting alternative. When such a situation develops, the group is confronted with the new task of resolving the group solutional conflict. This variation can be schematized as follows:

disturbing motive X *reactive motive*

group solutional conflict

group solution X *alternative solution*

modified group solution

Solutions may be successful or unsuccessful; in order to be successful, a solution must be unanimously accepted and must alleviate anxiety. Unanimity is necessary, for if one patient fails to accept such a solution as "all be alike," it cannot be effective. If one patient opposes asking the therapist to rule against a deviant patient, he is interfering with the solution. But unanimous acceptance does not imply that everyone must indicate overt willingness to abide by the solution. Most typically, acceptance is implicit, and some patients indicate through silent acquiescence that they will not interfere. Solutions also vary in the manner in which they deal with the associated conflict. Some solutions concentrate on the reactive fears; it is as if the patients are so concerned about their fears that they adopt a solution which copes with their fears at the expense of satisfying the associated wish. For example, the solution "all be alike" was established in response to this focal conflict: "wish to be unique and singled out by the therapists for special gratification" versus "fear of retaliation." This solution dealt exclusively with the fear. It reduced the fear of retaliation by renouncing the wish for a uniquely gratifying relationship with the therapist. Other solutions alleviate reactive fears and still allow some gratification or expression of the disturbing motive. The solution in which the patients banded together to express angry compliance was of this type —it relieved fears of abandonment by making it impossible for anyone to be singled out for abandonment or rejection, and, at the same time, allowed the disguised expression of resentment toward the therapists. In this case, the solution allowed for the disguised rather than direct expression of the disturbing motive. In other instances, one sees solutions which reduce fears and simultaneously permit the direct expression of the disturbing impulse. The most critical characteristics of group solutions are summarized in the following propositions:

Proposition 4

Successful solutions have two properties. First, they are shared; the behavior of all members is consistent with or bound by the solution. Second, successful solutions reduce reactive fears; individuals experience greater anxiety prior to the establishment of a successful solution, less anxiety after the solution is established.

Proposition 5

Solutions may be restrictive or enabling in character. A restrictive solution is directed primarily to alleviating fears and does so at the expense of satisfying or expressing the disturbing motive. An enabling solution is directed toward alleviating fears and, at the same time, allows for some satisfaction or expression of the disturbing motive.

We assume that, with time, one can observe the gradual emergence of a group focal conflict, along with concomitant efforts to resolve the conflict. Often, during the period when a group is struggling to find some way of dealing with its current focal conflict, several solutions are suggested before one which is acceptable to everyone develops. Some potential solutions are ignored or rejected immediately; others find support, then are built on and modified. By this process, a generally acceptable solution eventually emerges. One does not expect this process to be completed in a single group session, for the session is a convenient but arbitrary unit. The close of a particular session often finds a group still in the grips of some focal conflict without a successful solution having been reached. A series of sessions may revolve around the same conflict. Sometimes several sessions go by in which a group "plays out" a particular solution (for example, taking turns at recounting personal problems and getting advice from the others).

The basic unit in a therapy group can be defined as follows:

Proposition 6	*The group focal conflict is a unit of group life encompassing the period during which a single disturbing and reactive motive dominates the group situation. The unit is terminated by a successful solution.*

No single illustration can be expected to illuminate all aspects of the propositions stated thus far. The detailed illustration to be presented now should not be regarded as typical, except insofar as it demonstrates how the manifest material of a session refers to covert concerns and how a single group session may be summarized in focal-conflict terms.

The session to be described is the first of a reorganized inpatient group which included eight male patients, three female patients, and two female therapists. Only one patient was regarded as psychotic, two were alcoholics, and the rest were suffering from acute anxiety which had reached incapacitating proportions. Five of the patients had previously been in group therapy with Dr. T. The other six, as well as the other therapist, Dr. E., were participating in the group for the first time.

Dr. T. made a general statement about the purposes of the group. She commented that the group presented an opportunity for the patients to talk about whatever was important to them—events in the hospital, personal problems, or things that happened in the group. She introduced Dr. E. and announced the meeting schedule.

Such an opening offers little structure, yet communicates to the patients that they are expected to attend and to take responsibility for determining the content of the sessions.

Carl said that he would drop a bombshell into the group by asking Dr. E. how her hair could look like she combed it with an egg-beater and yet look so good.

When Carl uses the term "bombshell," he is calling attention to the daring and perhaps potentially dangerous quality of his comment. His comment has both an aggressive and a sexual flavor. It focuses the attention of the group immediately on the new therapist.

There was a brief silence. Tim said, "That was a left-handed compliment," and there was general laughter in the group. Carl said that his wife was too fussy about her hair, and Tim made some comment about his wife's hair. Margaret defended Carl's wife by saying that he should either compliment her or coax her into changing her hair style.

Apparently Carl was right, and his comment was really a bombshell, because the group seemed momentarily stunned into silence. Tim's comment seemed to provide tension release for the group by making explicit both the hostile and complimentary aspects of Carl's bombshell. Carl then felt impelled to take back the hostile elements of his comment by comparing Dr. E. to his wife, to Dr. E.'s benefit. With Margaret's attack on Carl, there is a suggestion of a battle drawn on sexual lines.

To this point in the session, several potential focuses have appeared, but it is difficult to see which way the group will move. There has been a direct approach to one of the therapists which seems to have both sexual and hostile elements to it, but in any case emphasizes the femaleness of the therapist. It certainly brought Carl to the forefront of the group and focused attention on him. There followed a retreat toward a discussion about outside persons and a hint of contention within the group. But so far, an underlying trend is not apparent.

Dr. T. suggested that there might be some feeling in the group because there were women patients present for the first time. The group did not respond to this comment but continued talking in a general way about hair styles.

This was a premature intervention—a guess at a focus which seems to have missed the point. Underlying this intervention was some assumption that the heterosexual problem being introduced had to do with feelings among peers. In a sense, the comment asks the patients to focus on their feelings for one another. The patients are not prepared to do this and continue their discussion of hair styles, which could be seen as a displaced and symbolic expression of sexual interests.

A trend toward focusing on sexual interests and impulses seems to be emerging, but neither the target nor the implications for the group are clear.

> Melvin, who had been silent up to this time, commented that he wanted a medal for being in a therapy group for the third time. Carl said that this was the fourth time he had been in a group, and Melvin said that he would have to back down.

On the face of it, this is an abrupt shift in content and focus. Although in a different area, this comment, too, has a bombshell quality. Melvin seems to be wanting to gain some kind of recognition or attention, either from the therapists or from the other patients, by pointing out that he is special. He points out the difference between himself and all the others and perhaps, secondarily, reminds the group that there are both old and new members present. Carl immediately attacks Melvin's claim to specialness and superiority. He is competitive and effectively gains the upper hand by implying that, if anyone is special and deserving of recognition, it is he and not Melvin.

> Jean commented that she was an alcoholic and therefore had different problems from all the other patients. Carl said, "We're all addicted," but Tim argued that this was not true. A discussion followed in which the patients tried to arrive at a definition of "addiction." Carl suggested that Tim might be addicted to sleep. Carl said that his wife thinks he is an alcoholic.

Jean makes her own claim to distinction. Like Melvin, she is immediately countered by Carl, who, this time, rather than suggest that he himself is superior, suggests that everyone in the group is the same and that Jean therefore has no claim to being special. It is interesting that it is always Carl who insists that everyone is alike and no one is special. Others in the group are not ready to agree with him.

At this point in the session, one might hypothesize that an issue is developing as to whether people are unique or the same. Two patients —Melvin and Jean—have made distinct bids to be singled out. Carl's first comment—the bombshell—might also be regarded in this light.

By that comment, Carl was clearly lifting himself out of the mass of patients and making himself conspicuous; in particular, he was bringing himself to the attention of one of the therapists. From a focal-conflict point of view, a disturbing motive may be emerging which involves a wish to be unique and to receive special attention. The object of the wish is not clear. For Carl, it is the therapist; for Melvin, it is probably the therapist (a medal from whom?); for Jean, it is less clear. The reactive motive—the force which keeps the wish from fruition—is not clear. All we can see is that one of the members, Carl, will not allow anyone to satisfy this wish. Whenever anyone makes a bid for uniqueness, Carl interferes. It is uncertain how the rest of the group feels about this issue. Perhaps they don't care; perhaps they care very much but are letting Carl fight their battle for them. In terms of focal-conflict theory, Carl is also suggesting a solution—"let's all be alike"; it is as if he is saying, "Let's not let anyone win this competition." But there is no evidence yet that anyone else supports this view.

> Tim and Melvin (both old members) began to talk about Dr. Y. (a psychiatrist who had been permitted to sit in as an observer of several previous sessions). They referred to an argument the group had had at that time about the cost of psychiatric treatment.

If one paid attention only to the content of this portion of the meeting, it might appear that these two patients are wondering whether the feelings stirred up in the group may be too much to handle. Perhaps they are indirectly questioning whether the group sessions will be worth while. However, the interactive characteristics of this episode suggest another line of thought.

Both Tim and Melvin were old members. By discussing a topic which was meaningless to the new people in the group, they excluded the new members from the conversation and brought sharply into focus the difference between the old and the new. Entirely apart from the content of their conversation, this behavior might be regarded as an interesting variation on the theme of claiming uniqueness. Before, each member has made a personal bid for attention or uniqueness. Now, two members collaborate in their attempt to establish a special place for themselves in the group. This behavior may be seen as a solution to the developing focal conflict. One might conceptualize such a focal conflict in the following manner:

disturbing motive	*reactive motive*
wish to be unique and singled out for special gratification from the therapists	interference by other patients

The behavior of Tim and Melvin partly involves giving up the wish to be unique, but still attempts to reserve a special place in the group for themselves as old members. The reactive motive does not involve feelings of fear or guilt, or the like, but simply indicates that, thus far, any bids for uniqueness have been blocked by another patient.

> Two of the new patients, Sam and Margaret, began to ask Dr. E. questions. Sam asked whether tranquilizing drugs would help him. Dr. E. asked whether they had helped him in the past. Margaret asked whether tranquilizers were sedatives. Dr. E. responded with medical information. At this point, both Tim and Melvin reacted with exaggerated pleasure. Tim said, "For the benefit of new personnel, doctors do not answer questions in this group, so this is really something."

Here, Sam and Margaret interrupted the conversation between Tim and Melvin. In effect, they did not permit reminiscences about special experiences. At the same time, they made their own bid for attention. These two new patients were seeking attention from the new therapist in the group. When it looked as if they were succeeding, Tim and Melvin interfered. Although they were ostensibly telling Sam and Margaret that they were getting something special, they were also implicitly telling both the patients and the new therapist that an old standard was being violated. Thus they are not only interfering with Sam and Margaret's bid to gain special notice from the therapist, they are also re-emphasizing the differences between the old and the new members. Here one sees a repetition of what has occurred earlier: a bid for a therapist's attention is blocked by other patients. Such repetition strengthens the hypothesis that a disturbing motive which involves a wish to receive something special from the therapists is operating. It also strengthens the assumption that the other patients will not allow anyone to be singled out in this way.

This interpretation re-emphasizes the interactive characteristics of the group. Turning to the content, one might wonder why the patients focus on tranquilizers rather than on something else. It is not clear whether this focus carries a symbolic implication, whether it expresses some wish to have things calmed down in the group, or whether it merely grows out of some private assumption that this is what doctors are for.

> Melvin referred to a discussion the group had had a number of meetings previously about automobiles. He then told Carl that this meeting would be a good opportunity to sell chances (again referring to something that had happened in a previous session). There was some talk among Carl, Tim, and Melvin about the cost of the chances and

about Ford, Mercury, and Lincoln cars (all these were topics which had been discussed in previous sessions).

This conversation involves strengthening the ties among old members and excluding the new members. Earlier it was suggested that in the group a solution was developing which would reserve a special place for the old members. It is as if the old members were saying, "Perhaps we cannot be unique and receive special attention as individuals, but at least let us band together to exclude these newcomers." The car conversation suggests that this solution is gaining adherents and being put into practice.

> Dr. T. suggested that the group was asking Dr. E. a lot of questions in order to find out what sort of person the new doctor was. The group responded with laughter. Dr. T. then suggested that the group was concerned about the new members versus the old members and pointed out that some of the conversation introduced by old members could not possibly be understood by new members.

The first portion of this comment appears irrelevant to the shared concerns which seem to be developing in this group. The reference to curiosity about Dr. E. does, however, touch on the wish, which several patients have revealed, to get close to Dr. E. and obtain special help from her. More clearly, however, the second portion of the therapist's comment directly confronts the old members with the alliance they are establishing and makes one aspect of the developing focal-conflict pattern—the solution—explicit.

> Tim said he really wanted an answer to the question he was about to ask and asked Dr. E. about a shot he had had which produced anesthesia in his arm. Dr. E. did not answer this question directly. The group began to discuss spinal taps. They expressed considerable apprehension about this procedure and wanted to know why it was used. The gist of the conversation was that spinal taps were about the most painful and horrible treatment that one could undergo.

Again, this constitutes an abrupt shift in topic. It might seem that the patients have not heard Dr. T.'s intervention or at least are not responding to it. But interactive characteristics show the patients turning away from Dr. T. and toward Dr. E. In terms of content, the discussion about injections and spinal taps may be a symbolic expression of the patients' feeling that doctors are potentially dangerous and capable of inflicting great pain in the guise of aid. It seems reasonable to suppose, then, that the patients actually are reacting to Dr. T.'s intervention. This intervention had blocked a developing solution by communicating disapproval. Perhaps it has elicited some covert angry reaction which the patients now express by turning to Dr. E. The content also suggests that the patients perceive Dr. T.'s intervention as a punitive one. Perhaps they are indicating indirectly and symbolically that the therapist's previous comment was as punitive as actually performing a spinal tap. Perhaps—although this is more speculative—they feel that their angry reaction deserves punishment. It is not clear which aspect of the therapist's comment they are responding to—whether it is the exposure of their solution to exclude the new members or whether it is the exposure of their curiosity about Dr. E. In any case, the reaction is a strong one, as is demonstrated by the primitive quality of the symbolism—spinal taps and anesthesia.

From a focal-conflict point of view, the therapist's intervention has led to a shift in the reactive motive. Previously the wish was held in check by an awareness that other patients would block any bid for uniqueness; now it is held in check by a fear that the therapist will punish the patients. It is as if the therapist will disapprove of not only the wish to be special, but even of the modified solution—a special place in the group for the old members.

It is interesting to note, parenthetically, that in this instance Dr. E. did not respond directly to the patients' questions. She appears to be responding to the earlier suggestion that to answer questions is to violate a custom of the group.

> The group began to talk about the value of their meetings. Alan said that he might learn to get along with this group, but added, "What good will it do me with friends and relatives?" Jean said, "I am a stranger, and yet you talk to me." Carl said, "This is because we've been through the same thing." Jean talked about Alcoholics Anonymous and said that the value of the group was that "you think you are alone, but you're not." Carl said that he would feel free to talk about anything in this group.

This portion of the session displays a drop in morale and then a recovery. The first part, in which the group is devalued, may express veiled anger toward the therapist; it may also suggest the patients' sense of despair when confronted with difficult issues and feelings. Then, rather abruptly, there is a shift in mood. The patients become more friendly to one another. For the first time, they begin to break down the barriers between the old and new members. (Jean, a new member, tells Carl, an old member, "I am a stranger, and yet you talk to me," and Carl responds, "This is because we've been through the same thing.") There is a new emphasis on the value of peers and the possibility of closeness among them.

From the point of view of the group's focal conflict, this shift suggests a renunciation of the wish to be unique (the disturbing motive), as well as the adoption of a new solution. The patients' friendly overtures may indicate that they will no longer insist on being unique, nor will the old members insist on being a special subgroup. It seems reasonable to suppose that the shift in the reactive motive—from the threat of active interference by other patients to the fear of punishment by the therapist—has led to this change. With such intense, primitive fears involved in the reactive motive, it seems that the only solution is to renounce the wish.

> Dr. T. responded to Carl's comment by saying that an important issue in the group would be what people felt that they could talk about and what they felt they could not talk about. Alan said that the group might be a place where he could learn to understand himself. Tim said he did not know what his problems were, but he did know his symptoms. He described them as eating, sleeping, and indefinitely postponing any attempt to do his job. Jean said she felt the same way and described a drinking pattern in which she drank alone until she was stuporous, ate nothing, and sipped straight whisky for weeks at a time. There was some conversation between Jean and Tim, identifying common problems.

The therapist's comment seems to be an attempt to slow down the headlong rush into complete trust and suggest to the group that it is appropriate to move more slowly. The interaction between Tim and Jean is a continuation of the previous friendliness but has now shifted to sharing the content of problems. In part, the patients seem to be turning to one another for support; in part, they may be mollifying the therapist by doing what they assume the therapist wants them to do. In either case, this portion of the session may be seen as a solution which focuses largely on the reactive motive. It is an attempt to deal with fears about the therapist's displeasure.

> Melvin brought up the subject of hypnotism. He said that he trusted his individual therapist, Dr. J., and would let him do anything, even hypnotize him. Jean said that Dr. J. had tried to hypnotize her once and that it had not worked. Ella said the same thing. Several patients asked Melvin about hypnotism, expressing a good deal of skepticism. Sam asked whether the pills he took produced the same effect as hypnosis. Alan suggested that sleeping was really like being hypnotized. Dr. T. asked, "You mean that everyone has been hypnotized?" Alan described blackout spells he had had. Jean and William were asking him questions about his spells as the session ended.

This portion of the session begins with Melvin indicating that he cannot accept the group solution—finding common ground and renouncing the wish to be unique. He is indicating that, if he cannot get what he wants in the group, he will turn to his individual therapist for a special relationship. He thus rejects the possibility of finding strength through relationships with peers. In effect, he says to the group, "You can trust one another if you want to; I will trust my own doctor." From a focal-conflict point of view, Melvin is disavowing the group solution. More importantly, he is also reintroducing the disturbing motive and making a bid for special attention. He is telling the others that he refuses to settle for giving up the wish as they seem willing to do. The others apparently think Melvin's comments will upset the applecart. They attack and depreciate Melvin's supposed special relationship with his therapist. Then the group copes with the anxiety which Melvin's comment has aroused by reconfirming their earlier solution: they insist that everyone is alike and no one, certainly not Melvin, has any claim to uniqueness. They claim that pills and sleep and blackout spells are all the same as being hypnotized. They end the session reaffirming the earlier solution: "We are all alike—friendly people with a great deal in common."

It is now possible to trace the detailed development of the focal-conflict pattern and to summarize the session in terms of a single focal conflict. The detailed development takes the following form:

disturbing motive		*reactive motive*
wish to be unique and singled out by the therapists for special gratification	X	reality factor: bids for uniqueness are blocked by other patients
angry and competitive feelings toward newcomers on part of old patients		

solution

old members band together to exclude newcomers

(Therapist's intervention exposes the solution and the competitive feelings and indicates disapproval.)

new reactive motive

fear of punishment from therapist

new solution

give up the wish entirely; turn to one another for support and

find similarities among old and
new patients

(Melvin's comment makes a new bid for a special relationship, thus reactivating the wish and threatening the solution.)

solution

all be alike; tolerate no individuality or uniqueness

This formulation identifies some of the details of the interaction. The following summary captures the most significant elements of the session in terms of a single focal conflict:

disturbing motive		*reactive motive*
wish to have a uniquely gratifying relationship with the therapist	X	fear of punishment from the therapist

solution

all be alike

With reference to the disturbing motive, the evidence about the nature of the wish is clearer than the evidence about the object of the wish. Yet it seems reasonable to suppose that the wish for uniqueness is associated with a wish to have a special, perhaps exclusive, relationship with the therapist. It also seems clear that the character of the reactive motive changes markedly. At first, it involved the recognition that attempts to achieve a special place in the group would be interfered with by the other patients. The level of anxiety during this period was relatively low. Later, it shifted to fear of punishment by the therapists. Here the anxiety mounted. Eventually, a solution emerged around the implicit agreement to give up the wish and insist that everyone in the group was alike.

Subsequent sessions suggested that this solution became a basic group standard and held sway for some time. However, eight or nine sessions later, the solution was altered. The patients agreed that they were basically alike but different in superficial ways. This modified solution allowed some differentiation in the group and perhaps a partial satisfaction of the disturbing motive; it was also consistent with reality, as the solution achieved at the end of the first session was not. This development is discussed in detail in Chapter 5, where we examine the culture of therapy groups and the manner in which group solutions become modified.

Methodological Considerations

The analysis of a group therapy session involves certain judgments about the meaning and relative importance of events in the session. At times, the content is interpreted as having a symbolic reference to the here-and-now situation. For example, in the illustration we assumed that the discussion about spinal taps implied some fear that the therapists might harm the patients. At other times, the characteristics of the interaction carry greater weight than the specific content. At one point during the session, for example, the most significant fact seemed to be that an old and a new patient were finding things in common. Sometimes much is made of a rather minute bit of interaction; at other times, a broader sequence of interaction may be summarized and regarded as relatively less important.

These comments suggest some of the methodological difficulties inherent in making complex judgments about a multitude of overt events with reference to assumed covert issues. Questions arise as to whether standard procedures are really possible, whether the bases on which judgments are made can be explicitly defined and communicated, and whether one can expect agreement among independent analyzers. An appropriate, reproducible procedure for making a focal-conflict formulation of the group-therapy session is required. Two choices are available: the holistic approach, which we have adopted, in which a global judgment is made about the import of the material, and a molecular approach which is based on a rating procedure. A molecular approach requires that judgments be made about successive, equivalent units of the interaction, that each unit be placed in one of a limited number of categories, and that the results be summed to characterize the session as a whole. Bales' "interaction process analysis"[5] and Leary's "interpersonal reflex"[6] are examples of molecular procedures applied to therapy groups. A molecular approach is preferable because it lends itself to concise definition, reproducibility, and statistical treatment. Agreement between independent raters can be easily measured; the bases for the judgments are relatively clear and can be communicated. In contrast, the bases on which judgments are made in an holistic approach are harder to define and communicate. It is more difficult to guard against subjective judgments.

Despite the fact that a molecular approach has many methodological advantages, the assumptions underlying our theory make such an approach inappropriate to our task. We assume that all of the varied elements of a session—the content, sequence, rhythm, mood, context, and non-verbal behaviors—are relevant to the group focal conflict. These elements differ in kind: the content of specific comments, for example, is easily specified and occurs within a narrow time limit; in contrast, context and sequential characteristics refer to broader aspects of the situation. Content can be summarized easily, but non-verbal behavior must be interpreted and involves more inference. Mood frequently must be grasped rather than measured. Because of these differences, the elements of a session cannot be regarded as equivalent and cannot be treated additively. Nor do we believe that the various elements are always of equal importance. Sometimes content may outweigh other aspects; at other times, context or sequence may provide the basic cue. The final decision about the character of the group focal conflict requires an integration of these non-equivalent elements. Thus the concepts of "unit," "category," and "summation" become inapplicable.

Our task, then, requires an holistic approach in which the various elements of the session are considered simultaneously and a general judgment is formed. We have tried to minimize the problems of such an approach by making the analytic procedure as explicit as possible and by relying on the combined judgments of two independent analyzers. By identifying the cues used for making judgments, by detailing specific problems, and by breaking the procedure into discrete steps, we have attempted to ensure that the judges are working on the same task in the same way. We have found that making intervening steps explicit allows independent analyzers to pinpoint disagreements and identify the source of their differences within narrow limits. Although we do not intend to provide a detailed procedural manual here,[7] we would like to outline certain procedures which we regard as appropriate.

The first consideration is the kind of data from which to work. We have found it most useful to work from a written summary backed by a tape. The summary is made by someone who has been present at the session—the therapist or an observer—so that important non-verbal behaviors can be included. If an analyzer listens to the tape with the summary of the session before him, he can familiarize himself with such details of the interaction as pace and tone, which cannot be communicated by the printed word. This method also makes it possible for the analyzer to correct any omissions or wrong emphases in the summary.

A second consideration involves keeping certain relevant cues in mind. Most obvious is content. We assume that the manifest content of successive associations has some relevance to the here-and-now interaction of the group; so, when examining content, we attempt to be alert to symbolic or displaced references to the current group interaction. For example, a complaint about the therapist's white coat might suggest a complaint about the type of relationship the therapist is maintaining with the group. Another important cue is the kind of interpersonal interaction going on in the group, quite apart from the content. Occasionally, a group will permit or even encourage one patient to dominate the discussion. This in itself might be of greater importance than the details of the patient's conversation. Or a therapist's intervention might be followed by a change in the topic or a shift toward more general conversation. Again, the interactive characteristic might be highly relevant. Non-verbal behavior is often very revealing. In one group session, the patients lined themselves up along one wall and jokingly referred to this as "the line-up." This was the first indication that the major preoccupation of the session involved guilt. In another session, a wish for help was expressed behaviorally—the patients consistently addressed themselves to the therapist rather than to one another. In an adolescent group, horseplay in which a boy pretended to snatch a purse from one of the girls expressed a preoccupation with sexual feelings. The context in which a session occurs is sometimes of such importance that an adequate formulation cannot be made without taking it into account. For example, a particular session might be understood only if one knew that the therapist had changed the meeting time or that this was the first session after an interruption or that the previous session had ended on a note of frustration or suppressed anger. A somewhat related aspect is the sequence of associations during the session. A comment which comes as a shift in topic might have very different implications from one which fits into the preceding train of association.

In assessing these cues and weighing their meaning, an analyzer should be alert to the distinction between idiosyncratic and group-relevant material. One of the special problems related to defining covert concerns in group therapy, as contrasted with individual therapy, is the presence of a number of patients. The question arises as to whether all comments are relevant to the group focal conflict or whether certain contributions are truly idiosyncratic—that is, the property of the individual and not the group. We feel that neither is strictly the case; any comment has both a personal meaning and an implication for the total group. The clue for the group meaning is the manner in which the other patients react to the comment. A particular aspect of a contribution may be reacted to while other aspects are ignored. When three or four patients react to a topic or a story introduced by one, it is relatively easy to see how individual comments contribute to a developing group theme. In other circumstances, the judgment is more difficult. For example, if a patient tells a long story about a personal experience and elicits no response from the others, it is difficult to know which aspect of his story has group relevance or, indeed, whether the most relevant aspect might not be the fact that he has been permitted to talk at such length. Here one must be more cautious in making assumptions about the implications of individual comments for the group.

In summarizing a session in focal-conflict terms, we wish to avoid, on the one hand, a mere summary of overt content and, on the other, an overly speculative formulation. We attempt to formulate the group focal conflict in terms specific to the session being studied. A formulation which is too general may be relevant to the group focal conflict but has probably missed the unique quality of its expression in that particular session. Such a formulation is not wrong, but it has lost its usefulness since it is likely to be equally applicable to a number of group sessions.

In general terms, the analytic process involves building, testing, and revising hypotheses until a formulation is achieved which satisfactorily accounts for all aspects of the session. Two major steps are involved. First, two independent analyzers produce group focal-conflict formulations of a session, aided by work sheets which (1) help the analyzer to attend to all relevant material and cues, (2) require him to move through the material noting general themes and making tentative hypotheses, (3) require him to trace the detailed development in focal-conflict terms, and (4) ask him to produce a summary of the entire session. Thus, each analyzer records not only his final conclusion, but also the details of his formulation and the evidence he has utilized in making it. In a second step, the two analyzers compare their formulations, noting discrepancies and arguing out their disagreements until they have achieved a final "official" formulation which satisfies both.[8] Although the analytic process is made as explicit as possible, some steps must remain implicit and uncommunicable. The procedure can be specified up to a point, but the crux of the matter is the final integration of the elements into a focal-conflict formulation. The achievement of such a Gestalt is essentially a creative act in which the steps and ingredients are difficult to specify.

In this analysis, the most crucial criterion of reliability is that of reproducibility by independent investigators. Ideal agreement would occur if two analyzers produced not only the same final formulation, but also agreed at every step along the way. Thus far, perfect agreement has not been achieved by any pair of independent analyzers; but, on the other hand, neither does gross disagreement occur. What is likely to happen is that the analyzers agree on the final formulation of the focal conflict but emphasize somewhat different aspects of its detailed development. Or they might agree on the significant elements but build these into the focal-conflict formulation in somewhat different ways. We have found, however, that it is almost always possible for two independent analyzers to resolve such disagreements by sharing and discussing the steps they have followed in producing each formulation. Although too many clinical judgments are involved to expect perfect agreement, we believe that the procedure described permits the maximum possible specification of points of disagreement and aids their resolution into a final joint formulation.

Notes

[1] In any small face-to-face group, whether it be a committee meeting, a staff meeting, or a cocktail party, one can observe "illogicalities" which suggest these covert levels. However, it is not the business of such groups to attend to such aspects of the interaction (unless, perhaps, they become grossly disruptive). In fact, the members are likely, without realizing it, to fill in gaps and ignore irrelevancies that are not too intrusive.

[2] For a discussion of the associational process in groups as compared with individual therapy, see Chapter 11.

[3] Henry Ezriel, "A Psychoanalytic Approach to the Treatment of Patients in Groups," p. 63.

[4] These terms are adopted from the work of Thomas French, who developed them for application to individual psychoanalytic sessions and dreams. See Thomas French, *The Integration of Behavior,* Vols. I and II (Chicago: University of Chicago Press, 1952, 1954). We have modified and extended this approach for application to group processes. The application of these concepts to the individual is discussed in Chapter 7.

[5] Robert F. Bales, *Interaction Process Analysis: A Method for the Study of Small Groups* (Cambridge, Mass.: Addison-Wesley, 1950).

[6] Timothy Leary, *Interpersonal Diagnosis of Personality* (New York: The Ronald Press, 1957).

[7] A full discussion appears in a previously published paper, from which some

of the materal in this section is adapted. See Dorothy Stock and Morton A. Lieberman, "Methodological Issues in the Assessment of Total-Group Phenomena in Group Therapy," *International Journal of Group Psychotherapy,* 12 (1962), 312–325.

[8] The full procedure has not been illustrated here. To avoid repetition, we have condensed several steps in our example.

3

Equilibrium and Change

The group focal conflict is an abstraction which defines a unit of group life. As an abstraction, it omits any detailed account of the actual sequence of events. The group focal conflict does not, however, spring into existence ready-made; rather, it emerges during the course of the session. The group is in a different state with reference to the group focal conflict at each successive point of the session. The disturbing and reactive motives may shift in character or in the manner in which they are expressed. At one point, the patients may focus their attention on their fears and, at another, on shared impulses or wishes. Solutions may appear, be discarded, or modified. The direction of movement is toward the establishment of a successful solution. The disturbing and reactive motives oppose one another; the solution copes with the opposing forces. We have also postulated that the group moves toward the solution by a series of steps. In attempting to conceptualize the manner in which events evolve during this process, we have found it convenient to think in terms of an equilibrium model. The group situation at any given moment can be understood in terms of forces in equilibrium, and the group's movement within the session can be seen as successive shifts in equilibrium.

Every session of every group differs in the details of its movement. To illustrate both the uniqueness of each session and the common process by which movement occurs, we shall describe two therapy sessions. The first occurred in an inpatient schizophrenic group. During the fourth session of this group, there was continual shifting between a wish to talk about oneself and one's problems and intense fears about the potentially damaging effects of the group. Panic mounted, and the group found no way of coping with this conflict.

The second illustration is taken from an inpatient group of nonpsychotic patients. Most of these patients were suffering from acute anxiety or long-standing character problems which were currently intensified and incapacitating. In the first session, the patients showed concern about being criticized or harmed by one another if they revealed themselves. They attempted to deal with this conflict by agreeing that, since everyone had faults, no one should criticize. One patient abruptly interfered with this solution and forced the others to turn their attention to him and find some other way of dealing with the dilemma. Both groups were conducted by co-therapists. The two therapists who conducted the second, nonpsychotic group were familiar with focal-conflict theory; the two therapists who conducted the schizophrenic group were not.

An Unsuccessful Escape from Panic

This illustration describes the fourth session of an inpatient group composed mainly of patients diagnosed as schizophrenic. In previous sessions, this group had been dominated by a paranoid patient who described his fears and details about his personal life. The other patients were more cautious about revealing themselves, but seemed eager to encourage the paranoid patient to talk.

> As the session began, Larry said facetiously, "We've talked about sex and liquor, now we can talk about politics and then close the group up." He added that there were three doctors against five patients. (He was referring to the two therapists and a non-participating note-taker.)

The session begins on an uneasy note, with an immediate emphasis on fears. One patient "jokingly" suggests that the patients adopt flight as a solution; the therapists are seen as antagonists and sources of threat.

> A paranoid schizophrenic patient, Bill (who had dominated earlier sessions), asked about the purpose of the group. He said he knew it had something to do with getting well but did not understand it. John

said he also had difficulty understanding it and was not convinced that group therapy could be helpful. Bill wondered, "Does the group make us comfortable for some purpose, or are we being observed or studied?"

Again, reactive fears predominate. Two patients express doubt and suspicion about the group. Yet there is also a dim expression of hope—a doubt-laden wish to be helped. This hope, however dim, may constitute the counterforce which prevents the solution of flight from taking hold. A focal conflict something like the following might be emerging: "desire to be helped by the group" versus "fear and suspicion of being harmed by the therapists or the group." The reactive side of the focal conflict is heavily emphasized.

John said that he was embarrassed by listening to other people's troubles and was disturbed by them. He wondered what he was going to get out of the group. He said, "Listening to other people's troubles upsets me and looks dangerous. There are very few times when I come out of here and say it's done something. I'm not objecting to that, because I don't expect anything. What's been done, I've done myself." Larry agreed with John and said, "I associate to others and feel afraid like him. I'm beginning to feel good physically and yet am afraid of leaving. I feel miserable when others are miserable, yet it helps me understand myself."

Two patients indicate that, for them, the important aspect of the reactive motive is the possibility of being harmed by contact with other sick people. The primitive quality of this fear underlines its intensity (and, of course, also reflects the degree of these patients' illness). The balance again favors the reactive fears although, again, a hint of hope appears. Still, there has been an essentially unrelieved intensification of reactive fears.

Bill said that he felt that, in a few more meetings, everyone would be able to talk more easily. "We feel something is wrong with us, and we should talk about it. I think we're on the right track."

At this moment of peak intensity in reactive fears, Bill introduces a solution which ought to relieve the patients' fears by postponing self-exposure; at the same time, however, he indicates that the road toward being helped will involve talking about what is wrong with oneself. He is throwing his weight on the side of the disturbing motive in a way likely to reduce the anxiety of the group.

Dr. N. commented that talk seemed to be both good and bad.

In general terms, the therapist's comment accurately reflects both the reactive and the disturbing motives. This comment gives equal weight to the patients' wishes and fears and fails to recognize the potential solution just introduced by Bill.

> John commented, "When you do find something out, it shakes you to the bone. I'm afraid of probing; I want to get away." He asked whether there was a way of getting at problems piecemeal. Larry wondered whether it happened all at once—"like 'Eureka!' and you get well." Both Bill and John said that they now felt a little freer in the group than they previously had.

These comments support the hypothesis that the movement toward a solution has alleviated reactive fears to some degree. The anxiety level is now probably at its lowest point since the session began. Along with a reduction of fear (reactive motive) comes a greater sense of the possibility of expressing oneself (disturbing motive).

> Larry said that when the meeting started he was really scared. Even the aides did not understand the patients, and he wondered whether the doctors did. He said, "I guess that if the doctors felt like us, they couldn't take it."

At this point, Larry feels free to discuss rather than merely express his fears. He locates his fears in the past and seems ready to talk about them.

> Bill said that, at first, he had been disturbed by the yelling in the wards but that he understood it now. The hospital was a place to blow one's top. "If you don't blow your top here, you won't anywhere."

Bill, too, locates his fears in the past. He introduces a solution which is clearly more enabling than those which have appeared previously. To regard the hospital as an appropriate place for the expression of impulses is a solution which permits feelings to be expressed without fear. The appearance of an enabling solution bears fruit:

> There was a general discussion about violent patients in the ward.

Following Bill's lead, others discuss hostile feelings through a conversation about violent patients. Expression of the disturbing motive dominates the group. Reactive fears are held in abeyance.

> Howard, who had not previously talked, said reprovingly, "That's not the right attitude for therapy."

Apparently the increasing expression of the disturbing motive stirs up anxiety in a previously silent patient. His introduction of a punitive remark may shift the balance toward a renewed emphasis on fears. He suggests a restrictive solution which would deal with the fear by giving up the wish.

> Dr. N. pointed out that everyone was saying that the living pattern in the hospital was both strange and terrifying.

By emphasizing reactive fears, the therapist may contribute to the intensification of the anxiety of the group.

> Bill said that he became frightened when he did not understand, but, when he knew people well, he was not afraid.

Bill deals with the renewed emphasis on the dangers of the group by suggesting a solution geared toward lowering the intensity of the reactive motive.

> Howard asked what was going to keep him from getting a breakdown and wondered how group therapy was going to help. Larry said that he was in the same boat. He knew he placed too much emphasis on work, and yet he could not give it up. He asked how he could get better and said that he was afraid.

Howard and Larry voice their fears. The group continues to move toward the reactive motive.

> Dr. O., talking to John, said, "It's a hell of a grind to get somewhere, and what guarantee do you have that you'll stay better?"

Here the therapist refers to both sides of the conflict, but the emphasis is again on the reactive side—the difficulties, problems, and discouragements.

> John agreed, saying that he had been working with therapy for six months and had not improved much. "I understand better, but I can't do anything with it. I can't break the pattern, even if I'm aware of the pattern. I've been analyzing all my life."

In response to the intensification of the reactive fears, John says, in effect, "Don't try so hard; it's not worth it." He is suggesting a restrictive solution which would reduce reactive fears by reducing the pressure to talk (disturbing motive).

> Marvin asked what John's problem was, and John answered, "Not a thing. I just get a little nervous. Don't you?" Marvin said that his problem was different.

Marvin is attempting to deal with the conflict by urging someone else to talk about his problems (express the disturbing motive) and ignore his fears. This solution cannot work because it necessitates doing the very thing the patients fear without in any way coping with their fears.

> Dr. N. said that many of the patients seemed to be saying, "There is a lot of frightening stuff here. Should we expose ourselves?" He commented on how John had "frozen up" just now. Larry and John agreed with Dr. N., and Larry pointed out how hard it is to talk about problems one feels deeply about. Tom mentioned the time several sessions previously when he had broken down and begun to cry in the group. John said that he was very nervous about talking about himself and added, "It's hard to convince myself that it's worth it."

The therapist refers to both the disturbing and the reactive motives, emphasizing the reactive motive as a fear of exposure. Two patients follow by discussing their anxiety about talking.

> Dr. N. said that John seemed to be saying that, despite what common sense tells you, these fears are real and painful.

The therapist reflects the reactive fears, underlining their powerful quality and communicating his understanding of the patients' feelings.

> Larry and Richard nodded agreement. Larry said that when he gets close to the real problem, he freezes up like John. "Nobody knows as well as I that it's foolishness, and yet it's as real to me as anything." Dr. N. asked him if he were ashamed. Larry said it wasn't that exactly: "Although I know my problem is made-up and foolish, it's very real to me." He said he didn't understand the purpose of the group. "I could never talk about my basic problem in the group no matter how long I sat here."

Here, there are further attempts to clarify the character of the fears about the group.

> Marvin asked Bill whether he felt he could talk about his problems if he stayed long enough. He pointed out, "Here in the group, everyone empties his mind and sees that he has common sex problems and deep-seated fears." Larry said regretfully that the group only talked about surface facts.

Here, Marvin suggests two solutions: first, the passage of time and, second, the recognition of common problems. His comment is a move to lower the intensity of the reactive motive.

> Dr. N. asked whether the group was talking about whether they could trust one another.

The therapist continues his attempt to clarify the reactive motive.

> Larry said, "So far, only one man, Bill, has talked about surface facts, and nobody else has talked at all. How can we ask John to talk?"

Evidently the possibility of further exploration of fears is frightening to Larry, for he expresses hopelessness about ever achieving a solution to the dilemma.

> Bill said (referring to a long personal story which had much paranoid material and which he had told in an earlier session) that people didn't believe him and that he couldn't talk about his story. He said, "What I want is to get away from the real problem and forget about problems." He added, "I never dream." He then bent over to Larry and said, "I appreciate what you said." (He was referring to Larry's comment that Bill had been the only person to talk at all.)

Bill, the one patient in the group who has talked freely in a previous session, emphasizes the dangers of expressing the disturbing motive by saying, in effect, "If you talk, you will be hurt by not being believed." He is re-emphasizing fears and suggesting that the solution is to keep quiet. Here, Bill reiterates previous suggestions by Larry and John that the only way out is to renounce the wish to get help through talking about oneself.

> Dr. N. wondered whether the others were frightened by Bill's having talked about his problems. "Are all of us wondering whether we have to do the same thing?"

The therapist is pressing the patients to define their fears more specifically. This re-emphasis on analyzing the reactive motive is introduced when reactive fears are intense and the patients are moving toward restrictive solutions.

> Bill told about his experience in an outpatient clinic, where he had wanted to cover up everything. As he talked, his comments became more disjointed and psychotic. He talked about war experiences and his "real problem" and ended by saying, "I want to get rid of this

> woman." Dr. N. said to him, "You are going to get fed up and get away." Bill said that he was afraid he was going to hurt him (he seemed to be referring to his young son) and then went on to say, "I'll be a bum when I fight with bums."

Bill responds with an outburst of anxiety in the form of an outpouring of psychotic material. This nonstop production of psychotic material is a demonstration to the others of the dangers of the group. Bill's outburst implies a solution of flight, which the therapist makes explicit.

> Two patients, Seth and Richard (neither of whom had spoken), left the room.

Two patients adopt the ultimate solution of physically leaving the group. They are coping with the conflict by totally renouncing the disturbing motive. That their departure occurs at this particular point in the meeting suggests that anxiety has reached a high point.

> There was a brief exchange between Marvin and Bill about the latter's problem, and Dr. O. interrupted by asking Larry whether this was what he meant by only one person talking. Larry said, "Yes; others refer to their problem, but never talk about it." He then asked, "Why should we work on John and myself? You saw what happened. It seemed that everyone turned on John." (He was referring to an incident earlier in the session when Marvin had asked John about his problems and John had nervously evaded this probing.) Bill commented that, if people asked him about his war experiences, he would "freeze up" too.

The therapist interrupts Bill's psychotic productions. He thus introduces a new solution by demonstrating that he can cope with the situation when it gets out of hand. His intervention is successful: Larry cooperates, and even Bill demonstrates his capacity to recover from his psychotic outburst. One would expect anxiety to lower at this point.

> Dr. O. commented, "By God, when real feelings are involved, we won't get caught with our pants down." There was considerable laughter and nodding of heads.

The therapist communicates to the patients his awareness of the intensity of their feelings, and this leads to a reduction of anxiety. During this period, a solution seems to be building up: the therapist can be relied upon to understand us and protect us from danger.

> Marvin said that they, like ordinary people, were reluctant to ex-

pose their feelings. Bill asked John why he was afraid. John denied being afraid and said something about being jumped on. Dr. N. made a comment about the purposes of group therapy and finished by saying, "If we feel attacked, we won't talk."

Marvin suggests a new solution: "Let's accept our fears as normal." If generally accepted, this solution could reduce the intensity of the reactive motive. But Bill immediately demonstrates one of the dangers of the group by attacking John. The therapist's comment reflects both sides of the focal conflict in rather general terms.

John said, "Next week I'll work myself up again. It's too painful. If I become a blithering idiot and know it, that's no damn good."

John, by expressing his primitive fear of the consequences of continuing with the group, again intensifies anxiety.

Marvin told Bill that he has to find out why he has the feelings he has. Bill replied angrily with psychotic material: "You'll never understand me if you don't have a problem. Don't judge me. You don't go to sleep with a girl just like that. People think it only takes five minutes. I don't have a problem, and you have no right to say I'm nervous because of my prisoner-of-war experience. I just don't want to pay a price to get in a gutter like the other bums. I'm also guilty and afraid that I may have acted like a baby. Yet sex is important." He laughed. "I wouldn't be in a hospital if it weren't for this girl, but I would have had to come back sooner or later."

Again, Bill exposes himself in a psychotic manner and displays a panicky amalgam of shame and fear—fear of being judged and fear of being contaminated or degraded.

Dr. N. closed the session by saying that the patients seemed to be wondering whether, because there were no guarantees, they were willing to try to get better. "Therapy can be helpful or not helpful, but, to the extent that we try to understand others and ourselves, we may get help," he said.

In his closing comment, the therapist restates the conflict. He makes explicit the dilemma on which the group has been dwelling throughout the session, but, by his choice of words, does not do justice to the intensity of the conflict. He does not refer to any of the potential solutions which have been suggested. The session ends with an upsurge of fears—the affect is close to panic—and with no adequate means of coping with the conflict. The session can be summarized in terms of the following focal conflict:

disturbing motive		*reactive motive*
wish to be helped through revealing one's personal problems	X	fear of being attacked, harmed, and made sicker through contact with other sick patients
	(no solution)	

Successive Efforts to Deal with a Deviant Patient

This illustration is taken from the first session of an inpatient, nonpsychotic group of ten men.

> Dr. T. began by saying that the group-therapy sessions were a chance for patients to talk things over among themselves. "We might talk about things that happen on the ward, in the hospital, outside the hospital, or in the group. The group will be informal, and we will talk about anything that seems important to you."

This comment may be regarded as a precipitating event; it presses the group to develop its own content and talk about "important" matters.

> Casimir asked, "What is a problem?" and added that a problem was something that someone could not solve. He said that what was hard for one person might be easy for another. Dr. T. replied that most people would probably agree with this. Casimir suggested, "We are being observed, not helped."

In the first few moments, a number of feelings about the group are communicated: that it is necessary to discuss problems, that in so doing inadequacies will be revealed, and that the therapists will observe but not help. Thus, one immediately sees the seeds of a potential focal conflict in which a wish to talk about one's problems (which is equivalent to revealing inadequacies) is opposed by a fear of eliciting critical reactions.

> Arnold asked, "What is a friend?" He then supplied a definition: "Someone who will cut your throat." Ronald said that a friend was someone who knew you and could accept your faults. The group then talked about trust and sincerity and wondered whether one could really trust others. Arnold said that he had no friends. His standards were very high, and no one came up to them. The people in the group were not his friends.

Arnold's comments vividly emphasize reactive fears. In response, Ronald suggests a solution which shifts the equilibrium toward the possibility of expressing the disturbing motive. If the patients can agree that they are friends who can tolerate one another's faults, they will have established an enabling solution which relieves fear of criticism and permits the revelation of problems. Arnold interferes with the development of such a solution by making it clear that he cannot accept it. Arnold's stand serves to intensify the fears of being depreciated or hurt by other patients if one reveals one's problems.

> A long discussion followed. Casimir said that he wanted others to tolerate his weaknesses. Arnold said that he himself had no weaknesses. He added, "Problems are not weaknesses." When Casimir asked what his problems were, Arnold said angrily, "I am not going to sit here and tolerate you fellows. This is sickening." Arnold then continued to insist that he was looking for perfection in others. A number of patients (Casimir, Ronald, Dave, and William) argued that this was a good ideal but could never be realized in life. William said, "You can expect it in science, but not in people." Arnold continued to insist that he expected perfection in others, was always disillusioned, and that he himself was perfect. When the others questioned this, he insisted, "I don't think so, I *know* so."

Here, the group is in a state of solutional conflict. Most of the patients are ready to accept a solution: "Agree that no one is perfect and that all should tolerate one another's faults." Arnold refuses to go along with this. Instead, he insists that he is perfect and has no faults. The group tries to deal with the solutional conflict by putting pressure on Arnold to change. This effort fails. Throughout this period, the group is in a state of high tension. Arnold's reactions to successive efforts to get him to change show that he will not (or cannot) change his position.

> Arnold went around the room asking each patient whether he felt that people could be perfect. All disagreed with him except John, who seemed uncertain, and Pete, who said, "No comment." Dave told Arnold, "We are still your friends." Arnold said he hoped that what went on here would have no relation to what went on outside the group.

Arnold is seeking support for his point of view. His effort fails, and Dave attempts to cope with the heightened tension and the feelings of irritation with Arnold by insisting that friendship and unity still exist in the group.

> The discussion about perfection continued, with Ronald questioning Arnold. Ronald asked Arnold what some of the things were which annoyed him. Arnold burst out with, "Everything about *you* annoys me—the way you are sitting, the way you have your finger in your mouth." (Ronald was sitting in his chair with his legs up and under

him.) Arnold said that he felt like choking Ronald but wouldn't because of the laws of society.

The group as a whole is still caught in its original conflict and is still attempting to work on Arnold. In part, the other patients are trying to reinstitute their original solution by pressuring Arnold to change. In part, they may be trying to understand why Arnold has assumed his deviant position. The group's consistent pressure on Arnold pushes him to an angry outburst, with a consequent increase in tension.

Dave suggested that Arnold, in his talk about perfection, was "pulling the group's leg," but Arnold denied this.

Dave again tries to deal with the solutional conflict by denying the reality of Arnold's deviant position in the group. However, Arnold insists that he is serious. The group can neither get Arnold to change his position and allow the group to solve the original focal conflict, nor can it relieve the added tension generated by the solutional conflict.

Arnold said that, if only he could get rid of his bitterness and hatred, nothing would stop him. Ronald asked if Arnold would help if someone were choking him. Arnold said, "I would choke you both." There was considerable laughter during this discussion, as if it were amusing.

Ronald attempts to take the force out of Arnold's anger by getting him to admit that there are limits to his aggressive feelings. This is similar to Dave's previous effort, because it attempts to deny the reality of Arnold's anger. The group's laughter may be an expression of tension, but it may also constitute an attempt to deny the reality of Arnold's strong feelings. The focus is not on the solutional conflict, but on the tension generated by this conflict.

Someone asked Arnold if he had ever had to admit that he wasn't perfect. Arnold said, "That's it. You put your finger on it."

The focus is again on an attempt to cope with the solutional conflict. However, the tactic shifts. Rather than trying to get Arnold to change his mind, one patient makes an explicit effort to understand his position. The previous attempts to pressure Arnold, to get him to change, have failed and have elicited dangerous, angry feelings on his part. Here, we see an attempt to explain Arnold's deviant position and thus make it more palatable to the group.

Arnold turned to Pete and said, "With all this tension, some music would help." (A piano, which Pete played occasionally, stood in the corner of the room.) Arnold then asked William (an older patient who was a lawyer) if, with all his experience, he could help. William denied that he could help, although Arnold kept after him.

Arnold signals the group that he has had enough. He switches from truculence to an appeal for help, thus reducing the anxiety associated with the anger generated by the solutional conflict. Yet there has been no resolution of the conflict itself.

Dr. T. asked what would happen in the group if people were not always perfect. Arnold misunderstood this as, "What if people were perfect?" and said that nothing would surprise him.

The therapist focuses on the solutional conflict by an attempt to get Arnold to explore his fear. This comment implies a renewed pressure on Arnold to admit to imperfection. The therapist is lending his weight to the group's efforts to change Arnold's position—an error, since it is already clear that this will not succeed.

Casimir said that Arnold was looking for utopia, and John said, referring to the world situation, "If we don't find it soon. . . ." Dave, Casimir, and Ronald agreed that no one person could be important enough to significantly improve the world situation. But Arnold insisted that someone could.

Perhaps because of the support offered by the therapist, several patients renew their effort to change Arnold's position and thus solve the solutional conflict. Although the content refers to the world situation, the interaction involves the patients lining up on the issue in exactly the same way they have lined up on the here-and-now issue. Three of the patients argue that no one can be important enough to change the world situation, but Arnold insists that someone could be perfect and important enough to do so.

Jack said that the trouble with Arnold was that he wanted everyone to be a chief and no one to be an Indian. There was some joking about this. Casimir began to laugh and said, "Stop it; I've been laughing for three days and can't stop." Arnold replied good-naturedly to this.

Here one patient introduces the idea of equality—a variation on the previous group solution. Jack is suggesting that, if the group cannot get Arnold to agree that everyone is an Indian, perhaps they can get him to agree that everyone is a chief. The solution of all being alike would be maintained. At this point, the group is attempting to deal with the solutional conflict in a new way. First the patients tried to get Arnold to change. Then they tried to deny the reality of his deviant position. Then they tried to explain Arnold's behavior to themselves in a way which would make it possible for them to accept him. Now they are trying to revise the original group solution to encompass Arnold's position.

> Casimir asked if any good had come of the session. Arnold said that it had made him feel better, and, as soon as the others opened up, it would help them, too. Al asked Arnold if he would "fall apart" if he found that he was imperfect. Casimir summarized by saying that Arnold was looking for perfection, but most of the others didn't think that perfection was possible.

Casimir implies withdrawal as a solution to the dilemma with Arnold. Arnold, perhaps encouraged by the possibility of a group solution that would encompass his position, reassures Casimir of the usefulness of the group. This seems to raise the hopes of a previously silent patient: Al probes Arnold to uncover Arnold's fantasies about the consequences of admitting imperfection. Casimir quite accurately sums up the solutional conflict. Only Arnold supports Jack's solution, and the group returns to attempting to change Arnold's position.

> Arnold asked each person how he felt about the Little Rock demonstrations then going on. Ronald said that he thought they were a crime against humanity. Jack said that he thought Negro children should be allowed to go to school with whites but that "a few restrictions should be put on them. I wouldn't want to live next door to them." Ronald said that some Negroes were good people and others weren't. Phil and Pete said they had no comment.

Here the group has made an abrupt shift in topic, initiated by Arnold. Perhaps Arnold's purpose is to divert the group from their direct discussion of him, but again the off-target content can be seen as relevant to the group situation. Using Little Rock as a symbol, the patients are discussing the appropriateness of excluding or discriminating against people. The mood has improved, and there is a greater sense of unity. It is as if the patients are making some efforts toward healing the breach caused by the solutional conflict by finding a neutral area for agreement. The emphasis is on the tension generated as a result of the solutional conflict.

> Casimir asked Arnold whether he was Greek, and Arnold said that he was American born. Casimir amended this to "of Greek extraction" and then said that there was a time when the world was divided be-

tween Greeks and barbarians. At that time, people sometimes said that someone was "worthy of being Greek." Casimir told Arnold that he should respect the group's opinion. Dave agreed.

Through the symbolism of nationality and the distinction between Greeks and barbarians, Casimir is pointing out the division in the group between Arnold (the Greek) and the others (the barbarians). He is suggesting that Arnold should be willing to regard the other patients as "worthy of being Greek." The emphasis is again on attempting to modify Arnold's position so that the solutional conflict can be resolved.

Dr. T. asked why it was important to convince Arnold. Casimir said it was important for the group to have a standard. He added, "We've agreed on some things; we have agreed to disagree."

The therapist's comment is an attempt to reduce some of the pressure on Arnold and to encourage the group to find some other way out of their dilemma. Casimir makes explicit the heretofore unspoken goal of the group—to arrive at some standard which will permit unanimity.

Arnold said it was important for everyone to talk and referred to Pete and Phil as people who had been silent.

Arnold again attempts to take the spotlight off himself and his deviant position.

Ronald said, "We haven't heard what Arnold thinks about the race problem." Arnold said that the colored man was a human being. Jack said, "If one moved next door to you, you'd be the first to move out." Arnold said rather bitterly that there was nothing worse than white trash, and several people agreed. Dave asked, with a note of challenge, why Arnold had said this. Jack said that Casimir was right: Negroes must prove themselves.

The patients again try to establish unanimity as a way of coping with the tension generated by the solutional conflict. This effort fails because, when the subject shifts to racial equality, several patients other than Arnold emerge as potential disrupters of group unanimity. Arnold is quite ready to agree with the majority that Negroes are entitled to equality, but the issue has apparently elicited strong feelings in at least two other members. There is some suggestion that the effort to find equality on a distant and symbolic level will prove ineffective and perhaps create additional problems in the group. In the next interchange, the issue is dropped.

> Casimir said that maybe there was one thing all could agree on. "Here on the fifteenth floor (psychiatric ward) is where I belong. How about you, Arnold?" Arnold said, "There is nothing wrong with me." John turned to Casimir and said, "Maybe he is speaking the truth. People on this ward are more intelligent and better informed." He continued to develop his point at some length. He said, "Everyone here is introverted. There is more similarity among us than there is between us and the people outside." There was agreement that everyone in the group was a perfectionist in the sense that he was trying to get better. Dr. T. said that the time was up.

Casimir attempts conciliation and tries to get Arnold to admit to imperfections, this time by agreeing that he himself belongs on a psychiatric ward. Arnold, extremely alert to this kind of pressure, immediately resists it. Through John, the group turns to another approach: "If you can't beat 'em, join 'em." John suggests that rather than everyone's in the group being imperfect, everyone is actually superior. As the session ended, the patients agreed that they were all alike—perfectionists in the sense that they were trying to get better. The final resolution can be regarded as an ingenious way of dealing with the group's solutional conflict. The group has redefined Arnold's insistence on perfection in such a way that it can accept his stand and incorporate it into its own position. Thus Arnold does not need to continue to resist the group.

The group has finally achieved a solution which all, including the deviant member, can accept. This solution—unanimity in perfection-seeking—seems pertinent to the solutional conflict in two ways. First, it brings Arnold back into the fold. Second, it copes with the anger and frustration which have been generated by the solutional conflict. The relevance of the solution to the original focal conflict is less clear. It is conceivable, however, that "faults" could be revealed and accepted by all, including Arnold, because such revelations could be perceived as seeking after perfection. The solution seems rather fragile. Yet, at least in part, it resolved the group's dilemma, for, in the next session, Arnold no longer occupied a deviant position and the group continued its slow movement toward expressing faults.

In focal-conflict terms, this session can be summarized as follows:

disturbing motive		*reactive motive*
wish to reveal one's faults to the group	X	fear of exposing oneself to attack and criticism from other patients

solutional conflict

agree that no one is perfect and all should tolerate one another's faults (maintained by majority of group)	X	insist that "I am perfect, and all others should be perfect" (maintained by Arnold)

solution

agree that all are perfectionists in the sense that they are trying to get better

In both illustrations, the patients are acting as if they were struggling to achieve a particular goal. In the first illustration (schizophrenic group), the patients went through a series of unsuccessful attempts to alleviate the anxiety generated by being forced to interact despite fears of contamination and profound personal damage. In the second illustration (inpatient neurotic group), the patients acted as if the shared goal were, first, to achieve a solution and, second, to maintain it in the face of challenge. In neither case was the goal explicitly or publicly stated. The term "as if" is used to emphasize the fact that the goal is not directly perceived by the patients, yet functions effectively and consistently to channel the interaction.

In terms of our theory, the patients act as if their goal is to achieve a solution to the prevailing group focal conflict or to maintain such a solution once it is established, especially if it is threatened. The group's goal is to reduce anxiety while achieving the maximum possible satisfaction of some shared wish or impulse. Groups construct solutions which are, in effect, compromises between strong opposing forces (the disturbing and reactive motives). They work toward a solution which allows some expression of the disturbing motive and also copes with the fears involved in the reactive motive. The goal may concentrate primarily on relieving anxiety, or it may emphasize gratification of the disturbing motive. At other times, the goal may be to maintain a solution which is threatened by another member or the therapist. But here, too, the underlying motivation is to prevent the eruption of anxiety; thus the primary goal is the alleviation of anxiety. The group will try to achieve this in a way which will also allow some gratification of the disturbing motive. If anxiety is very high, the group may be forced to give up its attempt to gratify the disturbing motive and may concentrate solely on anxiety-reducing maneuvers.

We are using the term "goal" in a rather special sense—the end product of a process of which the termination is marked by a reduction in anxiety. Volition or conscious awareness is not implied. Perhaps the term "need" would do as well. The group acts as if its need were to reduce anxiety by achieving a solution or maintaining an established solution. Whatever the term used, there is a process the end product of which is a balance between anxiety-reduction and impulse-gratification.

Because the goal is outside the awareness of the patients, one cannot utilize conventional techniques to identify it. One cannot, for example, rely on consensus to define the group goal, since each patient can state only his personal, public goal. In the special sense in which we are defining the group goal, it can only be identified in relationship to the group focal conflict.

The goal structure of any group, including a therapy group, is complex. Goals may be public or private, recognized or unrecognized, shared or idiosyncratic. Here, we are speaking of shared, covert goals. Conscious and unconscious individual goals are discussed in Chapter 7. Shared public goals, in the sense of an imposed or an agreed-on task, are not relevant to therapy groups.

Proposition 7 | *During a focal-conflict unit, the group moves toward the shared, covert goal—alleviating anxiety by establishing a successful solution to the prevailing group focal conflict.*

Movement toward the shared, covert goal is not characterized by a systematic progression, but by continual shifts in intensity and emphasis with regard to the prevailing group focal conflict. Every remark made in a session is relevant to the disturbing motive, the reactive motive, the possible solutions, or, sometimes, to several of these. Comments which refer to solutions may emphasize the reactive side of the conflict (the fear) or the disturbing side (the wish). Shifts in emphasis occur continually—one might find several comments which refer to the reactive motive, several to a solution which favors the reactive side, then a single comment which refers to the disturbing motive, and so on.

In the first illustration—the schizophrenic group—the very first comment refers to a possible solution ("let's disband the group"); the next refers to an aspect of the reactive motive ("the doctors are the source of danger"), the next to the disturbing as well as the reactive motive ("the group is supposed to help us get well, but perhaps we are only being observed and studied"), the next to the reactive motive plus another possible solution ("one can be made sicker by listening to other sick patients—perhaps it is better to give up trying"), the next to the disturbing motive and a third possible solution ("we should talk about our problems; perhaps time will help"), and so on throughout the session.

Over-all, this group moved in the direction of increasingly more intense fears. During the first half of the session, several patients attempted to stem the fear by proposing solutions which would mitigate the reactive motive and prepare the way for some expression of the disturbing motive. These attempts did not succeed, and, in the last half of the session, fears predominated and tension increased. In the second illustration, the initial emphasis was on the disturbing motive ("we should talk about problems") and, by implication, inadequacies. This was immediately followed by an emphasis on the reactive motive ("there is something dangerous about the group—we are being observed, not helped"), then by an even stronger emphasis on the reactive motive ("we will get our throats cut"), and then by an attempted solution ("we should get to know one another and accept one another's faults"). The group proceeded in this fashion until it became very clear that one patient had assumed a deviant position. At this point, the patients were confronted with a solutional conflict.

Following this, there were successive attempts to deal with the split which had developed in the group. At first, the patients tried, on logical grounds, to argue Arnold out of his position, but he would not give in. Arnold then tried to get support for his stand but failed. The patients then tried to "understand" Arnold in an apparent effort to make his position more palatable, but Arnold frightened them by becoming angry. The others tried to pretend that Arnold was only joking, then tried to explain his position to themselves by understanding him better. Next, they tried to escape the whole issue by distracting themselves, and so on. In general, the pattern consisted of various attempts to deal with the solutional conflict, interspersed with indications that the conflict had not been resolved and that the attempts were leading to even greater problems. Finally, a solution was achieved.

Taken as a whole, this session involved the rather rapid development of a focal conflict and the rapid development of a solution which would have adequately dealt with the conflict. When this solution was blocked by the inability of one patient to accept it, the patients turned their attention to this split and devoted their time and energy to finding some way of dealing with it.

The characteristic detailed movement which occurs in a session can be summarized as follows:

Proposition 8

At any given moment, the group situation can be described in terms of an equilibrium in which the disturbing and reactive motives and the solution exist in dynamic relation. Movement in the group consists of successive shifts in equilibrium.

This characteristic shifting is a consequence of the manner in which individuals react to the relative intensity of the disturbing and reactive motives at any given moment. Each patient experiences the focal conflict differently and so participates differently. Although we assume that all patients share in experiencing the focal conflict, the wish may be of greater importance for some; others may experience the fear more intensely. As the group moves in one direction, anxieties may be aroused in a particular patient, impelling him to counteract this move. For example, there may have been a number of comments which suggest that the wish is in the ascendancy and that the group may be ready to put the wish into action. This may intensify anxiety in a particular patient and lead him to reintroduce the reactive motive. This, in turn, may elicit a tentative solution directed to allaying the fear involved in the reactive motive. With the reactive motive reduced in intensity, another patient may feel free to re-emphasize the disturbing motive. Perhaps a solution will then emerge which emphasizes the disturbing motive and implies that it may find expression. As this pattern of action and reaction unfolds, the patients' anxieties are continually elicited and allayed. New and subtle aspects of the reactive motive are elicited, and gradually solutions which "cover" all aspects of the disturbing and the reactive motive emerge and find support. Sometimes a patient will be silent, permitting the group to move toward some solution. This occurs when the group focal conflict or particular aspects of it are not relevant to the individual's concerns. He can permit the group to develop without interfering only as long as he is not personally threatened. (See Chapter 7 for a more extended discussion of the motivation underlying behavior in the group.)

Thus, in the last analysis, the characteristic movement of a group and the ways in which a specific group moves can be understood only in terms of the varied manner in which the group concerns touch each person in the group. If individual differences did not exist, the group would quickly establish a common solution without the back-and-forth movement characteristic of both illustrations. (Implications of this point for decisions about the group composition are discussed in Chapter 11.) This view of the factors underlying successive shifts in equilibrium is summarized in the following proposition:

Proposition 9	*Movement of the group occurs as a function of individual differences in the position which each member takes with reference to the immediate relation among the disturbing motive, the reactive motive, and the solution.*

It can be assumed that all the members of the group—patients as well as therapists—continually experience internal reactions to the prevailing group forces. Only some of these reactions are expressed through comments or observable non-verbal behavior. For example, in the first illustration, Larry made the first comment, though others were undoubtedly experiencing a variety of reactions to the initial silence. When Larry suggested disbanding the group and added that there were three doctors against five patients, he influenced the group focal conflict by introducing a new stimulus. Rather than being confronted with silence, the patients were confronted with a statement which portrayed the therapists as sources of potential danger, attack, or persecution. It was Bill, a paranoid patient, who responded to the new stimulus. He revealed his feelings of suspicion about the group and, in so doing, shifted the equilibrium toward a still greater emphasis on reactive fears. John was then stimulated to introduce his fears and worries about the group. This pattern (eliciting situation, response, new eliciting situation, further response) continued throughout the session.

Again, in the second illustration, there was a sequence in which Ronald asked Arnold what annoyed him. This comment attempted to deal with the group solutional conflict by pressuring Arnold into admitting that he had faults and into yielding his former position. This situation elicited a strong angry reaction from Arnold. Arnold's behavior, in turn, altered the group equilibrium by emphasizing the dangers associated with the solutional conflict—dangers having to do with the management of angry feelings. In response to confrontation with such angry feelings, Dave attempted to depreciate these dangers by suggesting that Arnold was "only kidding."

This relationship between group situation and successive behaviors can be stated as follows:

Proposition 10

The immediate equilibrium constitutes a stimulus situation which elicits overt behavior from a member of the group. This behavior, in turn, has an impact on the balance of forces within the group focal conflict, changing the equilibrium. As a result, the group situation constitutes a different stimulus for the next act.

Like the patients, the therapist reacts internally to successive shifts in the equilibrium. Like them, he is sometimes stimulated to make a public comment, thus altering the balance of forces in the group. The manner in which the therapist intervenes and the points at which he intervenes are of great importance in influencing the course of the group and the character of the therapeutic milieu.

4

Group Themes

In therapy groups, the patients often struggle with a particular issue through a number of successive sessions. Such an issue may center around sexual feelings about one another, angry impulses directed toward the therapist, wishes to form a dependent relationship with the therapist, or competition and revenge. Sometimes a theme appears in one session and is dropped in the next. More often, a single theme persists for two, three, or more sessions, although it may appear in various forms during the sequence. A theme which is dropped is very likely to later reappear and preoccupy the patients for several more sessions.

In focal-conflict terms, a theme is defined as a series of focal conflicts in which the disturbing motives are closely related. For example, a series of focal conflicts all might include disturbing motives which involve a wish for an exclusive relationship with the therapist. A shift in theme occurs when a new disturbing motive becomes dominant in the group. The new disturbing motive might involve a shift in the person or persons to whom the feeling is directed or a shift in the feeling itself.

We have defined group themes in terms of the disturbing motive because we have found that the disturbing motive is the most stable aspect of the group situation, changing less quickly than the reactive motive or the solution and recurring in essentially the same form throughout the life of the group. The disturbing motives which emerge during group therapy refer to basic, persistent wishes and impulses. Reactive motives, on the other hand, are more susceptible to change. Although some reactive fears recur, others are dealt with during the early part of the group's life and seemingly are resolved, for they do not reappear. For these reasons, we have chosen to define the group theme as follows:

Proposition 11 | *A series of focal conflicts linked by similar disturbing motives constitutes a group theme.*

The focal conflicts which constitute a single group theme may differ from one another in reactive motive and/or solution. From the illustrations and discussions in Chapter 3, it is apparent that variations occur in a single focal conflict, and, of course, variations can also be expected to occur in a theme. In order to understand the manner in which a theme develops, progresses, and terminates and how shifts in theme occur, it is necessary to examine a series of group sessions. We have selected two illustrations—one is drawn from the beginnings of an inpatient group in which the prevailing theme was the impulse to reveal negative aspects, especially hostile feelings, of oneself; the other is drawn from the thirtieth week of sessions of an outpatient adolescent group in which the prevailing theme involved sexual feelings about the therapists.

The Wish to Express Hostile Impulses

The first session of this all-male inpatient group has already been described in Chapter 3. During the first session, a focal conflict developed which involved, on the one hand, a wish to get help by revealing one's faults and, on the other hand, a fear of exposing oneself to the criticism of others. Early in the session, the patients began to encourage one another to endorse the solution "agree that no one is perfect and all should tolerate one another's faults." This solution could not be established because one patient, Arnold, was unable or unwilling to go along with it. The rest of the session was devoted to attempts to get Arnold to change his mind, to pretend that his protests were not serious, and so forth. Finally the patients agreed that all of them, including Arnold, were perfectionists in the sense that they wanted to get better. The session was summarized as follows:

disturbing motive		*reactive motive*
wish to reveal one's faults to the group	X	fear of exposing oneself to criticism from other patients

solutional conflict

agree that no one is perfect and all should tolerate one another's faults (maintained by majority of group)	X	insist that "I am perfect and all others should be perfect" (maintained by Arnold)

solution

agree that all are perfectionists in the sense that they are trying to get better

In this session, the disturbing motive can be conceptualized only in general terms. In the group, there is some pressure to reveal "faults," but there is no indication of what these faults might be. The reactive motive appears more explicitly: the patients are afraid of criticism from one another. In order to understand the group at the close of the session, it is necessary to consider the relevance of the final solution to the solutional conflict as well as to the original focal conflict. It is difficult to evaluate the potential effectiveness of the final solution to the solutional conflict. Arnold permitted this solution to be established, which suggests that he was willing to accept it. On the other hand, the solution emerged at the very end of the session, and there was little time to test it or to be sure of Arnold's reactions. As a means of coping with the original focal conflict, the modified solution seems less successful than the original solution. At the close of the session, then, the patients are left in an equivocal position with reference to the original focal conflict; with reference to the solutional conflict, there is insufficient evidence to know whether the solution will prove adequate to deal with the deviant patient.

In the second session, Casimir began with a story about a man who had been misunderstood when he used the word "intimate." When Dr. T. asked whether such a thing could happen in the group, Casimir said that it could, and William added that the previous session's discussion about perfection was a good example. Casimir commented, "We sometimes let emotion rule our lives." Ronald and Al, in a long discussion, agreed that lack of understanding was inevitable because it was hard to communicate.

After a pause, Casimir asked, "How many here think it's smart to wisecrack smutty in front of the nurses?" He added that patients should treat nurses like honest working girls—"It's not smart to embarrass them." The others agreed with him in principle, but argued that "kidding around" was inevitable and didn't hurt the nurses. Casimir asked Arnold for his opinion, and Arnold said that he didn't think such talk hurt the nurses because they had heard it all before. Casimir continued to insist, "We are taking advantage of the nurses."

Al suggested, "Maybe we have been wanting to say bad things for a long time." Ronald reminded the others that this was a new experience, "In the process of adjusting, much strange behavior comes out. Furthermore, they've got a lot of talent here."

Ronald said that it was easy to misunderstand people and told about a violent patient whose aggressiveness was phony—he had never really hurt anyone. He added that profanity and so forth might be necessary. Casimir said that, when he ran a saloon, he threw out people who didn't behave properly, but Al said that Casimir couldn't do that here. An argument developed about whether people who went to saloons were low-class or whether their behavior could be understood as a sickness.

In a long discussion, the patients agreed that any overindulgence was wrong—drinking, cursing a lady, overeating, or even spending too much money. They concluded that moderation was the answer. Jack asked, "Who determines excess?" and then answered his own question by saying that everyone has to decide for himself. An argument developed about whether a person who indulges in excesses can control his behavior by will power. Casimir thought that he could, but the others disagreed. Dr. T. asked why most people did not want to accept the will-power theory, and Ronald said, "A place like this kicks the theory."

Ronald said that the business of understanding was very hard. Al said, "We need to see ourselves through other people's eyes." He told why he was in the hospital and finished by saying, "I am going to go out of here still hating my mother-in-law." He said that the main thing to watch out for was a dramatic change. Casimir said that he felt ashamed of himself for having problems—after all, it was not as if there were something physically wrong. Ronald argued, and several agreed, that the handicaps of people in the group might not be visible, but were very real.

In this session, Arnold no longer occupies a deviant position; he no longer actively interferes with the group. This suggests that the modified solution established at the close of the preceding session was accepted by Arnold and was successful in coping with the solutional conflict. The initial material of this session indicates that the focal conflict which developed so quickly during the first session is still an issue in the group. Though the language is different, the issue is much the same. In the first session, it was "anyone who reveals faults will be criticized by others"; in the second session, it is "anyone who tries to communicate runs the risk of being misunderstood." But, as the session proceeds, it becomes clear that the focal conflict has shifted. The disturbing motive still involves a wish to reveal one's faults, but "faults" are now defined as overindulgence. The nature of this overindulgence differs for each patient (hostile-sexual, oral, acquisitive). The reactive motive has changed more markedly and now appears to focus on the therapists rather than on the patients. If it is assumed that the comments about nurses are an indirect way of referring to the two female therapists, then a concern is being expressed about the possibility of harming the therapists by expressing bad impulses. A reactive fear which does not seem to develop as a shared concern is the fear of being ejected from the group if bad impulses are revealed. The change in the reactive motive indicates that the patients have been able to set aside their fears of being criticized by one another. This suggests that the solution which was established at the close of the first session functioned not only to deal with the deviant patient, but also to allay the fears involved in the original reactive motive. The patients move through a series of solutions. One of these—an agreement to express impulses only in moderation—seems to permit freer expression of the disturbing motive. It is at this point that Al is able to reveal personal material. This is the first time anything personal has been revealed in the group; what was feared has been accomplished, at least by one patient. In response to the indication that the disturbing motive can be expressed, Casimir expresses his fear of shame. He thus presents himself as a potential deviant for whom the established solutions are not functional. The other patients forestall a solutional conflict with Casimir as the deviant by agreeing to treat psychological handicaps in a serious manner. For the session as a whole, the group focal conflict can be summarized as follows:

disturbing motive		*reactive motive*
wish to express "bad" impulses freely	X	fear of harming the therapists

solutions

agree that the therapists can take it

make strange behavior a part of the group's expectations

define "bad" impulses as phony feelings that are harmless

agree to express impulses in moderation

This session differs from the preceding one in that (1) the disturbing motive is expressed in more specific terms; (2) the character of the reactive motive has changed—rather than fearing criticism from one another, the patients fear that their impulses may harm the therapists; (3) the activity during this session concentrates on solution-seeking, and the patients appear to be successful in developing solutions which allow a more direct expression of the disturbing motive. In contrast, the preceding session focused on the reactive motive and the necessity of dealing with a deviant member. By the close of the second session, the group had developed several solutions which reduced their fears and made it possible for them to express the disturbing motive more freely. The anxiety level is relatively low. The balance within the focal conflict favors expression of the disturbing impulse. The patients seem less dominated by their fears, and one of them has demonstrated that he is ready to talk about himself.

In the third session, reactive fears emerged in a primitive, overwhelming form.

> As the patients entered the room, they placed their chairs in a row against the wall, saying jokingly that this was a "line-up" and commenting about their "uniforms" (all were wearing hospital greens). Arnold commented scathingly about Pete's late arrival. Dr. T. commented, "You are scolding Pete the way you expect us to scold you."
>
> John told a joke about a sailor who had been alone on a desert island for three years. A girl who was washed ashore told him, "I am going to give you something you've missed for three years—some beer." The others laughed at his joke, but John turned to Dr. T. and said, "Why don't you say something? Otherwise, there's no control." He added that he didn't know what the group hoped to accomplish and wondered what was behind it. Dr. T. restated the purpose of the group. Miss O. (co-therapist) asked what they thought might be behind the group. Phil said that he would like to get something out of it, but, he added, "We just come here and argue, and everyone goes away teed off."
>
> Casimir suggested that the purpose of the group was to see ourselves as others see us. Al criticized the sessions by saying that they were just confusing battles of words. William added that it was difficult to articulate one's thoughts. Miss O. asked whether the patients felt that they were in a line-up because they were stupid. John said, "I'm guilty. I feel that this is a police line-up." Several patients asked what he was guilty of, but he did not respond. Al complained that the group was on too high a level—"We should use plain words."
>
> After a silence, John asked Miss O., "Do you differentiate between good and bad psychology? Or maybe you don't judge at all?" Miss O. replied that it was not so much a question of good or bad as it was of understanding. She added that the patients seemed to feel that what they do would be judged and asked, "Is this why it's hard to get started?"
>
> After another long and painful silence, John said that he was not

sure that therapy was doing him any good. Ronald urged patience. William suggested that the group discuss the theory of group therapy, but Dr. T. said the best idea would be to discuss the ideas that the patients had about therapy. Ronald said, "All of us have been subjected to therapy." He gave an example of a boy who had been mean to his sister and who, as a consequence, was shunned by others so that he finally "had to change."

Dave said that the bull sessions around the ward were more helpful than group therapy because everyone was relaxed. "We are not watched," he said. Dr. T. said that, apparently, the presence of staff members made the patients feel uncomfortable. Ronald said that, although he realized no one was here to judge him, it was still hard to express himself.

After a pause, Dave said that even a schoolroom was not this quiet, but Ronald added, "Except when a new teacher walks in." When Dr. T. asked why this occurred, Ronald said, "To make a good impression." Dave said, "You don't know what to expect, so you watch the teacher for a while." Ronald said that each teacher had her own set of rules and that the best way to find out what it was was to keep quiet and "wait till someone falls prey to the teacher." Dr. T. asked, "Are we waiting for a victim here?" Dave said that everyone was pretty self-conscious, and John commented, "No one is going to make us go to the gas chamber." Dr. T. wondered why it had been easier to talk during the first session than it was now, and several patients suggested that it was because the patients knew one another better now.

At this point, John walked out of the room. After a pause, Al commented that, although he was sweating, he wasn't going to run. Dr. T. said that it was hard to believe that it was really all right to talk about what one wanted to in this group. Al said that he felt very tense and was afraid to "stick his foot into something." Dr. T. said that everyone was afraid to "push the panic button." Ronald asked, "What better place to have a panic?" and added that, with a few shots or pills, one would be all right again.

Ronald asked what was being written down (referring to a nonparticipant staff member who sat outside the circle and took notes). Dr. T. answered factually; a long argument ensued about whether the patients minded and whether the notes were likely to be used against them. When the therapist said that time was up, Arnold said that this was the time that everyone had been waiting for.

The beginning of this session differs dramatically from the close of the preceding one. From a state in which fears were allayed and personal material could be revealed, the group has shifted to a state in which fears are intense.[1] Furthermore, the character of the reactive fears has again changed. Fears of harming the therapists have shifted to fears of being punished. These feelings were initially expressed by non-verbal behavior—the line-up. Apparently, the hints about the character of faults and bad impulses displayed in the second session and one patient's direct disclosure of problems have heightened anxiety. It is as if the patients felt that they had gone too far. The second session ended with the balance of forces in the focal conflict favoring the expression of the disturbing motive; now there is a dramatic swing toward the other direction—domination by associated reactive fears.

At the beginning of the session, the therapist commented on the patients' expectations of punishment, but was not punitive and so may have countered the patients' expectations. In the next contribution—John's joke—the previous disturbing motive reappears. Quite literally and concretely, John puts the disturbing motive into action: he "talks smutty in front of the nurses." His joke also carries the implication of an attack on the therapists for not providing what is needed. When the therapists do not react to his joke, John's anxiety is immediately aroused, and he turns to Dr. T. with the challenge: "Why don't you say something? Otherwise there is no control." John apparently feels that he has gone too far in expressing the disturbing motive and is seeking reassurance and control. At this point, the therapist fails John and the group. Failing to understand the implications of John's having told the joke and perhaps disconcerted by the directness of John's challenge, the therapist falls back on a sterile restatement of the group's purposes. Very probably, this comment indicates to the patients that the therapist is not only unable to provide control, but can also be harmed (e.g., disconcerted) by the patients' impulses. It is as if their worst fears are being confirmed. The rest of the session consists of reiterations of the shared fear of eliciting punishment from the therapists. The interaction is marked by intense anxiety, long and painful silences, and a depressed feeling about the group's potential for giving help. There are repeated indications that the patients felt like prisoners who deserved punishment: the use of such stark terms as "line-up" and "gas chamber," the comment about being "subjected" to therapy, and the shared image of the teacher who is likely to pounce on the pupil who violates her unknown rules. During the remainder of the session, the therapists try to get the patients to explore their reactive fears, but, clearly, the patients are so caught up in their fears that they can only experience them, not investigate them. A few comments attempt to reassure the patients that their fears are not justified, but these verbal reassurances have no apparent effect. The session is dominated by a reactive motive—massive, primitive fears of retaliation and punishment from the therapists. Although a number of solutions are introduced by various patients, none gains general acceptance, and the intense anxiety is relieved only by the end of the session—as Arnold says, "the time everyone has been waiting for." The session was summarized as follows:

disturbing motive		*reactive motive*
none apparent[2]	X	fear of punishment from therapists; guilt

unsuccessful solutions

ask for reassurance that the therapists will not make judgments

discuss group therapy in intellectual terms

get one person to provoke the therapists' wrath

accept punishment as deserved (John)

try to reassure oneself that the therapists will be helpful, not punitive (Ronald)

This session differs from the preceding one in that (1) it is dominated by the expression of reactive fears, (2) the reactive motive has shifted to fear of punishment from the therapists, and (3) the anxiety level is far higher than at any previous point in the group's history. At the close of the session, the reactive fears have reached a nearly intolerable level of intensity, and there is no solution in sight. At the beginning of the fourth session, however, the situation is much changed, and the reactive fears are markedly diminished.

> All the patients were present, including John, who had fled from the group during the previous session. Arnold asked about the World Series. (A game was scheduled during the time for the group's next session.) Dr. T. said that, if a game was played, the group would not meet. Arnold teased Pete, saying he was glad to see that he was on time. When the staff note-taker came in, someone said, "Here's the court reporter." Arnold announced, "The meeting has come to order," and someone said that the minutes should be read. Pete made an announcement about a Yom Kippur service.
>
> There was a long discussion about smoking. The patients speculated about why people smoke and pointed out that doctors disagree about its harmfulness. Arnold said that he neither smoked nor drank, and Casimir argued that moderate drinking was all right. In a further discussion about whether it was bad to smoke, Casimir said, "Why don't

we ask the doctors?" but Arnold said, "We don't want to embarrass them; one smokes, and the other doesn't."

Casimir suggested that Arnold felt hostile toward him because he saw some of his own bad traits in him (Casimir). Dr. T. asked whether this could be one reason why people get angry at one another. Arnold agreed, saying that he didn't like the way Casimir refused to back down from his opinions. Dr. T. suggested that Arnold had shown this trait the first day, during the discussion about perfection, and Miss O. commented that Casimir had shown this trait during the discussion about drinking. Arnold and Casimir agreed, and then began to argue about which of them had a closed mind. Dr. T. commented that sometimes it was hard to have an open mind and that Arnold's stand against smoking and drinking must be important to him for some reason.

The discussion returned to smoking, with Arnold arguing that it was a sign of weakness for doctors to smoke. Miss O. commented that some people thought it was all right to be weak. Arnold said, "All of us have our weaknesses," and there was a discussion about how the patients would feel if they knew other people's weaknesses and if other people knew theirs. Arnold said that he felt good when he knew about the weaknesses of others, but bad if people found out about his. Then he insisted that he was in a class of his own, superior to others. Dr. T. said, "You are telling us that it is important to you to believe that you are strong and in a class by yourself." Dave, Casimir, and Al questioned him rather sympathetically about this, and Arnold told a long story about his father, saying that he hadn't been able to make any mistakes as a child because his father used to beat him. Dave suggested to Arnold that deep-down he knew he had weaknesses, and Arnold agreed. But when Casimir pushed the point by saying, "You admit it yourself," Arnold said, "No." Dr. T. said, "He is telling us, 'Don't pin me down too much,' " and Arnold agreed. Arnold said that he had no friends, and several others argued with him. Dr. T. said to Arnold, "It'll be a great day when you admit to yourself that people are important to you and you're important to them." Arnold agreed.

The patients discussed a violent patient (not in the group) who had improved after shock treatment. Arnold said, "Because of his example, I trust the doctors." He added, "Up to now, I've been afraid to talk in the group about my problems."

Casimir, Al, and Arnold shared experiences about fathers. Casimir said that his father had beaten him, but that it hadn't bothered him; Al said that his parents had used psychological warfare. Casimir said that he had "told his father off" when he was eighteen, but Arnold said he had never been able to do that. In a discussion about relationships with their own children, Arnold said that he was a stern father, but his children were not afraid of him. A discussion followed as to whether people outgrow their childhood feelings about their parents. Casimir argued that one has to "will" oneself to forget. There was general acceptance of angry feelings toward fathers by all except Casimir, who said angrily, "Maybe your parents didn't know any better. Would you hold a grudge against a blind man?" Both angry feelings and hope for a good relationship were expressed by Arnold, who said,

"My feelings toward my parents are bad—I hope that the time will come when they come to visit me and we can sit down and have coffee and feel good. That coffee will taste like honey." The meeting ended at this point.

Again, a dramatic change has occurred in the group. The close of the preceding session found the patients gripped by fears and without a solution which could cope with them. Yet, at the beginning of this session, there is no apparent sign of intense anxiety. Even John, who experienced the fears most intensely, has returned to the group. It seems reasonable to suppose that something has occurred in the interval between sessions to account for this change. If we assume that each patient shared in the focal conflict which dominated the third session, then each patient was faced with a similar dilemma between the third and fourth sessions. To return to the group under the same conditions which prevailed at the close of the third session would mean re-exposing oneself to intense, almost unbearable anxiety. However, to fail to return meant not only exposing oneself to the censure of the therapist and the other ward personnel, but also giving up the wish to get help from the group. At this juncture, the patients chose to return to the group and run the risk of anxiety. In the opening moments of the session, the patients ask about the World Series, and the therapist tells them that, if a game is scheduled, the group will not meet. By this interchange, a new solution is introduced into the group. In this almost casual and highly symbolic way, the patients test whether their own needs and preferences are likely to be respected by the therapists and whether they will be forced to say in the group under any circumstances. The therapist's response reassures them on both these points and provides a potential mechanism for escape. It is as if the therapist is reassuring the patients that the group can be disbanded if the need to do so becomes sufficiently great. The humor which follows is a sign of the patients' relief. At the same time, their attempt to turn the session into a meeting with rules of order indicates that their need for control is still considerable.

The solution established at the very beginning of the session ("get reassurance from therapists that the group sessions can be canceled in response to the patients' needs") allays reactive fears so that the patients are able to explore their recurring dilemma—the consequences of expressing angry impulses. By the close of the session, a new and successful solution ("the therapists can be counted on to protect rather than harm the patients") which allows for a much freer exploration of both the wishes and fears in the focal conflict has been established.

The therapists' behavior is a crucial factor in this process. There are several indications early in the session that the patients still fear that the frank expression of their feelings may harm the therapists. For example, when Casimir suggests asking the therapists for their opinions about smoking, Arnold says, "We don't want to embarrass them; one smokes, and the other doesn't." A little later, Arnold attacks Miss O., the therapist who smokes, by saying that smoking is a sign of weakness. Miss O. replies that some people think it is all right to be weak, thus indicating to Arnold and the others that his attack has not harmed her and that she can accept weakness in herself and, by implication, in others. A later exchange involving the other therapist demonstrates that the therapists can and will protect the patients. This occurs when Arnold clearly, but not quite directly, admits that he, too, has weaknesses and one of the other patients tries to push him into making a more explicit statement ("you admit it yourself"). When Arnold refuses, he is, in effect, threatening to resume the deviant position he held during the first session and, at the same time, indicating that he feels threatened by this direct pressure. At this point, Dr. T. makes a comment which interprets Arnold's behavior to the group: "He is telling us 'Don't pin me down too much.' " This comment shields Arnold, but, more importantly, it probably demonstrates to the group that the therapist's strength will be used to help rather than to punish the patients. The therapist's comment also prevents Arnold from resuming his deviant position and protects the group from that threat. Thus, as the session progresses, evidence accumulates that, if necessary, the therapists can be counted on to protect both the individual and the group and that the therapists will neither retaliate nor fall apart if attacked. In effect, the therapists are responding to John's appeal in the previous session: "Why don't you say something? Otherwise there's no control." The therapists have collaborated with the patients in establishing a solution in which protection and control will be forthcoming when needed.

While this solution is being consolidated, the patients demonstrate a growing capacity to explore the disturbing and reactive motives in direct terms: angry, destructive feelings toward parents, fearful feelings, and the hope for a good relationship with parents are expressed and shared. The session was summarized as follows:

disturbing motive		*reactive motive*
wish to express "bad" (hostile) feelings	X	fear of punishment from therapists

solutions

get reassurance from therapists

that the group sessions can be canceled in response to the patients' needs

introduce structure into the group sessions (attempt unsuccessful)

get reassurance that the therapists can be counted upon to protect rather than harm the patients

This session differs from the preceding one in that (1) the focus is on solution-building and the exploration of reactive fears, rather than on the contagious expression of the reactive fears which characterized the previous session, (2) a solution which allows the exploration of the disturbing and reactive motives in far more direct terms than before is established.

After this meeting, the therapists felt that the group had successfully passed through a crisis. We might conjecture that this crisis was the threatened disintegration of the group. The crisis was resolved through a solution which alleviated fears and allowed the patients to explore, rather than merely express or be swayed by, their angry impulses toward the therapists and parental figures.

This session marked the end of a four-session sequence in which the patients were preoccupied with the potentially damaging consequences of revealing supposedly unacceptable aspects of themselves, especially those having to do with angry, destructive feelings. The fifth session had a transitional character: the anxiety level was somewhat higher, and the session had a chaotic, unfocused quality which made it difficult to identify the disturbing motive. The situation became clearer in the sixth session, when it appeared that the patients were preoccupied with the wish to be cared for by parent figures. The focal conflict which emerged during this session was summarized as "the wish to have all needs satisfied by the therapists" versus "the fear of loss of control over angry reactions to deprivation." This is a new theme, since the disturbing motive now involves the wish for dependency-gratification, rather than the impulse to reveal unacceptable aspects of oneself.

Sexual Feelings about the Therapist

This illustration includes the fifty-ninth through sixty-third sessions of an outpatient adolescent group. In contrast to the group described in the first illustration, this group already had a long history. Worries about criticism from one another, which plagued the group just described, had long since been disposed of. Solutions had gradually been established which permitted relatively spontaneous expression of a variety of feelings. For example, the patients could express feelings about parents with relative ease. Particularly important for this sequence of sessions was a previous solution involving object-displacement. When affect toward the therapists became anxiety-provoking, the patients could explore an analogous affect toward parents and vice versa. They could also retreat in time; when the present affect here and now became distressing, they could explore related affect in past relationships. In other words, the group operated on a solution which allowed them to retreat judiciously at times from the here-and-now to the there-and-then. This solution kept anxiety within tolerable bounds and enabled the patients to explore important relationships between past and present, intra- and extra-group events.

At the time of the fifty-ninth session, the group consisted of two boys and two girls, eighteen to nineteen years of age, plus two therapists, one male and one female.[8] During most of this sequence, one of the boys was absent.

> Session fifty-nine opened with Arlene's expressing surprise that Bob had been friendly when she saw him on the street the day before, since they had had a fight during the previous group session. Bob said that he had just felt like talking to her. A long silence followed, broken only by a few brief remarks about exams. Dr. T. commented, "This sounds like 'don't-rock-the-boat' day." Arlene asked Bob whether he felt guilty about his attacks on her during the last session, and he said he did not, because he didn't care whether he hurt her feelings. After another silence, Dr. K. said that he felt that people were pulling back, although they felt uncomfortable about doing so. Bob said that, when he was younger, he feared that people would kill him if they found out that he thought he was better than they. Dr. T. reminded the group that, during the preceding session, they had discussed the issue of being successful—how it is sometimes frightening to be successful or to be better than others if it makes one the object of attack.
>
> Bob told about some experiences in which he had felt frightened because of anticipated success. Marian interrupted by saying that she was still uncertain about why she was holding back. Bob talked about his attacks on Arlene during the previous session, and Arlene said that his accusations that she was jealous of Marian had made her feel awkward with Marian. Dr. T. remarked that there had been strong emotions and hurt feelings in the preceding session. Bob said that his feelings hadn't been hurt; he had been shocked at his own behavior and yet wanted to see how much he could get away with. Arlene said that she had been hurt and made to feel guilty.
>
> Arlene and Marian discussed their common reluctance to smoke at home. Arlene explained this by saying that she did not want to act grown-up at home. Dr. K. said that it sounded as if it would also be

hard for Arlene and Marian to act grown-up in the group. Arlene agreed, saying that she always felt childish in the group. Marian said that everyone in her family was mixed up about his role. Dr. T. said that there seemed to be some fear that acting grown-up would incur adults' disapproval.

A discussion about parents followed. Bob said that his father was jealous of him. The patients compared notes on the social adequacy of their parents, and all agreed that one or both of their parents were socially inadequate in some ways. Bob said that he wanted to pick a fight with the doctors and asked them to criticize him. Dr. T. said, "It sounds as if you want *us* to pick a fight with *you*." She added that people had been pointing out differences between parents and had commented earlier that the therapists were of different religions. "I'm sure people have noticed other differences too," she said. Bob commented that Dr. T. looked older than Dr. K., and Marian told him he was being cruel. Dr. T. wondered whether pointing out a difference was necessarily cruel. Bob said that, if Dr. K. were younger, the relationship between the therapists would be mother–son, which didn't seem right. He added that he felt jealous of the private relationship between the therapists. Marian said she didn't go along with Bob in seeing the therapy group as a family. The session ended at this point.

This session opens on a note of evasion, as if the patients are unwilling to participate. As it continues, the focus shifts to feelings about parents and/or therapists. The patients express desires to be successful by being adult and "in on things" with parents and/or therapists. In the discussion about parents, there is some hint that the patients feel themselves to be, or wish to be, more successful socially than their parents. Against this, there are fears that parents and/or therapists will disapprove. Bob tries to ensure disapproval by inviting the therapists to attack him. Later, in the discussion about the ages of the therapists, the patients try to determine whether curiosity and direct comments about the therapists will provoke punishment. When the therapists demonstrate that they will not respond with attack or criticism, Bob goes farther in his expressions about the therapists, while Marian indicates the need to retreat. The session was summarized as follows:

disturbing motive		*reactive motive*
wish to be successful as adults, peers with parents and/or therapists	X	fear of retaliation

solution

gain assurance that the therapists will not be punitive

Neither the disturbing nor the reactive motive can be clearly specified, they appear to have different meanings for different patients. But, in general, this session shows the transition from one theme to another. The patients move from a disturbing motive involving angry feelings about one another to a disturbing motive which focuses on feelings about the therapists. They move into this new theme somewhat cautiously, operating on a previous solution which allows them to move back and forth between feelings expressed toward their parents and equivalent feelings expressed toward the therapists. Bob's challenging behavior toward the end of the session leads the therapists to confirm their non-punitive stance. Here, a solution which has been important in the past is resolicited and reaffirmed. At the close of the session, anxiety is relatively low, and solutions which allow some exploration of the disturbing motive are in effect.

The sixtieth session opened with Bob's remarking that he had seen Dr. K. outside the group and Dr. K. had ignored him. He had thought it funny to see Dr. K. "walking around in a fog with too much on his mind." When Dr. K. said that Bob seemed to be making excuses for him, Bob said that he should have been angry but wasn't. Bob went on to say that Dr. T. was a Christian and, until lately, he had had no Christian friends. Lately he had been dreaming about conflicts between Christians and Jews (Dr. K. was Jewish). In one dream, Christians and Jews were worshiping together, and the Jews started pushing the Christians out because they had something private to talk about. Arlene said that she, too, had seen Dr. K. on the street and that he had ignored her. She had thought that he was justified because she had been acting silly with some girl friends. Dr. K. said that he hadn't seen Arlene and then commented that both Bob and Arlene seemed to be making excuses for him.

Dr. T. suggested that Arlene may have felt rejected, and she agreed, but Marian said that she would have felt embarrassed. She said that she thought of Dr. K. as a father and a boy friend and that it bothered her that she could think of her own father as a boy friend too. A general discussion followed in which all three patients compared their early childhood experiences with their parents. Bob said that he wished his father had been more affectionate. Arlene and Marian discussed common experiences of having gotten into bed with their parents.

Marian interrupted this discussion to ask Dr. T. why she was looking at Dr. K. and went on to say that she thought it indicated some sign of approval or sharing of feeling. Dr. T. commented about the possible relation of this feeling to feelings about parents, and Bob expressed yearning for his childhood. Dr. T. said that it seemed easier to think of warm relationships with parents during childhood than currently. Marian said that she thought that her changed relationship with her parents was related to her maturing sexually. Her mother embarrassed her around her boy friends. The patients discussed feelings about boy friends' or girl friends' reactions to family members with "typical Jewish traits." Bob said everyone liked his girl friend except his mother, and Marian said that her parents were oversolicitous about her boy friends.

Bob mentioned a roommate of his who had left group therapy, and Marian asked in surprise whether there were other groups. Bob asked Dr. K. whether he had another "flock of children," and Dr. K. said that he did have another group. There was some joking to the effect that the patients no longer felt special. This led to a discussion of feelings about not having the total attention of parents. Marian said that she felt resentful of the attention her parents gave to one another. Bob said that he wished he were the only child, yet feared the responsibility of having to support his mother some day.

The beginning of this session is marked by an expression of reactive fears. An external event—the fact that two patients have seen Dr. K. outside and he failed to notice them—becomes the vehicle for the expression of fears. Arlene makes explicit the assumption that punishment from Dr. K. (being ignored) was deserved because of her "silliness." Both patients deny any angry reaction. Dr. K. indirectly reconfirms the solution of the previous session (assurance that the therapists will not be punitive) by pointing out that he had not ignored the patients but simply had not seen them. In spite of this initial expression of reactive fears or perhaps as a result of the further reassurance offered by Dr. K., the patients proceed to explore their feelings about parents and therapists. An atmosphere of freedom and a relative absence of anxiety prevail. Two solutions which facilitate free exploration appear to be operating: a continued sense that the therapists will not be punitive and the capacity to shift freely between parents as objects and therapists as objects. One patient's attempt to introduce a restrictive solution is quickly blocked by another. During the period in which the patients share feelings about parental attitudes toward boy friends and girl friends, Bob interrupts, mentioning a roommate who has left therapy. We assume that this represents a tentative effort to escape from the current material by introducing a restrictive solution. Marian immediately turns this comment back to the current issue by expressing surprise that Dr. K. might have other groups. Thus the continued free exploration of essentially Oedipal concerns toward both parents and therapists is made possible through the continued operation of several enabling solutions.

The specific feelings which the patients explore are rather different for different patients and revolve around sexual impulses toward therapists/parents, wishes for exclusive possession, jealousy of the parents' relationship with each other, and so on. Different patients also express rather different associated fears: concerns about achieving one's wish and then being burdened with an Oedipal success (Bob); fears of exposing oneself as a sexual person to one's parents (Marian); and expectation of rejection and a sense of deserving punishment (Arlene).

In the next session, the sixty-first, the sexual theme continues.

> Arlene told about a dream in which she was apologizing to her parents. She laughed when she said that she had nothing on "on top" in her dream. Marian complained that, during her visit home on the week end, her parents encouraged her to eat, even though they had also told her to lose weight. She felt bad because she had reacted with sarcasm. She couldn't decide whether they wanted her to be marriageable, which is what they said, or fat. Marian theorized that perhaps her parents didn't want her to succeed. Arlene complained about herself, saying that she had been bragging about foolish things, talking to boys, and degrading herself. Bob complained about his envy of his girl friend. There was a general sharing of feelings about being in a fog, being frightened about forthcoming exams, and so on.
>
> Bob said, "Something we talked about last week has taken the starch out of me." Arlene repeated her dream to Bob, who had missed it because he had come in late, and Bob reminded Marian that she had once had a similar dream of appearing half-naked before her father. Bob tried to change the subject to "something trivial" and said to Dr. K., "I like that tie." Marian angrily protested that she had been talking about something important to her. This flare-up quickly subsided, and the patients remarked about their depressed mood. Dr. T. said that, judging from the references to parents and Dr. K., she had the feeling that the patients might want to say something along these lines.
>
> After a long pause, Bob said sarcastically, "Yeah, how about being my mother, Dr. T.? My mother's far away, and, Dad, I like your tie." Marian denied that she felt toward the therapists as she did toward her parents. Bob told of a childhood incident in which he had bragged about being favored in something. A boy had told him that he would be punished, and he had caught the mumps. The patients shared feelings about punishments they had received as children. Marian said that her parents never punished her, but that she always had the feeling that they would get mad at her. Dr. T. asked whether the patients felt that they deserved punishment because of the things they had been talking about in the group. Bob mentioned feeling affection for his parents yet associating them with punishment. Marian and Arlene shared feelings of having feared that their parents would kill them. They agreed that they couldn't understand such fears, since they had seldom been punished at home. Marian went on to explain that, although she was seldom punished, she had an intense feeling of having to live up to her parents' expectations. She attributed this to her parents' need for everyone's admiration. She saw the same traits in

herself and felt she had to understand her parents in order to change herself.

In an abrupt change of topic, Bob and Marian shared complaints about group therapy. Bob felt that there were too many people in the group. He wanted private, intensive therapy. Marian could see improvement in herself but couldn't understand how it had come about. She wanted, as she put it, "predictability" about what was happening to her. Dr. T. suggested that the patients might fear that criticizing parents or therapists would elicit punishment. Dr. K. added that there might also be some reactions to the questionnaires in which the patients had been asked to describe the therapists.[4] A discussion about feelings toward the therapists followed. Arlene said that, as far as the questionnaire was concerned, she didn't know the therapists well enough to describe them, so she had given them characteristics which she would like her father and mother to have. Marian suggested that they needed more time to think about how they felt about the therapists, but Bob implied that Marian was afraid of being critical. He assured her that the therapists would not hurt them if they were critical: "I might bite you, but they're paid not to bite you." Marian talked about her sensitivity about hurting people, which she thought was based on a fear of retaliation. Bob admitted that he had the same fear. In response to Bob's probing, Arlene told about her current depression, frustration, and rejection. Bob then discussed his relationship with his girl friend, saying that he was excessively dependent on her. Marian suggested that Bob should not talk so much about his girl friend. Bob wondered whether he was using his girl friend to provoke the girls in the group.

In discussing her diet, Marian listed non-fattening foods which she hated. Arlene said that she especially liked such foods, and this amused everyone since Arlene was so thin. Marian interrupted the general laughter by saying that they were laughing because they were nervous or embarrassed. Dr. T. commented that, on the contrary, it had seemed to her that everyone was having a good time. Marian denied this, but Arlene reasoned that perhaps they were embarrassed because they were unaccustomed to sharing enjoyment with their parents. Bob wondered what kind of "shmucky" parents they must have to make them react with such embarrassment to sharing fun with the therapists. The session ended at this point.

This session opens with the continued expression of Oepidal feelings by the two girls. Arlene's dream indicates that she feels a need to apologize to her parents for her sexual feelings; Marian feels uneasy about her angry reactions to her parents' supposed suppression and disapproval of her sexual interests. Following this, a pervasive mood of tension and depression develops. This is in marked contrast to the previous session, which was marked by the relatively free expression of Oepidal wishes and fears. The balance of forces at the close of the previous session favored the free exploration of feelings, but that balance has now shifted to an emphasis on reactive fears. At first, these fears are expressed vaguely, in terms of being "in a fog," being frightened about exams, and being generally depressed. In response to some pushing from Dr. T., the patients move from their depression, but their discussion now specifically focuses on fears of punishment from parents. In other words, they move from vague to specific expressions of the reactive motive. Marian and Arlene share fears of being killed by their parents; primitive fears are being re-elicited. When Bob says that he wants private, intensive therapy, this suggests that he wants an exclusive relationship with a therapist and that he feels there is something in the current group situation from which he would like to flee. Marian's comment that she wants "predictability" over what is happening to her suggests that she wishes for greater control and is developing some fears about the direction in which the group is moving. The concern at the end about having fun with the therapists suggests a concern about developing closeness or perhaps a certain kind of equality with the therapists. Taken together, these indications suggest that the following focal conflict is operating:

disturbing motive		*reactive motive*
intimate, close, sexual feelings for the therapists	X	fears of retaliation and punishment

The most striking difference between this session and the previous one is that the reactive fears gain in intensity and begin to dominate the group. In contrast with the previous session in which there was an extended, relatively free exploration of both wishes and fears, here there is the resurgence of a reactive motive which involves anxieties about punishment. As the exploration of the theme proceeds, sexual wishes begin to be experienced more toward the therapists than toward the parents. This shift in object appears to intensify the patients' fears. Apparently, the capacity to move back and forth between parents and therapists as objects of sexual feeling, given the intensification of feelings, is no longer an adequate means of coping with intensified anxiety. Specific fears begin to emerge—fears of being "killed" or otherwise punished for their sexual daring. At this point, shared fears begin to build up, and support develops for the adoption of restrictive solutions. However, no restrictive solution is consolidated. Efforts toward being trivial or changing the subject (for example, Bob's attempt to swing the discussion to his dependent feelings for his girl friend) do not gain a foothold, yet it is also apparent that the patients are no longer able to sustain explorations of the sexual theme. The session ends on a note of increased tension; no new solutions have been established. It appears that the group is withdrawing from the exploration of the sexual theme.

In the sixty-second session, Bob asked specific questions about the sexual experiences of Dr. T., the female therapist. He added that he had once thought of asking his mother such questions and felt that, if he knew that his mother had had premarital sexual experiences, it would put them on an equal footing. The girls seemed startled at Bob's audacity and said that they themselves were not curious about the therapists.

Marian said there were many things she didn't know about her parents and that she had repressed any curiosity she might have had about such things. Whenever she thought that her parents had secrets between themselves, she didn't like it, but this didn't happen often, since she was usually her mother's first confidante. Bob changed the subject by asking, "Do you want to know what I said about you two girls?" (He was referring to the adjective check list.) In the discussion which followed, the patients compared notes about how they had described one another, the therapists, their parents, and their siblings. They discovered that, with few exceptions, they had described one another as selfish. Marian said that she was surprised to find she couldn't clearly describe her parents nor her brother, whom she had previously idolized. Bob spoke of feeling jealous of his brother. Then the patients mentioned positive traits that they had ascribed to one another.

Bob interrupted by saying that he wished Alex would return to the group. There was some agreement that they would like Alex to come back or the therapists to add a new member to the group. They complained that, with only three of them present, it was hard to think of new things to say. Marian said that the group was an "uninteresting and dead triangle." Bob said that he had mixed feelings about being the only boy. Dr. T. suggested that the patients might want a new member in order to distract them from the topics they had discussed lately. Bob said that he thought he had many unexpressed feelings about the people in the group. Abruptly, he asked Dr. K., "Do you like me?" He added that he wanted the therapists to like him and thought that they did. Marian said that she thought it would be unprofessional for the therapists to have such feelings about the patients. She added that she wanted one-third of the attention, "no more, no less," and said, "I persist very hard in not wanting you to have human characteristics and in wanting you just to be doctors." Bob said that he wanted his parents to pay more attention to him. There were comments about wanting the exclusive attention of parents and yet panicking at the thought of getting it. Tension seemed high. Marian expressed fear of being alone with the therapists. She felt that she might cry or that they might hurt her. The two girls shared anecdotes about feeling angry at mothers whom they had seen abusing their children. Arlene mentioned the disapproving looks of two old ladies when she was with some boy friends and girl friends on a bus. The feeling was

expressed that, if the therapists liked the patients, they could no longer be objective about them. Arlene talked of wanting to shock her parents and of describing her sexual experiences to her mother. All shared experiences of having stolen small things in their preteens.

The subject shifted back to the patients' feelings about the therapists' liking them or remaining objective. Marian took the lead in wanting the therapists to remain "clinicians." She said, "They have special knowledge about how to handle people in our condition." Bob scornfully questioned whether the therapists were handling things. The session ended on a note of intense conflict between Marian and Bob: "I just don't want them to be human beings," she said; "And I vote 'yes!' " Bob insisted.

The sixty-second session begins with further expression of the disturbing motive by Bob, who expresses curiosity about the sexual experiences of Dr. T., and a combination of both expression and suppression on the part of Marian, who refers to her repressed curiosity about her parents. There is a retreat from discussion about the therapists to discussions about parents and then a further retreat to discussions about one another (non-adults). The traits that they ascribe to one another are those of selfishness and jealousy, feelings which play an important part in the underlying focal conflict. Apparently, the patients are still uncomfortable and attempt to cope with the conflict by suggesting that another patient be added to the group. This appears to be a device for "diluting" current group feelings. The therapist's intervention at this point appears to block the restrictive solution. The patients are thrown back into the prevailing focal conflict, and conversation shifts to a concern and curiosity about the therapists' feelings toward the patients. Here, for the first time, feelings involved in the persisting disturbing and reactive motives appear to be experienced intensely in the here-and-now situation. Closeness, in the form of being liked by the therapists, is yearned for, yet regarded as dangerous. It is assumed that liking invariably carries with it a loss of "objectivity," which seems to imply either punishment or intolerable favoritism. The members of the group display conflicting feelings about closeness to the therapists. Bob appears more ready than Marian, who is very fearful. In focal-conflict terms, the session might be summarized as follows:

disturbing motive		*reactive motive*
wish to be close to therapists (involving a mixed sexual–dependent relationship)	**X**	**fear of the therapists being punitive or showing favoritism**

unsuccessful solutions

object-displacement—discuss feelings about one another

add a new member in order to "dilute" feelings in the group

These attempts to institute restrictive solutions are not successful. Tension is very high at the close of the session. The previous group solution (that the group can rely on the therapists' non-punitive stance and the utilization of displacement) has broken down as a *group* solution. Although one patient indicates that he still feels free to explore this area, another shows that her anxiety is building up to an intolerable pitch. What is possible for one patient is highly threatening for another. Thus, at the close of this session, the group is in a state in which a previously successful solution can no longer operate because of the intensification of the disturbing and reactive motives; attempts to institute new solutions fail, fears intensify to threatening proportions for at least one patient.

In the sixty-third session, Bob opened the discussion by saying to Dr. K., "I think I could be a better therapist than you," and then, after a pause in which no one said anything, added "Much better." Dr. T. said that she wondered whether Bob was trying to disconcert Dr. K. as he had tried to disconcert her during the previous session. He replied, somewhat drily, that there wasn't room in the group for him and Dr. K. "Going to scare him out of the group," Bob said. When Dr. T. asked whether he thought he would succeed, he said that he could try pretty hard but didn't know whether it was worth while. He added, "If we drive him out, that would leave you and me."

The others entered the room, including Alex, who had been absent for four sessions. Alex immediately began to explain his absences—he had had to be a poll-watcher on election day, and so on. When he had completed a lengthy explanation, Bob asked him for the real reasons. Alex said that he had just given the real reasons. Bob invited Alex to join him in driving Dr. K. out of the group, but Alex said that he didn't see the point in it.

Marian said that she had been thinking all week about her experiences in bed with her parents on Sunday mornings. Alex made fun of Marian's comments, and Arlene abruptly said that she felt like leaving the group. Arlene said that she felt more and more inhibited: "I dreaded coming here today; I just didn't want to. . . . I'm ashamed of coming here." There was a diversion while the patients supplied one another with matches and ash trays. Dr. T. commented that the group had been getting into difficult material lately and might find it somewhat frightening. Alex said that he sensed fright in the room, although he had not been feeling tense until the moment he had walked in.

The conversation became choppy. There was a brief attack on Alex, pressing him to give his "real" reasons for his absences; Arlene said that she had had a date, but added that it didn't count as a success because it was a blind date. Bob facetiously asked Dr. T. for a date, and Marian irritably asked him about his girl friend. Bob said that he liked variety, and Marian disconsolately said that she thought she might break up with her current boy friend because she was becoming more and more critical of him. Arlene said that she hated people's seeing her walk into the building where therapy was held. Marian talked of feeling inhibited with boys, especially near her home, for fear that her father would see her holding hands with someone.

Alex remarked that he was satisfied with his emotional state and didn't want to do anything to disturb it. Bob told him, "I think you're a wreck," and the two engaged in a mock fight in which neither seemed very involved. The others told Alex that they felt that the group was empty without him, and Alex protested that he didn't see why he should be important to the group. "I feel that the group has no right to feel it has any claim on me." He went on to say that he wanted to be able to come or go as he chose, but the others insisted he ought to make a decision one way or the other and that his reluctance to do so was selfish.

Arlene commented that she had found a new father image in a teacher. Bob said that he had dreamed that his girl friend had died. Alex said he had been feeling good since he had had a satisfying, give-and-take intellectual conversation without his usual need to argue for the sake of arguing. Marian told of success in losing weight and in an exam. Arlene said that she had gotten an A in a class but was afraid that she couldn't do it again. She didn't feel that she had deserved the A. The patients discussed feelings of personal failure even when they got good grades—feelings of having fooled the teacher, and so on. Arlene said that Mr. N., to whom she referred as her "new father image," wouldn't approve of becoming conceited over a good grade. Dr. K. pointed out that depreciating herself was a pattern of Arlene's. Arlene agreed: "I'm piling up all my bad traits." Dr. T. said the subject of being successful was a touchy one and asked, "What's so awful about being successful?" Marian said that she didn't know how to cope with success—that it was hard to keep success and hard to handle it in dealings with other people. "It's better not to have it," she concluded. Bob said that he was thinking of quitting school for a year, and Alex argued that, if he did, he would be sorry later. Bob said that he thought that life was sad because dreams of success never came true—for example, one might want to marry and be close to a woman, yet in marriage most people remained strangers. Arlene said that she thought of herself as the long-suffering heroine type. There was more mock fighting between Bob and Alex, and the session ended.

In the beginning of this session, Bob, after demonstrating that he does not share Marian's heightened anxiety, gives further expression to the disturbing motive—in this case, wanting to get rid of Dr. K. Marian attempts to institute a solution of displacement by changing the subject to a discussion of parents. However, such a solution seems unable to cope with the anxiety. Arlene expresses her fright and dread directly, and the other patients express anxiety by dwelling on depressed, hopeless feelings. Alex's re-entry, as well as his stand on wanting to minimize his involvement with the group, provides a handy escape from the conflict. The patients adopt a new, restrictive solution: "pretend that it is only Alex who fears involvement." They move away from the sexual theme, and, in the latter part of the session, feelings about intellectual success become the major preoccupation. This new theme is reminiscent of the fifty-ninth session, in which discussions of success preceded the current theme of sexual feelings toward the therapists.

In both illustrations, a typical movement in and out of the theme occurs. During the time that a single theme dominates a group, the group characteristically moves toward and away from the direct expression of the disturbing motive. Typically, the disturbing motive is initially expressed in vague, disguised, indirect, or incomplete terms. Later, the disturbing motive becomes more explicit and more specific. As the group begins to move away from the theme, the disturbing motive may again be expressed indirectly. Finally, as the group shifts to the next theme, a new disturbing motive appears. This sequence can be seen in both illustrations. In the inpatient group, the movement is toward and away from the revelation of "bad," angry impulses. The disturbing motive is first expressed as a wish to reveal "faults," but there is no indication of the nature of these faults. Later, the disturbing motive is expressed as a wish to release "bad" impulses. Still later, the impulses are perceived as destructive, and, finally, angry, hostile feelings are revealed. This group moves away from the theme as the disturbing motive shifts from a "wish to express 'bad' (hostile) feelings" to a "wish to have all needs satisfied by the therapists." In the adolescent outpatient group, the sexual theme first emerges as a wish to be successful as adults—peers with parents and/or therapists. In this initial expression of the disturbing motive, sexual feelings do not emerge as such. It is only later that sexual feelings toward the therapists are expressed directly. As this group moves out of the sexual theme, wishes for sexual success give way to wishes for intellectual success.

In our view, this intra-theme progression depends on the character of the solutions which the patients build to cope with successive focal conflicts. As long as the group is able to develop enabling rather than restrictive solutions, movement toward increased directness of expression occurs. The movement away from direct expression occurs when restrictive solutions begin to predominate. Enabling solutions have a freeing effect; they permit the patients to express and explore their impulses more directly. However, as this exploration proceeds and the patients are more directly confronted with the character of their impulses, associated fears may again become intensified, or new reactive fears may emerge. As the interaction progresses, reactive fears become so intense that the previous enabling solutions are no longer adequate to keep them within tolerable limits and, in order to cope with this mounting anxiety, increasingly restrictive solutions are introduced. These new, restrictive solutions are directed mainly to the alleviation of fears at the expense of satisfying the disturbing motive. Thus the disturbing motive is increasingly suppressed or disguised. This movement is not necessarily a smooth one. Although the over-all trend is first toward and then away from a more direct exploration of the disturbing impulses, the detailed movement is one of thrust and regression. In the movement toward direct expression, momentary reversals occur as restrictive solutions are temporarily invoked. In the movement away from direct expression, a restrictive solution may be abandoned temporarily. Despite these irregularities, it is usually possible to identify a turning point when the group begins to substitute restrictive for enabling solutions.

The process just described occurred in both illustrations. In the inpatient group, the initial disturbing motive (wish to reveal "faults") stimulated fears of eliciting criticism from peers. The group dealt with this by establishing a solution in which the patients were seen as alike in wanting to improve themselves and, therefore, did not need to fear one another's criticisms.[5] This was an enabling solution, for it alleviated the patients' fears and still allowed some expression of the disturbing motive. This solution allowed the patients to express the disturbing motive in more direct terms. In response to the increased expression of the disturbing motive, a new reactive fear was elicited—fear of harming the therapists. A series of solutions, most of which had an enabling effect, emerged in response to this new focal conflict. For example, the patients eventually agreed that the therapists "could take it," thus reducing their fears of harming the therapists and making it possible to express the disturbing motive even more directly. Here a temporary reversal occurred, for when the patients moved toward expressing the disturbing motive by actually attacking the therapists, the therapists demonstrated by their reactions that they could not "take it." This elicited a new reactive motive—an almost overwhelming fear of punishment. The patients were able to resume their movement toward a more direct expression of the disturbing motive only after the therapists demonstrated a non-punitive attitude and a capacity to withstand the patients' angry impulses.

The adolescent outpatient group moved toward the direct expression of the disturbing motive more rapidly than did the inpatient group. The adolescent group had a much longer history and had already established certain enabling solutions. For example, an established enabling solution (displacement in object and time) permitted this group to move relatively rapidly toward the direct exploration of Oedipal wishes and fears. Even here, however, the initial expression was somewhat blunted and disguised, and it was only when another solution (assurance that the therapists would not be punitive) was established that the patients seemingly felt free to express their feelings with greater directness. Even during the period of most direct and useful exploration, there were attempts on the part of certain patients to introduce restrictive solutions. However, such efforts were blocked by the other patients, and the general movement toward greater freedom and directness was interrupted only momentarily. Initial unsuccessful attempts to establish restrictive solutions heralded the movement away from direct expression. These efforts included attempts on the part of one or two patients to institute restrictive solutions: "talk about trivial things," "change the subject," or "add a new member in order to dilute feelings in the group." These were followed by a successful, but only temporarily maintained, solution which involved displacement: "talk about feelings about one another rather than about the therapists." Finally, the restrictive solution "assume that it is only Alex who fears involvement" became established.

The internal development which occurs during the dominance of a single theme can be summarized as follows:

Proposition 12

Within a single theme, movement occurs toward and then away from direct expression of the disturbing and reactive motives. Such movement is determined by the character of the successive solutions.

(1) *Movement toward direct exploration results from the establishment of successful solutions which emphasize gratification of the disturbing motive.*

(2) *Movement away from direct exploration results from the establishment of successful solutions which alleviate reactive fears while still permitting partial, indirect expression of the disturbing motive.*

Because a theme ordinarily prevails over successive sessions, several intervals between sessions do, of course, occur. These intervals, as such, do not introduce drastic shifts or reversals in the group focal conflict. The balance of forces within the group focal conflict and the prevailing solution at the close of a session are the significant factors in determining what is likely to happen during the succeeding session. Yet the fact that an interval has elapsed also has an effect. A particularly striking example of what may occur during an interval takes place in the all-male inpatient group; the third session ends on an apparently intolerable level of anxiety, generated by intense fears of retaliation from the therapists. During the interval between sessions, some of the patients assume a different position toward the prevailing group focal conflict, for at the beginning of the fourth session, they enter the room with less anxiety and are immediately able to devote themselves to instituting a solution to cope with the reactive fears.

We believe that this occurs through a process in which each patient works over the session in his own way during the interval. Such working over may always occur, but it is especially likely to affect the course of the group when the previous session ends with an emphasis on reactive fears or on the expression of the disturbing motive. When the former occurs, all of the patients share, to some extent, in the intensified anxiety. Thus, if a session ends on a note of high anxiety, the patients' working over between sessions is likely to be directed toward alleviating this anxiety. It is not surprising, then, that the patients come into the next session ready to institute anxiety-relieving solutions. Nor is it surprising that individual efforts toward such solutions meet with general cooperation.

When a session ends with an emphasis on the expression of the disturbing impulse, a different reaction is likely to occur. According to our view, direct expression of the disturbing impulse can occur because a successful enabling solution which alleviates reactive fears and simultaneously permits the undisguised emergence of the disturbing motive is in effect in the group. But any solution is effective only while the group is assembled and in operation. Once the group has dispersed, the individual patient may react with the feeling: "I've gone too far." This kind of reaction occurs in the adolescent group, sixty-first session, when Bob says, "Something we talked about last week has taken the starch out of me." In other words, during the interval, the patient may experience intensified fears in response to having participated in the expression or exploration of some disturbing motive. He may then mobilize certain defenses which lead him to display more caution when the group next meets. If this is the case, it is not surprising that the patients come to the next session with reactive fears relatively more intense and with a readiness to support restrictive solutions.

This discussion of the continuity of group events and the potential impact of the interval between sessions has emphasized the individual's internal reactions. We have not considered how external events or experiences may impinge on the group as a whole. In the illustrations presented in this chapter, two such events occur. In the adolescent group, two of the patients accidentally meet one of the therapists outside the group, and he fails to notice them. A somewhat different kind of external event occurs in the inpatient group, when a violent patient is admitted to the ward. In both cases, the external event colors but does not abruptly transform the character of the group. In the adolescent group, the fact that the therapist failed to notice the patient on the street is perceived as a punitive act; it fits directly into the current reactive motive, which involves the expectation of punishment from the therapist because of sexual-competitive impulses. In the inpatient group, the external event figures in an attempt to cope with fears about losing control over angry feelings. The violent patient is described as displaying "phony" hostility. By agreeing that he really has control over his angry feelings in spite of his behavior, the patients establish a solution: "define bad impulses as 'phony' feelings that are harmless." Thus, external events are generally utilized in a way which is consistent with the character of the group situation.[6]

The character of the continuity between group sessions is summarized in the following proposition:

Proposition 13

The equilibrium of group forces at the close of a session heavily influences the events of the next session.

(1) *If the equilibrium at the close of a session is marked by emphasis on the disturbing motive, the patients are likely to mobilize defenses against the disturbing impulse during the interval. The beginning of the next session will be marked by the establishment of more restrictive solutions and/or greater emphasis on reactive fears.*

(2) *If the equilibrium at the close of a session is marked by emphasis on the reactive motive, the patients are likely to mobilize defenses against their fears during the interval. The next session will be marked by a reduced anxiety level and the establishment of solutions which cope successfully with reactive fears.*

All of the foregoing refers to movement which occurs during the period in which a single theme is dominant. Themes do not persist indefinitely. After two, three, four, or five sessions a shift occurs in the disturbing motive which is so marked that a new theme can be said to dominate the group. We have observed this shift to occur in two ways. First, an enabling solution may be established which permits the expression of some disturbing impulse which is related to the previous one but is sufficiently distinct to be judged a new theme. Second, and more typically, a change in theme occurs when the patients establish the kind of restrictive solution which requires giving up the disturbing motive. The first of these two processes occurred in the inpatient group. Initially, the patients were preoccupied with the wish to reveal "bad," hostile impulses. As enabling solutions were established, the patients were able to express and explore the original disturbing motive in direct terms. Along with this exploration, associated feelings of a rather different character were also expressed. The first hint of this occurred in the final moments of the fourth session, when, along with the expression of shared angry feelings toward parents, one of the patients also expressed the wish for a good relationship with his parents. A general shift to a new disturbing motive—"wish to have all needs satisfied by the therapists"—was established two sessions later. The second kind of shift occurred in the adolescent outpatient group. A series of enabling solutions not only permitted the patients to explore their sexual feelings toward the therapists with some directness, but also led to the generation of intense reactive fears. As these fears were intensified, the original solutions were no longer adequate to relieve anxiety. The patients seemed unable to generate new, enabling solutions; instead they dealt with their fears by establishing a restrictive solution which suppressed the sexual character of their desire for success and recast it as a desire for intellectual success.

The processes by which a group shifts from one theme to another may be stated as follows:

Proposition 14	*Movement from one theme to another occurs when (1) an enabling solution is established which permits a new disturbing motive to be expressed or when (2) a restrictive solution is established which prohibits satisfaction or expression of the prevailing disturbing motive.*

An unanswered question about the evolution of group themes concerns the effects of enabling solutions. Under some circumstances, the establishment of an enabling solution leads to further exploration of the same disturbing motive; under others, it leads to a shift in disturbing motives. We have been unable, as yet, to differentiate these circumstances.

Notes

[1] Patients vary in the stance which they adopt toward the group focal conflict and reveal their stances at different moments in the process. In this illustration, patients who were prominent in moving the group toward the more direct expression of personal material in session two subsided as active participants during session three. Patients who did not contribute actively to the expression of the disturbing motive in session two were active in expressing reactive fears in session three. Often, a shift in the balance of the focal conflict, as well as a shift from one focal conflict to a related one, is signaled by a shift in the participation pattern in the group.

[2] No disturbing motive was postulated for this session. The session was dominated by fears and solutions directed toward alleviating these fears.

[3] This group is utilized as illustrative material in Chapter 6, where the sequence of sessions described here is compared with an earlier sequence in which sexual themes also predominated.

[4] This refers to an adjective check list which the patients were asked to use to describe themselves, family members, and group members.

[5] We are omitting the details of the solutional conflict which developed in this group.

[6] The impact of external events on the long-term development of the group is discussed in Chapter 6.

5

Group Culture

We assume that a psychotherapy group, like any other social entity, will develop a characteristic culture. The culture includes the practices, standards, and mutual understandings which regulate relationships within the group and define the character of the group world. The culture which develops in the therapy group interests the group therapist because it forms the context of therapy; therapy groups characterized by different cultures may provide quite different therapeutic experiences for their members. For example, one can imagine a group in which the patients take turns being the center of attention and the object of help, in which the atmosphere is polite, and in which the patients spend a great deal of time talking about personal history or current outside relationships. In contrast, in another group, the patients might characteristically express feelings strongly and directly, interrupt and fight one another for the attention of the group, and spend most of their time discussing feelings about one another. Two such groups would provide very different settings for therapy.

The term "culture" is, of course, adopted from anthropology, where it is used to define the special characteristics of a society or segments in a society. When applied to such large groups, the term incorporates the total range of human experience and behavior. In contrast, the culture of a small group is limited to the special life of that group. The culture of a large society is functional; it regulates relationships in the society and provides a means of understanding and explaining the personal and natural universe. The culture of a small group is also functional; it defines appropriate behaviors and ways of thinking which are relevant to the life of the particular group.[1]

The following characteristics are primary to the concept of culture as it is generally defined: elements of the culture perform a regulatory and defining function; they are the product of the interaction of the group; they extend in time beyond the specific originating situation; and they have a powerful influence on the behavior of the members. In focal-conflict terms, it is the group solution which meets this definition. Accordingly, the culture of the therapy group is understood to consist of the successful solutions which a group generates to deal with successive focal conflicts.

The group's solutions regulate and define the group in a variety of ways. Some solutions may define the over-all character of the group. An outpatient group of adolescents constructed a solution in which they agreed that the group was not a serious enterprise. Or sometimes, in the early sessions, a group is defined as a "class" or a "bull session." Certain solutions define the relationship between the therapist and the patients. For example, the solution "punish the therapist by exclusion" temporarily excommunicates the therapist from the group world. In an outpatient group of schizoid men, the solution "band together to express angry compliance toward the therapist" developed. This solution not only defined relationships with the therapist, but prescribed a vehicle by which angry feelings could be expressed. In the first session of an inpatient group, the solution "all be alike" developed. Similar solutions appeared in other groups: "we are all alike in that we are sick"; "everyone here is in need of help." Such solutions define the character of the group by labeling the patients as certain kinds of people. They also suggest that such behaviors as insisting on uniqueness or denying sickness will be regarded as taboo.

In fact, many solutions function as taboos. During its first session, an outpatient group implicitly agreed that feelings about family members were not to be discussed in the group. In effect, they outlawed an area of discourse. An outpatient adolescent group developed the solution, "each have a turn at receiving the advice of others," thus outlawing the expression of hostile competitive feelings. At other times, solutions provide a vehicle for communication; they prescribe channels for the discussion of feelings or problems. In the second session of an adolescent group, the patients operated for a brief period on the solution, "talk about sexual feelings by means of discussing dreams." This constituted an agreement that sexual feelings could be discussed, provided that it was done in rather distant, intellectual terms. An inpatient group operated for some time on the solution, "talk about impersonal as well as personal things." This solution permitted the patients to utilize an impersonal mode of interacting when necessary. We have found that, in general, many solutions relate to group boundaries: what can be talked about, how it can be talked about, and with whom one can talk. Many solutions proscribe or prescribe areas or modes of discussion and deal with unacceptable affect by outlawing it or providing safe vehicles for its expression.

Because a single solution often refers to several aspects of the group culture, it is often difficult to categorize it. For example, a single solution which referred to a procedure ("each have a turn at receiving advice of others") also had implications for the nature of the therapy group and the kinds of relationships seen as appropriate within it. A solution which referred most specifically to relationships among members ("we are alike in that we are all sick") also defined an aspect of the group's character and permissible content areas.

As the group copes with various issues, a number of solutions are established. These solutions arise in response to the successive conflicts. Thus, each set of solutions is a direct outgrowth of interaction in the group. One does not see solutions which regulate the patient's behavior outside the group—solutions, for example, which attempt to regulate his behavior with parents or roommates. Solutions which refer to the general outside culture—modes of dress, food preferences, and so on—do not become established because they are not specific to conflicts within the group.

In Chapter 2, it was pointed out that each successful solution functions to alleviate anxiety and to permit some satisfaction of the disturbing motive. We are now suggesting another function. Seen from an external point of view and a broader time span, the group's solutions function to set limits, regulate relationships, and define the group world. In other words, the solutions function as the group culture. This view of the therapy-group culture can be stated as follows:

Proposition 15 | *Successful solutions to group focal conflicts, taken collectively, constitute the culture of the therapy group. The elements of the group culture define the character of the therapeutic enterprise, the relationships among patients and between patients*

> ***and therapists, the boundaries on the expression of affect, acceptable content, and acceptable modes of interaction.***

The culture of the group is subject to change over time. Some early solutions may persist; others may be modified or drop out entirely. If one views the group at any given moment, the culture does not consist of all successful solutions, but only of those solutions which were established and never modified and the most recent modifications of other past solutions. A successful solution, then, transcends its specific emergent situation. It emerges in response to a specific, current focal conflict but continues to hold sway even after that conflict has subsided. For example, an outpatient adolescent group developed a solution which involved taking turns at "being the patient." One of the patients would present a problem; the others would question him about it and offer advice. Then, it was someone else's turn, and the group would go through the same procedure with another patient. This solution arose out of a focal conflict which involved angry, competitive feelings toward peers versus fears that these feelings would get out of hand and become destructive. The solution—in which the patients "leaned over backward" to be fair—sternly suppressed the disturbing motive in order to deal with anxiety over potential destructiveness. This solution continued for four or five meetings. Even though there were no concomitant signs of the original focal conflict and other issues became focal, the patients continued their turn-taking pattern.

Because many solutions involve prohibitions or omissions, evidence of the continuing persistence of a solution is often difficult to obtain. If a solution involves avoiding talking about sexual feelings, the absence of such talk does not constitute evidence that the old solution persists. Or a solution may involve a complex pattern of behavior. For example, a group may establish a solution which permits them to veer off into impersonal or ostensibly irrelevant content. But they may exercise this prerogative only intermittently, and it is difficult, during the intervals, to determine whether the solution is still operative. Conventional sources of evidence are unavailable. One cannot poll the patients to find out what solutions are operative in the group, since solutions are not necessarily explicit. Rather, they are agreements which may exist outside of awareness. Although the patients may become aware that "we always take turns," they are not likely to see this as a group solution or an aspect of their culture.

The clearest demonstration of the persistent influence of group solutions occurs when a past solution is violated or threatened. The patients mobilize to protect the solution, often attacking the member who has threatened it. In the following illustration, a group solution which was established during the initial sessions of the group was threatened during the seventeenth session. Though the solution had not been in evidence during the interval, the patients exerted strong efforts to protect it.

Reactions to an Inadvertent Attack on a Previously Established Group Solution

During its first sessions, an inpatient group had established the solution "talk freely, but bring up impersonal as well as personal material." This solution developed in response to a focal conflict which involved a wish to please the therapist by responding to the therapist's desire that the patients talk freely and bring up topics on their own versus the fear that such freedom could lead to loss of control and other dangerous consequences. The solution allowed free discussion but, at the same time, mitigated anxiety by providing an escape to impersonal topics when matters threatened to get out of hand.

After seventeen sessions, two new patients were added to the group. During the first session which he attended, one of the new patients, Simon, unwittingly threatened the long-established group solution.[2]

> Very soon after the session opened, Simon began talking in a rapid and headlong way. He said that he had marital and working problems. "Most of my problems are due to the Army. Everyone dislikes the Army," he said. Several patients disagreed, but Simon continued with a long and progressively more confused monologue. He said that in the future, society would not need an army or police because everyone would be able to regulate himself. When some of the others argued this point, Simon overrode them, insisting that police were only necessary to control things and that, in the future, people would be well and be able to control themselves. While the patients were still involved in a heated argument with Simon, he was called out of the room. A long silence followed.

Simon's behavior can be regarded as a threat to the group's previously established solution. Simon was talking about impersonal matters—the very behavior which, up to this point, had adequately served to prevent loss of control in the group—yet Simon was clearly out of control. In effect, he was demonstrating to the patients that their solution was ineffective. This threat was of sufficient importance that the remainder of this session and all of the succeeding session were devoted to efforts to cope with it.

After a long silence, someone commented that Simon sounded like a Communist, but others disagreed. A rather intellectual discussion about the distinction between freedom and license followed, and there was agreement that people couldn't really do what they would like to do. The discussion turned to how to handle troublesome neighbors, and the group considered but rejected the ideas of complaining to the neighbor or threatening him with the police. During a discussion about food, the patients agreed that one shouldn't eat food that one didn't like. They agreed that it was extremely annoying when someone kept offering you food even after you had said that you didn't want it.

The first portion of the next session was devoted to discussion about examinations; one patient said that, although he had recently failed an examination, he intended to try again. Simon was rather silent but then began to talk rapidly and disconnectedly about how first impressions were always wrong. An argument developed as to whether first impressions were always wrong, and someone suggested that Simon must feel that he had made a bad first impression on the group. He admitted this, and others agreed that they had felt this way at times. Later, when Simon began to repeat his position about policemen, the therapist asked the group what was really being talked about. One of the patients suggested the real issue was the patients' attitude toward authority. The therapist agreed and added that there was also a concern as to whether each person could control himself or whether he needed outside control. One or two patients indicated their understanding of this point.

After Simon is called out of the room, the patients spend the rest of the session attempting to deal with the feelings aroused by his behavior. All of this work is carried out in indirect, symbolic terms. The patients' discussion about freedom and license can be seen as an attempt to reassure themselves that they, at least, know the difference and can exert controls. Through the talk about troublesome neighbors, they symbolically consider alternatives for dealing with Simon; later, in the discussion about food, they express some of their resentment toward the therapist who has forced Simon "down their throats." In the next session the patients are again confronted with Simon's behavior and, this time, utilize two new ways of dealing with it: first, they are able to empathize with him, realizing that he is not so different from them, and, second, they interpret his confused talk as relevant to the group discussion. The patients cope with the threat presented by Simon's behavior by perceiving it as relevant to the group situation rather than as out of control and thus preserve the original solution.

In this illustration, a past solution retains meaning for the group. The amount of time and energy devoted to coping with the patient who threatens the solution is proof of its importance.[3] Thus, even though other issues intervene and the solution does not appear active, a threat to its existence arouses concern. The persistence of such a solution can be understood in terms of its defensive-enabling function. If a solution is abruptly undermined, the anxieties associated with the original focal conflict are likely to re-emerge. It is this re-emergence which constitutes threat.

Solutions are, however, subject to modification. Modification occurs through an extended process—shifts occur in the focal conflict, and the associated solution gradually becomes less necessary to the group. When the solution is no longer required in order to protect the patients from re-experiencing the anxieties associated with the focal conflict, conditions are ripe for change. The crucial shift involves the reduction of reactive fears. Although the process cannot be regarded as automatic, certain characteristics of the group process do make it likely that these changes will occur. A solution is a compromise. It may cope with anxiety, but always at the cost of the partial or, sometimes, complete inhibition of the wish; all solutions involve some restriction of the disturbing motive. Thus, the achievement of a successful solution copes with the associated focal conflict but does not permanently render it a dead issue. The patients vary in their experiencing of the disturbing and reactive motives. Because of these individual differences, there will always be those who push for satisfaction of the disturbing motive and those whose anxiety is ready to break out despite the solution. The focal conflict is, therefore, inherently unstable. Although conditions exist in the group which make for the stability of the solution, conditions also exist which push the patients toward re-experiencing or re-expressing various aspects of the group focal conflict, thus paving the way for a concomitant shift in solution.

Modification of a Group Solution

In order to illustrate the processes which lead to cultural change, relevant material from the first seven sessions of an inpatient group will be described. (The first session of this group was discussed in Chapter 2.) In this group, six new patients were added to a group of five patients. The first session of this enlarged group was summarized in focal-conflict terms as follows:

disturbing motive		*reactive motive*
wish to have a uniquely gratifying relationship with the therapist	X	fear of destructive punishment from the therapist

solution

all be alike

Several characteristics of this solution might be pointed out. First, it is one-sided, dealing with anxiety but precluding any satisfaction of the disturbing motive. Second, it is unrealistic. To insist that everyone in the group is alike is, in fact, a fantasy. Third, the therapists are likely to view this solution as anti-therapeutic. The solution outlaws the expression of unique personal material. The patients might talk about personal matters, but only in reference to common characteristics or problems. Such a solution could restrict the patients' ability to utilize the group situation therapeutically. Finally, the patients themselves might become aware that they are inhibiting the expression of personal material and so defeating their own desire for therapeutic help. On all these grounds, then, one would expect the solution to be an unstable one. Yet, although this solution was challenged almost immediately, it persisted for some time and gave way only during the sixth and seventh sessions of the group.

Very early in the second session, one of the patients, Clifford, behaved in a way which violated the group solution "all be alike":

> During a discussion about another matter, Clifford abruptly stood up and began to pour out his personal problems. For three or four minutes, he uninterruptedly told how a prized possession of his had been destroyed. He said that he had owned an automobile. On his wedding night, his wife was driving the car because he had felt that he had had too much to drink. She had had an epileptic seizure and wrecked the car. The group reacted with considerable tension during this highly charged recital, and, finally, one of the patients told Clifford to "sit down and make himself comfortable."

Viewed against the background of the established solution, Clifford's behavior can be seen as a challenge to the group solution in two major ways. Entirely apart from the content of his remarks, his behavior is a bid for special attention. By standing up, he literally raises himself above the crowd. In addition, he communicates highly personal, unique experiences. On both accounts, he violates the solution which requires being alike and suppressing unique material.

> After Clifford sat down, the initial reaction of the others was to criticize him and depreciate his problem. The patients expressed disapproval of his behavior toward his wife and doubted whether he had really been drunk. They agreed that he should not have permitted his wife to drive and that the accident had been his fault. Following this, the patients became depressed. They devaluated the group, wondered whether they were brought together to be studied or helped, and were scornful of psychiatrists' knowledge. This note of hopelessness continued until the end of the session.

Clifford's behavior engages the attention of the group for the rest of the session. First, the others try to punish Clifford for his deviant behavior by depreciating his problem and withholding sympathy or support. Following this, they become depressed and express hopelessness about the group. Perhaps they are angry at the therapists for permitting Clifford's behavior to occur; perhaps they can think of no way out of their dilemma other than to reject the whole idea of group therapy. There is no evidence that they are re-instituting the original solution "all be alike." All that is apparent is that the group has been very much disconcerted by Clifford's behavior.

> The third session continued the mood of hopelessness. Through a discussion about the book, *The Fifty-Minute Hour,* the patients wondered whether anyone was really helped by therapy. Paul asked what the relationship between a doctor and his patient should be when they met socially—what if the patient was doing something he was not supposed to be doing, like drinking? He described, in vague terms, an encounter in which a doctor had been unfriendly and wondered if "an unfriendly attitude is the policy in this hospital." Melvin said that his doctor "kidded" him when he saw him in the hall, and Sam said, "But you are the pet." There was a good deal of confusion as to what the relationship with the doctor should be, but most felt the doctor should maintain some distance.
>
> Tim told about a dream in which he was driving a car at high speed with a passenger beside him. Unexpectedly, he came to a steep cliff, could not stop in time, and went over the edge. He was angry at his passenger, who had not warned him even though he had known about the cliff.
>
> A long discussion followed in which patients shared childhood experiences of punishment. All who spoke described themselves as having been bad—or, perhaps, good on the surface, but "bad underneath." The general theme was that they had deserved the punishment that they had received.

There are a number of indications that the reactive motive which developed in the first session is still present. The patients still expect the therapists to be punitive or, at least, unfriendly. In addition, resentment is expressed toward the therapists. All of this is expressed in quite indirect terms and has a somewhat different flavor for different patients. For Paul, the expectation is of unfriendliness and disapproval; the resentment is rather mild. For Tim, the whole issue is experienced more intensely. In his dream, the passenger (therapist), who knew about the dangers of the road (group), failed to warn the driver (Tim). For Tim, the resentment seems to focus on the therapist's failure to protect the patient against the dangers of the group. This exploration of feelings about the therapist-patient relationship is apparently threatening to the patients, since they immediately turn to content which suggests that they deserve punishment. The discussion about childhood "badness" also suggests that the patients are reinstituting their earlier solution, "all be alike." Through the vehicle of childhood reminiscences, they are reaffirming that they are all alike in deserving punishment for their "badness."

From the point of view of modifying a group solution, two things are important: first, there is evidence that the original solution is still in operation; second, the group devotes considerable time to working on the reactive motive involved in the original group focal conflict. They symbolically explore their relationship with the therapists: the feelings which the therapists have and should have about the patients and the resentment which the patients feel toward the therapists. As for the original disturbing motive—the wish to be unique and have a special relationship with the therapist—only a fleeting sign of it occurs, when Melvin is accused of being his individual therapist's pet. In sum, the original focal conflict is still operative, and the patients are still behaving in a way that indicates that the original solution is in the fore. However, a new characteristic is apparent; the group is beginning to explore the reactive motive.

> At the beginning of the fourth session, the patients found it hard to get started, and the mood was again one of dejection. They talked about occupational therapy projects which had failed. During a discussion about music, Tim asked whether anyone had taken advantage of the opportunity to borrow records from the public library. Then, in a discussion about sampler records, Ella said that they were cheap, but Tim argued that, although they were inexpensive, they were worth a lot. The therapist suggested that the discussion had to do with the patients' mixed feelings about the worth of the group, but this was denied. Tim said, "It's a good thing I wasn't talking about the city dump."
>
> In sharing Army experiences, several patients agreed that officers were inefficient or had poor judgment. Margaret wondered why American women were never in the front lines as soldiers, and a discussion followed as to whether women could tolerate combat. After comparing the strength of American versus European women, several patients agreed that American women were strong.

The first half of this session concerns the patients' ambivalent commitment to the therapy group. There is still a good deal of skepticism about the potential value of the group (the patients discuss projects which do not turn out well), but at least one patient, Tim, suggests that the group (public library, sampler records) might be worth something. The feeling that the therapists are potentially dangerous and that the patients must take care persists. When the therapist suggests that the casual discussion about records refers to mixed feelings about the group, this is denied, and Tim expresses the feeling that he is glad he has said nothing more critical about the group. The implication is that, if he had, he would be in trouble with the therapists. Later, the group appears to be assessing the strength of the therapists (both are women) when they wonder whether women can handle combat conditions. The session ends on an optimistic note, with some agreement that women can handle tough situations.

There is some indication, through the third and fourth sessions, that the reactive motive (concern about the therapists' punitiveness) is shifting. Much of the material focuses, in an indirect way, on the therapists. There are persistent expectations of unfriendliness, disapproval or more drastic punishment, resentment of the therapists, mixed feelings about their capabilities, and finally, some agreement that the therapists are strong. Although the reactive motive which developed in the first session persists, the fear appears to be diminishing in intensity. The therapists are still regarded as powerful, but some of the patients begin to see the therapists as a source of strength and control rather than as a source of punishment.

> The fifth session began with the patients wondering why they didn't talk about their problems, since this was the purpose of the group. Clifford suggested that it was like a log jam and that, if one person started, others would join in. Paul told about feeling angry toward his individual doctor because the doctor had refused to give him a pass. (Paul, like all the other patients, was also receiving individual therapy.) He had told the doctor how he felt. The others seemed amused and shared stories about defying officers in the Army, getting around them, and breaking rules. Paul said that he had expected to be punished for some infraction in the Army but hadn't been.
>
> The patients shared stories about childhood mischief in a lighthearted way. In the course of this discussion, they wondered why girls are afraid of snakes and mice and boys are not. After a slight pause, Clifford said that he had been worried about his job, but had talked to his supervisor and found that it could be arranged to his satisfaction. The others supported Clifford. There was general agreement that what each person needed was sympathy. They shared feelings of shame about being psychiatric patients and wondered whether, for example, the hospital chaplain knew what went on in the group. Alan scornfully commented, "A minister would stand next to a man in a pool of quicksand and tell him to have faith." Margaret said, "Ministers have their approach, and psychiatrists have theirs."

For the first time in several sessions, the patients consider talking about personal problems. Clifford's analogy about the log jam is interesting in view of the group's solution of "all be alike." He is pointing out that, if the group moves toward the discussion of personal material, someone has to start. Perhaps the group cannot get into personal problems at this point because it would require violation of the solution "all be alike." Someone would have to start and thus make himself different from the group. In any case, no one responds to Clifford's suggestion, and, instead, the patients reconsider their feelings about the therapists. They express a much increased capacity to argue with, challenge, and be angry at persons in authority and even to let such persons know about their feelings. When Paul says that he expected to be punished and wasn't, he indicates that he no longer shares in the previous reactive fear.

Expressing feelings through a discussion about childhood mischief is a device which has been used earlier, in the third session. Here, it is utilized to confirm the "we are all alike" solution. But there are important differences. Now, the group can discuss childhood mischief with an air of lightheartedness and without the earlier emphasis on deserving and receiving punishment. This suggests that, for the group as a whole, the concern about punishment has diminished. Second, the patients are willing to accept differences—in this case, between boys and girls. (It will be recalled that in the previous session they had agreed that women were just as capable of combat as men.) What begins here is a diminution in the intensity of the reactive motive, as well as some yielding in the solution "all be alike."

Later, when Clifford indicates that he found his employer helpful rather than punitive, he is doing two things: he is underlining the new feeling that persons in authority need not be punitive, and he is testing out the possibility of bringing in personal material. He is doing so in a more modulated, less demanding way than in the second session, and his contribution is more in tune with the group's concerns. In contrast with their earlier punitive reaction toward Clifford, the group now supports him. Further, they agree that everyone wants sympathy. Here the group is modifying the earlier solution. Differences in some areas are acknowledged (girls, but not boys, are afraid of snakes) but not in others (everyone wants sympathy). In contrast with the earlier insistence that everyone is alike, this view is more realistic: girls *are* afraid of snakes, and everyone *does* want sympathy.

During this session, there is evidence of a general reduction in the intensity of the reactive motive. Although there are indications of uneasiness about the potential punitiveness of therapists, there is increasing support for the view that they may be tolerant and even helpful. Along with this shift, there is some indication that the earlier solution of "all be alike" is being modified.

> In the sixth session, the patients again had trouble getting started. Alan said that he had something on his mind but couldn't remember what it was. After a pause, Paul wondered how the clocks were set: "Is there a central place, or do they pay attention to each clock?" Alan said that he thought that they were set by hand. Desultory conversation was interspersed with long silences. Paul suggested the group break up for the day or play cards. Clifford reminded the group that he had tried to break the ice the second day by talking, but no one responded. Carl told a joke about psychiatrists who went to burlesque shows to watch the audience. Paul asked several others to tell jokes, but they said that they couldn't in front of ladies. This led someone to tell Paul that Paul's problem was that he had never married. Paul said that he had come close but had probably been frightened. After another long silence, the patients complained that they had no trouble talking outside the group sessions, and Paul said, "It's because of the doctors." Clifford said that he had been afraid to talk to his supervisor but that it had turned out all right. Alan said that, if you talked in school, you were punished. Dr. T. asked him whether he thought that he would be punished here, and he said, "No."
>
> Paul mentioned that he had had dreams that bothered him. Alan told of a recent dream in which he had bowled a 300 game and nobody had looked at him. Paul told of a dream in which a beautiful woman had wanted to adopt him and marry him. During a social hour in the hospital, he had picked out a woman whom he wanted to talk to, but later he couldn't find her. Dr. T. said that both patients were talking about not getting enough attention and being disappointed. Carl said that he had had lots of similar experiences. Paul told about having made a lamp and having got no recognition, but when Dr. T. suggested, "You were disappointed," Paul denied it.

What is most notable about this session is the reappearance of the wish to be unique, followed by a resurgence of anxiety and a more specific expression of the reactive motive. At the close, anxiety has been controlled, and the disturbing motive is again dominant. The events of the preceding session have paved the way for this development. The reduction of fears in the fifth session and the modified solution allow the re-expression of the wish for special recognition for the first time since the first session. The first hint of this occurs in a symbolic way, when Paul wonders how the clocks are set: "Is there a central place, or do they pay attention to each clock?" Even this tentative and symbolic expression of the disturbing motive intensifies the group's fears. There is greater anxiety than has occurred at any time since the first meeting. Following the initial diffuse expression of fears, the reactive motive comes to the fore in specific terms. The patients find it hard to talk "because of the doctors." It is important to note, however, that the reactive motive is expressed differently than before. Rather than insisting on the damaging, punitive behavior of doctors, the patients express their fears directly or in terms of social interactions involving authority figures. The patients recognize that their comments refer to the here-and-now situation. When Paul says that their fears are due to the doctors' presence, and Clifford responds with a comment about his supervisor, it is generally acknowledged that he is talking about the therapists. Following a period in which the patients reconsider whether they need to be frightened of the therapists and seem to agree that these fears may be unfounded, the disturbing motive is re-expressed through discussions of dreams and hospital experiences.

In terms of the flow of sessions, the reactive motive appears more intense during the sixth session than during the fifth. The reduction of fear during the fifth session paved the way for the partial breakdown of the original solution and the re-emergence of the disturbing motive. However, the very fact that the patients permitted the wish for uniqueness to re-emerge apparently provokes sufficient anxiety to produce tense silences, indicating the resurgence of reactive fears. Toward the end of the session, however, after they have reassured themselves to some extent that the therapists will not be punitive, the patients again express their wish for uniqueness. During this session, a progression toward more direct expression of the wish to be unique and receive special attention occurs. At first, it is expressed in symbolic terms, then through dreams, and then through experiences in the hospital. What is important in terms of the prevailing focal-conflict pattern is that the wish involved in the disturbing motive can be recognized and discussed. The solution "all be alike" has shown signs of yielding, and the reactive motive is experienced far less intensely. Thus, the disturbing motive can be recognized and discussed far more directly than before.

> At the beginning of the seventh session the patients wondered whether the therapists, like all the patients, had been "in the War" like all of them, and Jean said, "Next time, we will all be in." Paul told of a dream in which he owned a troupe of actors. Someone rushed up to him to tell him of an accident to the troupe, and he became frightened and shouted for help. Jean said that another patient had dreamed that she had taken his ice cream away from him. She reported a dream of her own in which she had had five husbands.
>
> Later, Bill told about his sister, who had everything she wanted and still was not happy. Paul suggested that perhaps she didn't have everything—"only she knows that." There was general agreement that many

people put on a front and that the hardest thing in the world was to reveal one's own feelings. While talking about Bill's sister, menopause was mentioned, and there was agreement that both men and women experienced emotional problems about growing older. In a discussion about food, the patients noted that they had differing tastes in food and that many of them had changed their food preferences over the years. There were complaints about hospital food, but, when Sam said that he was usually offered more than he could eat, several others agreed.

This session involves a sorting of the patients' similarities and differences. Initially, there is a reiteration of the solution "we are all alike." Paul's dream can be seen as a statement of the original conflict: he expresses the wish to be the sole survivor of an accident to the troupe (group) and, at the same time, experiences the fear and anxiety which the wish elicits. The discussion about Bill's sister leads the patients to make a distinction between surface behavior and inner feelings. In the ensuing discussion, the group rallies around an agreement that, although surface behavior is different, people may experience the same underlying concerns—for example, both men and women experience distress about growing older. Toward the close of the session, the patients talk about their differences in terms of food preferences. At the end, they recognize that they are demanding, but suggest, for the first time, that satisfaction is possible.

During this seventh session, the revised solution hinted at earlier is more clearly defined. There are similarities among people, but there are also differences. The group is beginning to agree that "we are different in surface ways, yet basically alike." In later sessions, this new solution replaced the previous solution. During the following eight sessions, it enabled the patients to explore the disturbing motive in direct terms. They maintained that they were basically alike in wanting attention and recognition. Such needs and wishes were expressed freely, in ways which ranged from laughingly caricaturing their demands ("each patient should have a single room"; "or a suite of rooms with a blonde") to reminiscing about childhood ("my biggest wish was for a barrel of ice cream that I could dive into and eat my way out of"). With the new solution, tolerance for individual differences increased, as did the opportunity to explore individual concerns. The patients were able to tolerate any kind of surface difference as long as they maintained the idea that they were all basically alike.

From both the patients' and the therapists' point of view, the new solution was far more satisfactory than the previous one. For the patients, the new solution allowed partial gratification of the disturbing motive. Although no patient could have an exclusive relationship with the therapists, each could have a special relationship by virtue of his uniqueness as an individual. By developing a sense of basic sameness, the patients could tolerate superficial differences and allow each person to achieve a special and somewhat different place in the group. From the therapists' point of view, this modification in the group solution allowed a broader range of material and feelings to be expressed. Feelings and experiences which previously had to be suppressed for fear of violating the group solution could now be revealed.[4]

In order for the original solution to be modified, certain changes had to occur in the balance of forces within the focal conflict. Initially, the group put most of its time into working on the reactive motive—the fear of the therapists' punitiveness. From the third to the sixth sessions, the group's major efforts were turned toward an exploration of their relationship with the therapists. This occurred on a symbolic level, through discussions about Army officers, supervisors, and unidentified "doctors." Later, the reactive fear was discussed directly. Following this rather extended concentration on the reactive motive, other aspects of the focal-conflict pattern came into the foreground. The solution began to show signs of yielding, the wish for exclusive attention re-emerged, the fears were briefly reactivated and again dealt with, and a modified solution was established. The crucial factor was a shift in the character of the underlying group focal conflict which involved a reduction in tension and, hence, a reduced need to maintain the original solution. This view of the manner in which a group solution is modified can be stated as follows:

Proposition 16	*A shift in a group solution can occur only when modification occurs in the group focal conflict with which the solution was originally associated. This modification consists in the reduction of reactive fears, which renders the original solution less necessary to the group as a device for binding anxiety and allows the solution to be modified or dissolved.*

Different patients play quite different roles in this process. In our illustration, it is Clifford who is the challenger. We assume that Clifford is less bound by the group solution and/or feels a greater need to push for gratification of the disturbing motive than do the other patients. It is Paul who often spearheads work on the reactive motive. Perhaps he is able to do this because his fears are less intense. Tim has an impact on the group in the fourth session because he is less willing than the others to deal with the dilemma by becoming cynical about the group as a potential source of help. Paul, Alan, Jean, and Tim may be more touched by the group focal conflict than others, for they are the ones who bring in dreams which are highly relevant to the shared group concerns. Other patients are far more passive. In some cases, their contribution is merely silent acquiescence. Sometimes, differences in role cannot be observed and all the patients participate in the same way. For example, everyone seemed willing to use the device of reminiscing about childhood experiences to explore their fears and revise their solutions. These examples emphasize the point made earlier —that the factor which moves the group is the different way in which each patient experiences the focal conflict and, consequently, the different way in which each person is stimulated to participate.

In theory, a reduction in the intensity of the disturbing motive could also lead to the modification of the group solution. A reduction in the disturbing motive would lead to a reduction in reactive fears and again render the solution less necessary to the group. However, this does not occur. Perhaps the explanation lies in the contrast between the character of a wish and the character of a fear. Disturbing motives express basic human needs; people do not renounce the wish to gratify such needs. Changes do occur in the disturbing motive, but these involve the manner in which it is expressed, the degree of delayed gratification which is tolerated, or the extent to which reality is taken into account in its gratification. The intensity of the wish remains the same. The changes that do occur in the disturbing motive are a consequence of shifts in the solution.

Direct attacks on a group solution are ineffective in producing change. Such an attack appeared in both the illustrations presented in this chapter. In the first illustration, the new member, Simon, inadvertently challenged an established group solution. In the second illustration, Clifford's behavior challenged the group solution "all be alike." Behavior which challenges a group solution is abrupt, startling, and disturbing to the patients. Because such challenges are dramatic and typically elicit a strong response from the group, they can be easily recognized. They generate an upsurge of tension in the group, and the subsequent interaction focuses on the challenger and the challenge. His behavior threatens the prevailing solution and is a potential force for effecting change in the group solution. However, such direct attacks on a group solution are not likely to lead to change.

When a direct challenge to a group solution occurs, the other patients make every effort to protect the original solution. Usually, the patients try to get the deviant to change his position. Such efforts generally fail because the deviant, for reasons of his own, cannot change.[5] The patients often continue to pressure him long after he has shown that he cannot or will not yield. Then, as alternative ways of protecting the solution, the patients may attempt to exclude the deviant, re-interpret his behavior, or excuse it so that it can be encompassed in their previous solution. One of these devices usually succeeds, and the patients are able to retain the original solution. Occasionally, all these efforts fail, but only then is the group forced into some modification of the solution.

Likewise, the character of the original solution is not a significant factor in determining change. For the primary feature of all successful solutions is that they function to reduce anxiety, and it is this which gives them their staying power. Some solutions might be regarded as inherently more satisfying than others, for they not only alleviate reactive fears, but also allow some gratification of the disturbing impulse. Yet the solution which gratifies the wish seems no more immune to change than the solution which does not gratify the wish. Or an unrealistic solution may also be maintained over a considerable period. For example, the solution "all be alike" was a fantasy. The patients were not all alike and were continually confronted with evidence of the fact. Yet, as long as the solution was necessary to the group, the patients were apparently willing to deny reality in order to maintain it.

The therapist may regard some solutions as therapeutic and others as anti-therapeutic. But this factor, too, cannot affect the tenacity with which the patients cling to an established solution. For, from the point of view of the patient, the primary function of the solution is to alleviate anxiety, and this can be performed equally well by therapeutic and anti-therapeutic solutions. Finally, the passage of time does not, in itself, guarantee change. The process by which change occurs is an active one which requires exploration of the reactive motive associated with the solution. It is only with this groundwork that change can occur. Without it, a group solution may persist indefinitely.

Proposition 17

Changes in the group culture do not occur through (1) direct challenges to the group solution or (2) a reduction in the intensity of the disturbing motive. Likewise, the properties of the solution itself, (satisfying or unsatisfying, realistic or unrealistic, therapeutic or anti-therapeutic) do not render one solution more subject to modification than another.

Our illustrations have dealt with single solutions. Over a period of time, a series of solutions, each one tied to a particular focal-conflict issue, develops in a therapy group. Some of these solutions persist over long periods; others yield quickly. At any given point, the culture of the group can be described in terms of the solutions currently in operation. But a group's total culture is continually being added to and modified, and the process of culture formation goes on throughout the life of the group.

Notes

[1] In large societies, cultural transmission between generations and diffusion between contemporaneous cultures are relevant processes. In the therapy

[2] This example, as well as a portion of the second illustration, has been re-
group, such considerations are not relevant.
ported previously in a paper on deviancy in therapy groups. See Dorothy Stock, Roy M. Whitman, and M. A. Lieberman, "The Deviant Member in Therapy Groups," *Human Relations,* 11 (1958), 341–372.

[3] As an alternative explanation of the group's reaction to Simon, one might argue that such behavior would be threatening and frightening to any group, regardless of the character of past solutions. In this case, both alternatives seem equally plausible, but other cases can be cited in which certain behavior, innocuous in itself, still appears threatening to the group. This occurs in the second illustration in this chapter, where Clifford is attacked for demanding the center of attention when the group solution "all be alike" is in effect. Or, previously acceptable behavior may suddenly be rejected when a new solution develops. In another inpatient group, a patient who consistently maintained that he did not need the group was not challenged until the patients moved towards establishing the solution "agree that everyone is in need of help."

[4] The new solution provided a new context for therapy. For example, one patient found himself able to reveal shameful facts about his past for the first time. Not only did the new group solution make this possible, but the others, acting in support of the group solution, were able to

offer him considerable support. This example and the general relevance of the group culture for the therapeutic process is discussed in Chapter 8.

[5] The meaning of the experience for a deviant patient like Simon or Clifford is discussed in Chapter 8.

6

Development of the Group

Observation of a therapy group over its life reveals, despite short-term variations, progress in particular directions. These observations suggest that certain basic issues recur during the life of a group. No matter how long the group goes on, the patients are recurrently confronted with such basic issues as how to manage anger constructively, how to be aware of emotions without being overwhelmed by them, how to maintain integrity of self yet enrich life through interdependence with others, or how to manage close personal relationships. These issues recur, and each time, they find expression through current material—the patients' experiences with one another and the therapist, their outside experiences, and aspects of the past brought into the group situation. A second observation is that the culture of the group changes during its life; the standards which govern possible content and permissible feelings are continually evolving. On the whole, these progressive shifts in group culture tend to broaden the group's boundaries. As the group goes on, solutions are likely to allow the patients to talk more directly about a broader range of topics and to express more frankly feelings about one another and the therapist. The recurrence of basic issues and the progressive expansion of group boundaries are the basic observations on which our developmental scheme is based. Our over-all view of group development is stated in the following proposition:

Proposition 18 | *The development of a therapy group from its inception to its termination is characterized by the recurrence of basic themes under progressively expanding cultural conditions.*

Phasing is de-emphasized in this view of group development. However, we do differentiate an initial or formative phase which is different from that which follows. The group begins with what might be thought of as a "first round" of certain basic themes, which differs from later recurrences of the same themes. In this sense, the formulation to be presented might be regarded as a two-phase theory of group development: a brief formative phase and a much longer phase during which the group can be thought of as "established."

When the group begins, it is unformed. The therapist has offered minimal structuring, for he has provided no agenda and suggested no topic. He is likely to restrict himself to brief introductory remarks which may or may not include patients' introductions. Thus, the patients are provided with no official guidelines and no signposts to tell them what to talk about or how to proceed. Yet, from the first moment that the group assembles, events are activated which generate the initial focal conflict of the group. Three factors are involved—prior expectations of the patients, the nature of the group situation, and the composition of the group.

Patients enter a therapy group with certain expectations about what the group may be able to do for them and what the situation will be like.[1] A patient is likely to experience certain hopes and fears about the group and make assumptions about what will occur in group therapy and about the way in which he can be helped. For example, a patient may fear that others will ridicule her when they find out how silly her problems are, or a patient may protest that others will not be experienced enough to help him. Sometimes certain assumptions, hopes, or fears are expressed quite indirectly. For example, one prospective patient could only repeat, with obvious anxiety, that he did not want to be in a therapy group. In the course of the interview, he mentioned that he always chose as friends people whom he regarded as superior, that he often became disillusioned and critical of others, and that he assumed that the other members of the group would be people with "defects." It did not seem far-fetched to assume that a major, though inarticulate, source of threat was the fear that his habitual way of relating to the world would be impossible in the group, thereby arousing intolerable anger or disappointment.

Some expectations reflect concerns which the person would have about any group or interpersonal situation. For example, a patient may expect that he will inevitably be rejected by others when they get to know him well or that, whenever he gets close to someone, he will end by hurting that person's feelings. Such worries are experienced in the job, in the family, and in other interpersonal settings, and the patient correctly anticipates that they will also come up in the therapy group. In addition to these general expectations, the patient may make some special assumptions about the therapy group. Although there are many variations, a very common assumption is that the patient's role is to provide data about himself and that the therapist's role is to provide help. The patient's assumption that he must talk about himself usually carries the implication that he must talk about personal problems and reveal secret, often shameful, feelings. With reference to the therapist's role, unsophisticated patients are likely to think in terms of advice, and more sophisticated patients in terms of the analysis of their problems. These expectations seem to persist despite a verbally expressed awareness that "you can't tell me what to do; I know I have to figure it out for myself." A related expectation is that the therapist is the sole source of help. The role of other patients is not so clearly defined. Some patients vaguely assume that the others will be auxiliary therapists who will provide ideas about their problems. Others assume that they will learn to get along with people by learning to get along with the patients in the group. Mostly, though, the other patients are regarded as an audience. For a few exhibitionists, the presence of an audience is anticipated with delight, but far more frequently the audience is feared as a source of potential criticism or ridicule.

These assumptions about the group can be stated more formally by saying that the patients have in mind a therapeutic contract which assumes that the patient's role and duty are to reveal personal problems so that the therapist can perform his role and duty, which are to utilize these data to analyze problems or provide advice. It is as if the patient, in his need to anticipate what the therapy group will be like, draws upon his previous experiences. He is likely to think partly in terms of the classroom and partly in terms of a doctor-patient relation.

The assumptions which the patient makes about the character of group therapy tend to intensify his fears or lead him to suspect that he will be robbed of his usual ways of coping with his fears. The patient who habitually fears that he will be rejected by others once they get to know him well also feels that in the group situation he will be obliged to reveal himself to others. The patient who is afraid that close contact with others is sure to lead to his hurting their feelings feels forced into a situation of closeness. The patient who utilizes withdrawal as a protective device fears that this will not be tolerated in the group.[2]

The second major factor influencing the character of the initial group sessions is the situation in which the patients find themselves once they enter the group. When a patient arrives for his first group session, he is confronted with one or two therapists and a large number of patients. This is a basic structural characteristic of the interpersonal milieu. The realities of the milieu and the patients' expectations are likely to generate conflict and uneasiness within each patient. In order to carry out his part of the assumed therapeutic contract, the patient feels he must reveal personal material not only to the therapist but also to an audience of peers. He is often uneasy about the group's ability to maintain a non-judgmental attitude. Further, if the patient assumes that help comes principally, if not exclusively, from the therapist, he is confronted with a number of competitors for the therapist's attention. Finally, very little experience in the group is required before the patient begins to suspect that the therapist is not going to live up to his side of the assumed contract. The patient quickly discovers that the therapist has some other idea about what the group is all about and that the advice or analysis which he was expecting is not forthcoming, at least not in the form or quantity that he might have wanted.

Immediately upon entering the group, then, the patient is beset with conflicting feelings. He is convinced that certain things must be done if he is to be helped, but at the same time these seem dangerous. Convinced that others will criticize and reject, how can a patient talk about his problems? How can he reveal secrets which will only be laughed at? How can he express angry resentment toward others if it might destroy them? The fact that these concerns are likely to be covert and only partially recognized makes them no less potent.

The precise character of the initial group focal conflict depends upon the composition of the group. Invariably, some patients are more vulnerable to certain issues than to others. Because of these individual differences, patients may express particular wishes or fears. Depending on how these expressions touch the others, they may or may not be picked up. If an expression is picked up, it will be elaborated by various comments, and, in a modified form, it will develop into the initial group focal conflict. Because of the individual differences and the resultant variations in group composition, one therapy group might emphasize concerns about destructive feelings' hurting others, whereas patients in another group might emphasize fears of punishment if they express impulses toward closeness. The therapist's style also has an impact on initial themes. For example, in groups in which the therapist suggests a procedure or topic, the initial material might be organized around a shared wish to comply with the therapist's wishes. A therapist who communicates to his group that he intends to focus on the specific problems of each patient may precipitate more competition for his attention than a therapist who encourages discussion among the members. These can be regarded as variations in the therapist's personality or theoretical orientation which find expression in variations in style. Sometimes therapeutic errors are made which have an impact on the initial themes. For example, a therapist taking on his first group communicated considerable insecurity during his opening comments. He concluded his rather lengthy remarks by saying that he, too, would be learning as the group went along. This group behaved as if its first task was to reassure the therapist. In another first session, the therapist broke the initial silence by saying, "We're wasting a lot of tape." This group became preoccupied with the therapist's potential punitiveness.

Of the three factors which have been postulated as significant in generating the initial focal conflicts, then, the first two (the patients' expectations and the structural characteristics of the group) are relatively stable from one group to the next. The third factor—the specific composition of the group—is always unique. Thus the patients' expectations and the structural characteristics of the group introduce similarities from one group to the next; yet differences in composition make every group different. Taken together, the factors which determine the initial focal conflict of the group can be stated as follows:

Proposition 19 | *The initial focal conflict of the group is a product of three factors: the patients' expectations about the group, the structure of the group, and the composition of the group.*

Certain focal conflicts—or, more correctly, certain disturbing and reactive motives—usually characterize the early sessions. Certain of these derive directly from the three factors just discussed; others arise in response to the solutions which the group establishes to the initial conflicts. For example, a group which deals with initial fears by developing a shared image of an all-powerful, protective therapist might then become anxious about the punitive ends to which the therapist might put his power. A group which has dealt with initial fears of criticism by focusing on one patient who has offered himself as a topic of conversation might then resent him because of the attention he is receiving.

Early reactive motives—the shared fears which emerge in the group—are likely to include fears of criticism or ridicule from the other patients; fears of harm through contact with other sick people; fears of hurting other patients or the therapist; fears of punishment, retaliation, or harm from the therapist; and fears of intolerable guilt and anxiety. The following reactive motives appeared during the early sessions of various therapy groups:[8]

Fear of retaliation or disapproval from the therapist.

Fear of abandonment and the therapist's angry reaction.

Fear of guilt about tattling.

Fear of punishment from the therapist.

Fear of attack, harm, and increased sickness through contact with other sick people.

Fear of exposure to attack and criticism from other patients.

Fear of loss of control over sexual feelings.

Fear of harming the therapist.

Fear of criticism and condemnation.

Fear of looking foolish.

Fear that destructive impulses will get out of hand.

Fear of being thought crazy by the therapist.

Fear of harming one another by destructive impulses.

Fear of destroying, thus losing, the therapist.

Such fears, of course, emerge in conjunction with specific disturbing motives or wishes. These include wishes to reveal one's problems in the group, to please the therapist by talking about oneself, to have an exclusive special relationship with the therapist, to be angry at the therapist for not providing help, and to form intimate relationships with others in the group. In specific groups, the following disturbing motives appeared:

Resentment toward the therapist.

Wish to reprimand a deviant patient who has used information gained in the group to hurt another patient.

Wish to reveal "faults" and "bad" impulses to the group.

Sexual feelings about one another.

Wish to be helped by revealing personal problems.

Anger at the therapist for punishing and refusing help.

Wish to be unique and singled out for special attention from the therapist.

Wish to destroy or exclude rival patients.

Wish to be the "favorite child."

Wish to comply with the implicit demand of the therapist to talk about feelings and problems.

Competitive feelings toward one another.

Wish to talk frankly about oneself.

Hostile impulses toward a fellow patient.

Just as certain specific disturbing and reactive motives appear during the early sessions, characteristic solutions develop. Perhaps a discussion of common initial solutions should open with a solution which does not occur: that of disbanding the group. The patients could protect themselves from the intense anxieties characteristic of the early sessions by disbanding. But although patients may discuss this possibility, we have not yet seen a group who did it. Perhaps the reason is that disbandment is a solution involving total surrender of any wish to get help from the group. Anxieties do not become so intense that the group as a whole uses the solution of mass flight. Before this point is reached, someone always comes forward with solutions which permit some alleviation of anxiety and at the same time maintain the group.

Thus, rather than agreeing to disband, the patients find other ways of coping with initial focal conflicts. Very often, a solution will involve disguising the disturbing or reactive motive so that the patients need not recognize its true character. Thus, the early wishes and fears may be displaced onto outside figures, discussed symbolically or intellectually, projected onto a member of the group, acted out, or denied. Although these mechanisms differ from one another, they have a common function—that of coping with the conflict by avoiding recognition of the fact that the feelings belong to oneself or that the conflict pertains to the present situation. The following are some examples:

Deny sexual feelings by insisting that feelings about one another involve only friendship.

Deny that anything bad exists within themselves.

Discuss the problems of an outside person and agree that he needs help.

Discuss competitive, jealous feelings about outside peer figures.

Act out competitive feelings in the group by intellectual arguments.

Get one person to admit that he has problems, then attack him.

Another type of solution involves recognizing the impulses involved in the focal conflict but admitting to them minimally or rationalizing them. Angry feelings may be rationalized by seeing their object as deserving punishment or as having brought the anger on himself. Angry feelings may be excused by being seen as a way of pleasing the therapist by virtuously expressing oneself directly. Some examples are:

Agree that everyone has *little* problems.

Agree that anger toward fathers is justified (displacement plus rationalization).

Justify anger by constructing fantasy that the therapist is making unreasonable demands.

A related type of solution involves safely expressing the disturbing motive so that the feared consequence will not occur—for example, by banding together to express angry compliance or expressing anger toward therapist by acting as if he is not there. In both cases, angry feelings toward the therapist are expressed in ways which do not look like anger, thus protecting the patients from the consequences they fear if they express their feelings.

Several of the above solutions involve seeing everyone in the group as alike in some respect. Some variation of the solution "we are all alike" often appears in early sessions. The frequency with which this appears may be related to the fact that it can operate as a solution to a variety of focal conflicts. For example, such a solution may develop in response to a focal conflict in which the reactive motive involves fears of criticism or attack from one another. If the patients can agree that they are all alike, then they have made themselves equally vulnerable. The same solution is sometimes a response to a focal conflict involving competitive impulses or a wish for a special relationship with the therapist. Sometimes this solution deals with threatened loss of self-esteem by agreeing that the patients are all alike in having had the good sense to seek psychiatric help.

Another common solution is the practice of "turn-taking." In a rough way, the patients each take a turn at being "patient," asking questions, while the others function as "therapists," offering explanations. This solution, too, can function in conjunction with a number of related focal conflicts. It can deal with competitive feelings by carefully providing each patient with equal time. It can cope with anger or disappointment about the therapist's failure to give advice by finding substitute therapists. By introducing structure and control, it can protect the patients against fears of loss of control over angry, sexual, or dependent impulses.

During the early sessions, patients often attempt to handle a stressful situation by trying to get the therapist to provide a solution. The following solutions belong in this category:

Demand a guarantee from the therapist that therapy will be worth the trouble and anxiety.

Demand that the therapists provide direction.

Get the therapists to control things.

Get the therapist to make an anonymous ruling against a deviant patient.

Ask for assurance from the therapist that they can talk about "unreasonable" things.

Sometimes the therapist feels that he can comply with these requests and will cooperate in establishing the solution. For example, he may be ready to assure the patients that feelings which they regard as "unreasonable" are within bounds. But more often the therapist does not cooperate with the patients in establishing solutions, either because the request is beyond human capacity or because compliance would violate his ideas about therapeutically useful behavior. Patients sometimes think that, if the therapist asked the right questions, all their problems would be solved. Not being capable of this kind of magic, the therapist cannot comply; if he gives the appearance of complying, he succeeds only in perpetuating the myth. Patients sometimes appeal to the therapist to punish a deviant patient. In this case, the therapist is being asked to do something of which he is capable, but which may violate his idea of appropriate behavior. For these reasons, patients' efforts to get the therapist to provide solutions are likely to fail.

The solutions which develop during the early sessions are likely to be restrictive rather than enabling in character. Solutions which involve displacement, intellectualization, projection, denial, or turn-taking reduce anxiety by avoiding or suppressing the feelings which have generated the anxiety. When the group is operating on such a solution, tension is reduced but the disturbing motive remains unsatisfied and inaccessible to exploration. Solutions which involve rationalizing or minimizing partially satisfy the disturbing motive, but may have the same eventual effect, since a feeling which is rationalized or minimized cannot be constructively examined.

Because these solutions restrict opportunities for the expression and exploration of feelings, they are likely to be regarded as anti-therapeutic by the therapist. Nevertheless, they perform a necessary function in that they alleviate initial anxieties and make it possible for the group to remain intact. Although restrictive, such a set of solutions facilitates therapy, because it constitutes a culture in which the patients feel sufficiently comfortable to commit themselves to the group.

The early sessions mark the formation of a group culture—the rapid establishment of solutions to a series of initial focal conflicts. The rapidity with which this develops is related to the level of anxiety during these early sessions. It is as if the patients must achieve solutions, structure the group, and form a culture in order to feel minimally comfortable. Nor can they pause to thoroughly examine the many issues which arise. Any impulse which arises is likely to bring with it, almost instantaneously, associated fears and counter-impulses. This occurs long before the impulse is expressed in a direct way, so that a disturbing motive expressed on a symbolic level is likely to be accompanied by a reactive motive similarly expressed. At the same time, there is likely to be a rapid production of potential solutions. Only a few of these are eventually established. A solution which does find general acceptance may persist, or it may undergo immediate modification. A solution to one focal conflict may generate another issue or may be challenged by a patient. These processes give the early sessions a choppy quality, and themes often seem to change or be interrupted before they are thoroughly developed. These characteristics of the early sessions can be summarized as follows:

Proposition 20

The development of a therapy group begins with a formative phase in which themes emerge and are dealt with for the first time. This phase is marked by the rapid establishment of a group culture which is dominated by restrictive solutions.

(1) *Restrictive solutions involving disguising, finding a spokesman for, or rationalizing the disturbing or reactive motives are associated with a broad range of group focal conflicts.*

(2) *Restrictive solutions involving turn-taking are associated with disturbing motives which involve anger at the therapist for failing to provide adequate direction or competitive feelings toward one another.*

(3) *Restrictive solutions involving implicit assumptions of similarity among the patients are associated with reactive motives involving fears of criticism or ridicule from peers or fears of threatened loss of self-esteem or disturbing motives involving angry, competitive feelings toward one another or a wish for a special relationship with the therapist.*

(4) *Restrictive solutions involving displacement or projection are associated with disturbing motives involving hostile or sexual feelings.*

We have suggested that a first round of focal conflicts and the establishment of an initial culture constitute the formative phase of the therapy group. What marks the end of the formative period? The crucial factor does not appear to be the number or variety of focal conflicts which have come up; groups vary in this respect. Rather, the close of the formative phase is marked by the establishment of successful solutions which cope with initial anxieties about criticism, ridicule, punishment by the therapist, and so forth. Hope for therapeutic gain is established so that patients can feel some commitment to the group. The process is not a complete one. What is important is that the group has generated a set of solutions—a culture—which permits it to function with reasonable comfort.

Therapy groups we have studied usually reach this point between the eighth and the twelfth sessions. A reliable indication that this point has been reached is the relief which accompanies it. There is some feeling that the group is now a group, for it has become meaningful to the patients and they are not likely to leave it. For the first time, the therapist may feel confident that the group will continue to develop in a useful way.

The exact time which marks the end of the formative phase is clear in some groups and vague in others. In some groups the therapist may recognize only in retrospect that the group has moved into a new phase. In other groups this point occurs more dramatically. The therapist may come away from a particular session feeling that the group has taken shape. Sometimes the turning point is marked by a ritualistic sign. For example, in several groups this moment was marked by a round of introductions although introductions had occurred during the first session. The repetition seemed to mark the point at which the patients were really willing to know one another. When the turning point occurs rather pointedly and dramatically, the accompanying feeling of relief is likely to be very noticeable.

Proposition 21 | *The close of the formative phase is characterized by a shared sense of commitment to the group and a subjective feeling of relief associated with the achievement of successful solutions to the initial group focal conflicts.*

Following the termination of the formative phase, the group enters a lengthy established phase which continues until the group terminates. The established phase is not internally homogeneous. Under the continuing push of impulses, old themes recur, sometimes leading to the utilization of previous successful solutions, sometimes to the modification of old solutions. Modified solutions, in turn, permit patients to express impulses, wishes, and fears in new and usually more direct terms.

Basic wishes and fears remain essentially the same throughout the life of the group. Both early and late, there are disturbing motives which involve hostile impulses toward peers and the therapist; impulses toward anger, revenge, and competition; sexual yearnings; wishes for intimacy; wishes to reveal oneself to others and find acceptance; impulses toward exclusive possession and a need to be taken care of. Similarly, there are reactive motives which involve fears of retaliation and punishment, of abandonment and loss, of arousing intolerable guilt and anxiety, of attack by others, and of losing self-esteem, of losing control over sexual and destructive impulses, or, more primitively, of losing control over one's sense of self. In contrast, the solutions by which the group operates—the group culture—show continued modification. The trend is toward the predominance of enabling solutions and toward fewer restrictive solutions.

As the group develops, the solutions which allow no satisfaction of the disturbing motive tend to be less predominant. Given a choice, the patients prefer to operate on a solution which satisfies the disturbing motive. For example, a solution which says "we are all alike in having felt destructively competitive toward siblings" might make it possible to directly express a disturbing motive involving competitive feelings without having to fear loss of self-esteem or blame from others. A solution which states "recognize that children can be cruel to one another" might free the patients to recognize angry, cruel behavior. Restrictive solutions do not disappear altogether and, in fact, serve a vital function for the group. They operate like safety valves or escape hatches which are utilized when anxiety reaches intolerable levels. Anxious periods are just as likely to occur during the established phase as during the formative phase. In the context of the progressively broadening group culture, themes are dealt with on a level which would not have been possible during the formative period. The new levels of exploration elicit reactive fears which are subjectively just as intense as those which were experienced earlier. This suggests that, from the point of view of the patients, focal conflicts which superficially look as if they involve differing degrees of intensity are experienced as equivalent. Because the patients continually operate on the limits of what is possible for them, the necessity for escape-hatch solutions persists. Thus, one does not expect any group to consistently operate on enabling solutions. Rather, even late in the group's development, one expects patients to resort to restrictive solutions, usually for limited periods.

It is relatively easy to list the solutions on which a group is operating at the turning point. The group's history is relatively brief, and the group has moved through a limited number of focal conflicts. As the group proceeds, concise description becomes more difficult because of the more complex and extended history and because some changes become apparent only through the absence of earlier solutions. To illustrate the kinds of changes in culture which may occur, let us consider a hypothetical group whose initial culture could be stated as follows:

> We are all alike in that each of us has problems; however, if the truth were known, we are superior to people outside psychiatric hospitals because we are intelligent enough to admit that we have problems and to seek help. If we are careful about what we say, we will not be criticized. The therapist can probably be counted on to use his power to protect rather than to attack us. Still, the group is a somewhat dangerous place. There are things the therapist and other patients will not stand for, but we can always protect ourselves by talking about outside subjects like baseball. Besides, George can always be counted on to talk about himself and thus protect everyone else from the dangers of self-exposure.

After meeting regularly for eight or ten months, the culture of this group might be something like the following:

> We are all alike in that each of us has problems; however, each person's problems are unique and make him a special person in the group. Still, there are some basic similarities; for example, we would each like to have the therapist for ourselves. If we stopped to think of it, we would still probably regard ourselves as superior to those not receiving psychiatric help, but this doesn't seem so important an issue any more, and we don't think about it much. It is possible to reveal a great deal more about ourselves than we thought it would be, since it has turned out that we won't be criticized. After all, each of us could be criticized for something, so there is no point in making judgments. The therapist is not so powerful as we thought he was. There are still times when the group seems dangerous, and there are still things which cannot be said. When the atmosphere becomes tense, we can always talk about some outside event like movies or television. We used to count on George to talk about himself so that no one else would have to, but people became angry because he was getting all the attention, so we don't do that any more.

A second group might initially operate on the following set of solutions:

> Although it is shameful to be in a therapy group, perhaps it is tolerable as long as no one sees us coming here and as long as no one gossips outside. The problems which are revealed are the fault of parents, and, therefore, there is no reason for any of us to feel ashamed or to criticize one another. The therapists are not a source of danger because, as professional people, they have no feelings about us. And we have no feelings about them—certainly not angry feelings, even though they are not doing their job properly. Although there are certain dangers in the group, they can be avoided as long as we stick to the proper

procedure, which is to take turns at presenting problems while everyone else asks questions and offers advice. It is all right to express feelings about one another as long as it is done toward the end of the session when the time is nearly up.

Later, the culture of this group might shift to the following:

> Feelings of shame and fears of criticism are not so prominent now, perhaps because we have discovered that no one can expect to be perfect and that some of our expectations for ourselves were unrealistic. It is all right to have feelings, even angry feelings, about the therapist because the therapist will not seek revenge, being a professional person who can be counted on to control his reactions. Lately, however, we have been wondering whether this is the case; the therapist may turn out to be human after all. It is no longer necessary for us to take turns at being the patient since we found out that it is possible to interact more directly without catastrophic results. However, certain things still seem dangerous, and, when things get tense and difficult, it is still possible to resort to turn-taking. This doesn't last so long as it used to, perhaps because someone is certain to point it out. Therapy doesn't take place exactly as we expected it to. Our hopes of understanding ourselves thoroughly have not yet been met. Still, some changes seem to be occurring, and we don't think much about this point any more.

These hypothetical cultures differ from one another, and each is different from and yet similar to its own initial culture. Because each group is unique in its composition, each group begins in its own way and develops a unique initial culture. The initial culture has an impact on what follows, and each group follows its own course.

The initial successful solutions appear to be an especially important aspect of the group's history. At the close of the formative phase, the group's history can be thought of as encompassed in a set of solutions which have a potent influence on the later development of the group. One solution might preclude the emergence of certain disturbing or reactive motives; another might facilitate their appearance. For example, if a group has established as one of its initial solutions the practice of turn-taking, this in itself will inhibit give-and-take in the group and may delay the emergence of competitive feelings. In contrast, suppose the group members have adopted the solution of protecting themselves by getting one patient to expose himself to expected punishment from the therapist. Such a solution might actually generate a focal conflict involving competitive feelings, and in such a group competitive feelings might emerge much sooner.

The group's history is a potent factor in influencing its later development, but we have avoided suggesting that the group's history determines its later course. Outside events do occur which have an impact on the group. Such events include changes in the group's composition or routine (absences, tardiness, interruptions for vacations, and the addition and loss of patients); outside personal experiences of particular patients (a patient's marriage or the death of a parent); and events in the outside world (the testing of an atom bomb or the admission to the ward of a destructive patient). At first glance, these events seem to stir up feelings which might not otherwise occur and merely divert the course of group events. Yet it is striking how often these outside events become integrated into the current focal conflict. For example, a student group was concerned about the hospitalization of a fellow student who was only casually known to the group members. This group had been involved in a focal conflict focusing on feelings about the therapists' omnipotence and whether their power might be used destructively against the patients. The solution to this conflict was a relatively unstable one. When a fellow student was hospitalized, the patients' fantasies were consistent with the previous concern. It is hard to say whether the external event elicited the concern or whether it provided a content vehicle for the expression of an unresolved concern. It seems clear that the same event could have stirred up quite different fantasies in another group or in the same group at another time. We have observed that essentially the same event can be utilized differently by the same group at different times. For example, consider the admission of a destructive psychotic patient to a psychiatric ward, a not uncommon event. At one point, an inpatient group was coping with a focal conflict involving destructive impulses versus fears of retaliation. A destructive patient on the ward was said to express "phony" hostility (see Chapter 4). Although he had thrown a chair through a window and stirred up considerable anxiety in the ward, the patients in the group referred to his behavior as harmless. The patients maintained that he knew what he was doing and really would not hurt anyone. At this point, this group was attempting to institute a solution that denied destructive impulses. In effect, they were trying to alleviate their anxieties by insisting that hostile impulses were not real and therefore not potentially destructive. The external event was brought into the group in a way which supported this emergent solution. It is clear that a good deal of distortion was required in order to use the event in this way. In the same group a similar event on the ward later had a different impact. This time, a destructive patient elicited fears about the potential loss of control over hostile feeling. Far from assuring one another that such behavior represented "phony" feelings, the patients expressed fears that they, too, might lose control over their anger. The fact that a very similar external event was utilized in differing ways can be explained in terms of the particular group focal conflict which existed at the time. It seems to be an oversimplification to say that, if some external event had not occurred, a particular issue would never have come up in the group. On the other hand, it is just as much an oversimplification to assert that external events have no impact on the group. At the very least, they provide an otherwise unavailable vehicle for expression. At times, they seem to re-elicit a theme which otherwise might not have recurred until later.

An unresolved issue with reference to the group's established phase is whether a therapy group develops to a point which can be regarded as group maturity or to a point where further development is unlikely or unnecessary. Put into our theoretical terms, a mature group is one which has achieved stable solutions to basic focal conflicts. In a work group, reaching a state of maturity means that it is in a position to work efficiently on its external task. But in a therapy group, which has no external task, reaching this state may mean that it has accomplished its business. We believe that therapy groups do not reach a state of ultimate maturity. They continue to work on recurring basic issues until the patients feel that enough has been accomplished individually so that terminating the group is appropriate. But group maturity per se seems an alien factor. The imminent close of the group is a precipitating event which is likely to call forth focal conflicts involving separation, abandonment anxieties, and feelings around accomplishment and achievement. But it is very unlikely that such themes arise for the first time during the closing sessions. Probably the final meetings are merely the final recurrence of issues which have been explored at various times. In fact, it is likely that a group is able to enter a closing period only because such issues have been worked on and much groundwork has been laid for coping with the feelings elicited by final separation. It is in this sense that we do not see the final series of sessions as dramatically different or separate in the life of the group.

Proposition 22

The development of a therapy group includes an extended established phase in which themes recur and are dealt with repeatedly. This phase is marked by the continual modification of the group culture. During the established phase the group culture includes both restrictive and enabling solutions, although the latter predominate.

(1) *Important enabling solutions are those which*

> *involve confidence that the therapist can be counted on to forestall grossly harmful or overwhelming affect in the group and implicit assumptions of basic likeness. These solutions may be utilized in association with a range of focal conflicts.*
> (2) *Restrictive solutions, such as displacement, intellectualization, and flight toward irrelevant topics, continue to be utilized from time to time and function as escape hatches for the patients. These solutions may be utilized in association with a range of focal conflicts.*

In order to point up the manner in which the same theme may be dealt with during the initial phase of a therapy group and during its established phase, we will summarize the manner in which an outpatient adolescent group coped with a theme which involved sexual impulses toward the therapists during the fourth and sixty-first through sixty-third sessions.

This group consisted of three boys and three girls eighteen to nineteen years of age and a male and a female therapist. Sexual themes, specifically sexual impulses toward the therapists, and attendant anxieties appeared early. These themes were important for the adolescents and recurred a number of times. In the second session, the disturbing motive involved sexual feelings about one another, and the reactive motive involved fears of such feelings getting out of control. In the third session, the disturbing motive again involved sexual impulses, but it was difficult to determine whether the primary target was peers or therapists. In the fourth session, the target of sexual feelings shifted more clearly toward the therapists. The following focal conflict was formulated to summarize the fourth session:

disturbing motive		*reactive motive*
wish to surpass others in achieving sexual success with the therapists	X	fear of some catastrophe (anticipation of loss of therapists because of their angry reactions)

solutions

emphasize one's intellectual impotence

insist on one's inability to compete as a male or female

express competitiveness through arguing about who is the most incompetent

express sexual interests only in terms of peer relationships, but even here insist on one's innocence or failure

The most striking features of the session can be summarized in five points. First, the disturbing motive was expressed in an exceedingly indirect, tentative manner. For example, one of the girls implied that she and Dr. K., the male therapist, had shared an enjoyable, private experience when she told the group that they had met at a lecture the evening before and had heard an exciting speaker. Competitiveness appeared only in the interaction and was expressed through continual interruptions and abrupt shifts of topic in which each person snatched the spotlight from the previous speaker. Second, even these indirect indications of sexual interests were quickly suppressed before any development or more direct expression could occur. Initial expressions of the disturbing motive were interrupted by individual attempts to divert the conversation to concerns about studying, a long intellectual explanation of problems, and so on. After some time, a topic on which patients shared feelings about incompetence caught on. Surface coherence was lacking, giving the session a choppy quality.

Third, initially the reactive fears were vague and unclear; later there were indirect and momentary indications that the reactive motive might involve fears of retaliation from the therapists if the patients were to succeed sexually. At first, one could only guess from the interruption of or immediate flight from any expression of sexual interests that some gross but undefined reactive fear was operating. Later, hints about the character of the reactive motive were expressed in shared admissions that the patients were more successful academically than their parents had been and in concerns about how their parents might feel about them. The reactive fear was most directly expressed by one of the boys, who "caught" the male therapist looking at him and wondered whether it was because someone had just implied that he was interested in one of the girls.

Fourth, the session was dominated by the extended spinning out of rapidly shifting related solutions. From the point of view of the time taken, the bulk of the session was devoted to expressions of the solution "we are impotent." This was initially expressed in terms of inability to study, failure to get into the college of one's choice, and so forth. This shifted into a discussion which referred more specifically to sexual incompetence. Several boys shared fears about possible homosexuality; theories were offered to account for failure to attract boy friends or girl friends.

Fifth, the predominant solutions alleviated reactive fears by giving up all hope of satisfying the wish. The patients insisted on their intellectual and sexual incompetence, thus denying the possibility of winning in sexual competition. They shared feelings of hopelessness about their intellectual equipment and later traded stories about their lack of success in dating. Thus, the patients dealt with the focal conflict by insisting that they need not fear the catastrophic consequences of their sexual interests since any effort on their part to win in a sexual competition was doomed to failure. The device amounted to "don't hit me; I'm helpless; I won't try." At the same time, this device allowed the expression of some competitive feelings, since each patient insisted that he or she was worse than the others. This solution, typical of those found during early sessions, dealt with the fears involved in the reactive motive by giving up the wish. By various solutional devices, the patients concealed from themselves the true character of both their sexual competitive wishes and the associated fears. Thus they relieved their anxiety but rendered the basic issue inaccessible to examination.

Related themes recurred a number of times in this group. Much later, the same issue reappeared and could be generally summarized as follows (for a more detailed account, see Chapter 4).

disturbing motive		*reactive motive*
sexual feelings for the therapist of the opposite sex	X	fears of retaliation and punishment from therapist of the same sex

It will be noted that, although the theme is essentially the same, there are differences in emphasis between the two focal conflicts. In the later recurrence, the competitive aspect of the disturbing motive does not appear, and the reactive motive can be stated more precisely. The fear of abandonment is gone from the reactive motive, and it now focuses more specifically on fears of retaliation and punishment from adults. Yet the two focal conflicts are striking in their similarity. The disturbing motive in both instances involves sexual impulses toward the therapist of the opposite sex; the reactive motive in both cases emphasizes the dire consequences of experiencing such feelings.

In summarized form, the two focal conflicts are very similar. Yet differences in the manner in which the conflict was expressed were striking. The most notable features of the later recurrence can be summarized as follows. First, the disturbing motive was expressed in relatively direct terms. For example, one of the girls recognized her feelings of rejection when she saw Dr. K. on the street and he failed to notice her. Another commented that she would have felt embarrassed and went on to talk about thinking of Dr. K. as a father as well as a boy friend. Later, a patient commented on a non-verbal exchange between the two therapists and said that she thought it indicated some sharing of feelings. In general, the patients were able to report such feelings with considerable freedom and directness. This directness sharply contrasts with the indirect manner in which similar feelings were expressed during the initial appearance of this theme in the fourth session.

Second, the group shifted, with apparent ease, from references to sexual interest in the therapists to similar interest in their own parents. They seemed to understand the emotional equivalence between therapists and parents. The content swung back and forth rather freely among explorations of here-and-now feelings about the therapists, current feelings about parents, and past feelings about parents. For example, the girl who referred to thinking of Dr. K. as a boy friend and a father followed this with speculations as to whether her increased interest in personal grooming was related to changing feelings about her own father; this in turn led into a general discussion about childhood sexual interest in parents. The comment about shared feelings between the therapists was followed by a general discussion about warm, sexually tinged feelings during childhood about parents and then by shared thoughts about parents' current reactions to boy friends and girl friends. Our impression that the patients were aware of the equivalence between therapists and parents is hard to document, but derives primarily from the ease with which the discussion shifted from therapists to parents as objects of sexual feelings and curiosities. The use of certain metaphors also supports this impression. For example, one of the patients asked Dr. K. whether he had another flock of children. (Although the patients had discussed feelings about parents during the earlier occurrence, the same capacity to move freely back and forth between parents as objects and therapists as objects could not be observed.)

Third, the reactive motive took much longer to gain ascendancy, but, when it did, it was highly specific. For example, the patients talked about feeling affectionate toward parents while, at the same time, associating them with punishment. Two girls shared feelings of having been afraid that their parents would kill them, which they found odd since they had never been punished at home. This led to a discussion of fears of the therapists' being critical of them.

Fourth, the sessions were dominated by extended discussions of the disturbing motive. The patients were able to explore sexual and related feelings about the therapists and parents in considerable detail before they began to show signs of uneasiness. As the sessions progressed, the balance between the disturbing and the reactive motives gradually shifted from an initial free expression of the disturbing motive with no signs of associated anxiety to the gradual emergence and eventual dominance of reactive fears. In the end, the patients adopted a restrictive, suppressive solution and abandoned the issue. But this process occurred slowly, so that a great portion of the sessions was given over to explorations of the disturbing motive. (This was in marked contrast to the initial occurrence of this focal conflict, in which even the veiled appearance of the disturbing motive immediately led to fears and the rapid institution of restrictive solutions. The fourth session was dominated by the spinning out of restrictive solutions rather than by the expression of the disturbing motive.)

Fifth, the solution which was eventually adopted dealt with intensified fears by giving up or suppressing the wish. Thus the group ended with a suppressive solution. In this respect, the later recurrence and the initial appearance of this focal conflict were similar. However, in the first occurrence, the suppressive solution involved a mutual agreement that the patients were impotent and incapable of competing successfully. In the later recurrence, the suppressive solution involved displacement into intellectual spheres. Another crucial difference lay in the pacing and the extent to which the solution dominated the material.

Notes

[1] This discussion of patients' expectations is based on the comments which patients made during the early sessions of several groups and on individual interviews conducted before the first session. The primary purpose of the interview is to become sufficiently acquainted with the patient to make a mutual decision about whether a therapy group might be appropriate. During the interview, considerable information is gained regarding the patient's expectations about the group.

[2] Frequently, in an exploratory interview, a patient may warn the therapist that he is likely to be silent at first, thus eliciting the therapist's assurance that time may be required before he feels like talking freely in the group. In effect, the patient warns the therapist that he may not be able to live up to the contract; the therapist, in turn, assures the patient that he does not regard initial withdrawal as a violation of the contract.

[3] This list and the discussion which follows are based on three sources: (1) a detailed formal analysis of the first meetings of three therapy groups (Dorothy Stock, "Interpersonal Concerns During the Early Sessions of Therapy Groups," *International Journal of Group Psychotherapy,* 12 [1962], 14–26), (2) a review of twelve additional groups conducted by ourselves and colleagues, and (3) a study of early sessions reported in the literature wherever these accounts included sufficient clinical data. The latter include six first sessions reported by Florence B. Powdermaker and J. D. Frank, *Group Psychotherapy,* pp. 115–129, 513–527, a sixth session reported by George Bach, *Intensive Group Psychother-*

apy, pp. 43–45, a first session reported by Henry Ezriel, "A Psychoanalytic Approach to Group Treatment," pp. 64–68, and a first session reported by W. R. Bion, *Experiences in Groups, and Other Papers*, pp. 29–39.

II

The Individual's Therapeutic Experience

7

The Patient's Experience

In this chapter, we shift our focus from the group to the individual and examine the experience and behavior of the patient in the context of the group. More specifically, we are concerned with the patient's reactions to the group situation, his impact on group events, and the manner in which he experiences and conceptualizes the group therapy experience.

When a person begins therapy, he can be described in terms of his current pathological state and his current susceptibility to change. In characterizing the individual at this point, we will utilize the theoretical terms developed by Thomas French.[1] The idea of conceptualizing group events in focal-conflict terms was originally stimulated by the work of French, who developed a conceptual scheme for understanding individual personality and the character of the two-person therapeutic process. French suggested that an individual's current behavior can be understood as the expression of individual solutions to currently experienced focal conflicts. These focal conflicts are rooted in long-standing nuclear conflicts which developed much earlier in the individual's life. Feelings consonant with basic nuclear conflicts are experienced in current interpersonal settings and take on a special character from the specifics of the current situation. Similarly, habitual individual solutions originally developed in order to cope with the nuclear conflict find expression in derived forms modified to suit the derived focal conflict. In this view, the individual can be understood in terms of (1) a limited number of related nuclear conflicts, (2) the solutions which he has evolved to deal with these conflicts, and (3) the derived expression of both the conflict and the habitual solution in terms appropriate to current interactive conditions.

To illustrate, an important nuclear conflict for a thirty-five-year-old patient, Paul,[2] was summarized as follows:

disturbing motive		*reactive motive*
need to be loved and cared for	X	fear of rejection and object loss

This nuclear conflict could be understood in terms of the patient's history, which included an illegitimate birth, early abandonment by his mother, and a childhood spent in a crowded institution. As a child, he established specific devices for coping with this dilemma. He befriended younger children even more bereft than he. In this way, he enjoyed maternal care vicariously by offering it to others; moreover, he established close relationships with children who needed him badly and were unlikely to reject him. Early in life, he developed a fantasy about his origin which he elaborated in fairy-tale fashion. In this fantasy, his father was a distinguished man, and his mother had reluctantly placed him in an orphanage under the pressure of very difficult circumstances. As Paul moved into adulthood and faced different tasks and situations, he experienced this nuclear conflict in various forms in many interpersonal situations. His need to be loved and cared for persisted but became elaborated and modified into a wish to be wanted and to have close contact with people. This wish remained a potent force and was experienced on the job, in the Army, in social life, and, currently, on the ward and in the therapy group. The fear of rejection and object loss which appeared in the reactive motive of the nuclear conflict also was experienced repeatedly in many current interpersonal situations. Major aspects of Paul's life could be conceptualized in terms of a series of focal conflicts rooted in the core nuclear conflict but influenced, in their specific character, by the nature of the interpersonal situation in which the conflict was re-elicited and re-experienced.[3] The habitual solutions which Paul had developed to cope with this persisting conflict were also maintained in modified forms. Although Paul's circumstances no longer permitted him to be helpful to younger children in the orphanage, he utilized various opportunities to be useful to those with whom he came in daily contact. As he grew older, he found he could engage and keep the interest of others through intellectual arguments about politics and social issues. At the time at which he entered therapy, Paul had a repertory of habitual solutions: (1) adopt a maternal role, making himself useful and necessary to others; (2) present himself to others in terms of a fictionalized life history; (3) gain contact through intellectual argumentation; (4) engage in sexual contacts with degraded women who would not leave him; and (5) occasionally drink alcohol to excess. Certain of these habitual solutions were related rather directly to solutions adopted early in childhood. For example, the solution which involved making himself useful to others first emerged when he was relatively young and persisted, with appropriate modifications, to the time of entry into the therapy group. Similarly, the solution of a fictionalized life history developed very early and persisted. The only modification was that, as Paul moved out of the orphanage setting, where others would have known that the story was made up, he made his private fantasy a public story. Paul did not begin to engage in sexual contacts with degraded women until he was an adult, but this solution may be a modification of the earlier one of helping persons more helpless than himself. Alcoholism was also utilized as a solution in adulthood.

An individual's life style consists of his repertory of solutions. Solutions are incapacitating to varying degrees. For example, Paul's solution of gaining contact with others through intellectual argumentation was appropriately rewarding. It enabled him to establish contact with others in a way which was acceptable to them and did not elicit the feared rejection or abandonment. Further, this solution did not cause Paul undue pain, nor did it interfere with other satisfactions. On the other hand, his bouts of alcoholism were maladaptive; they temporarily deprived him of association with job colleagues—an important source of rewarding friendships for him—and elicited disapproval from others. His fictionalized life story was also a maladaptive solution. In order to maintain this solution, he had to be constantly on guard. This wariness made it even more difficult to achieve the closeness he sought. Certain more adaptive possibilities for dealing with his dilemma were absent from Paul's repertory. For example, he was not married and was thus deprived of satisfactions which he might have gained from closeness with a maternal woman or with children of his own.[4]

Presumably, the patient enters therapy because some or all of his habitual solutions have begun to be non-functional. Perhaps some change in his life has robbed him of people who figured importantly in some solution; perhaps he is entering a new phase of life, and his habitual solutions are no longer adequate to cope with intensified impulses or fears; perhaps a breakdown of habitual solutions has led him to adopt more maladaptive, painful solutions. In any event, he feels sufficiently distressed to seek therapy. Ezriel has suggested that an effort to reproduce transference relationships is the source of the individual's unconscious motivation for seeking treatment.[5] According to this view, an individual in the ordinary course of his life seeks relationships which are adequate for his unconscious needs. Ezriel says, "A person's mental economy will remain in a state of 'healthy' equilibrium as long as he can find adequate outlets for his unconscious needs; this will depend on the quality, quantity and distribution of the object relationships of his unconscious fantasies, and on his resources and opportunities in his environment."[6] Ezriel sees these efforts as attempts to diminish tension arising from unconscious object relations. Further, he perceives the individual as operating in a state of relative comfort as long as these efforts meet with success or relative success. When something occurs to disturb this equilibrium, a person experiences heightened anxiety and may be motivated to seek treatment. Ezriel suggests that: "The transference relationship is therefore not, as was originally believed, something that gradually develops in the course of and as a *result* of treatment; rather, it is the patient's need for such a relationship which is the true, though unconscious, *cause* of his seeking treatment."[7]

This view, although expressed in differing theoretical terms, is consistent with our observation that the decision to seek treatment may correspond with some breakdown of a habitual solution or the exposure of a habitual solution as inadequate. This need not occur as a result of some dramatic incident or loss. It may occur simply because an individual, in the course of moving from one phase of life into another, finds his old solutions inadequate in the light of emerging impulses and concepts of himself. This can be seen readily in adolescent patients, who, in the course of maturing, can no longer settle for previously acceptable modes of dealing with persistent conflicts. Over the years, the individual has developed certain solutions for crucial focal conflicts. At some point, these solutions may no longer be adequate to cope with the anxieties involved in the focal conflict or the renewed push of the disturbing motive. For example, consider a patient who, for many years, has coped with a conflict—sexual impulses toward her father versus fears of punitive response from her mother—with extensive suppression of sexual interests and an outpouring of energy into artistic pursuits. Such a solution functioned adequately through childhood and middle adolescence, though at the expense of expressing sexual interest. On entering college, the push from within was reinforced by the observation that others in the environment did not seem to need suppressive solutions. Combined, these factors undermined the previous solution.

At the point of entering therapy, then, at least some of the individual's habitual solutions are in an unstable state. Although they still seem necessary, they are somehow not so acceptable as they were. Either the habitual solution is not functioning adequately, or the individual feels a sense of unrest because the solution can be maintained only at a high personal cost. The individual is in a state of ambivalence regarding certain habitual solutions: the solution which he would like to abandon seems absolutely vital to his continued existence. He maintains the maladaptive solution not because he wants to, but because he feels that he must. The solution seems the least dangerous of the available alternatives. This suggests that, in spite of the tenacity with which the individual holds to these solutions, he nevertheless is ready to abandon them whenever conditions permit.

Proposition 23

At the point of entering therapy, a person is characterized by a repertory of habitual solutions which cope with personal focal conflicts. Certain of these habitual solutions are maladaptive in character. The individual is ambivalent about certain of these habitual maladaptive solutions; he regards them as essential to his existence yet also wishes to be rid of them.

When a patient enters a therapy group, he inevitably finds himself in a threatening situation. As described earlier (see Chapter 6), the initial sessions of the group are characterized by certain inherent promises and certain inherent threats. Stated most generally, the individual is likely to feel that he can be helped if he reveals himself and his problems to the others. But with this, he experiences certain threats: the dangers of exposing himself to the ridicule and criticism of others, of discovering intolerable things about himself, of being drawn into expressing feelings which will get beyond his control. In short, the situation is a threatening one, yet one which the patient doesn't want to leave because he hopes for personal benefit.

During the first session, a group focal conflict emerges which includes certain of these wishes and fears. Rather than experience vague anxieties associated with expectations about the group, the individual feels threatened by events in the immediate interactive situation. The initial focal conflict is likely to bear some relevance to the patient's personal concerns. Perhaps the covert shared wish is one which he too experiences; perhaps the fears which develop in the group are like his own. As the group proceeds, solutions which are related to certain of his habitual personal solutions begin to emerge. Perhaps an emerging group solution directly supports a personal interactive pattern; perhaps it threatens or precludes a preferred interactive mode; perhaps it does not directly bear on the individual. As the group proceeds, a series of focal-conflict situations emerge which involve a range of emotional issues: intimacy, sexuality, dependency, hostility, trust, retaliation, shame, and so forth. Throughout the history of the group, such basic issues emerge and re-emerge. Many of these issues are likely to be relevant to specific areas which are at the heart of the patient's neurotic problems.

To illustrate: when Paul entered a therapy group, he found himself in a situation which was immediately threatening to him because of its implicit challenge to one of his habitual solutions. The general assumption was that the patient must talk and reveal his secrets if he was to be helped. For Paul, this might have meant admitting that his fictionalized life history was false and revealing the painful facts about his early abandonment. His initial behavior indicated how important it was for him to protect this solution. He sat in a corner, away from the others, arms folded, and said, "I'll come, but I won't talk." He did, however, listen, and soon a group focal conflict emerged which closely touched his personal concerns. The focal conflict "wish to have a uniquely gratifying relationship with the therapist" versus "fear of destructive punishment from the therapist" developed. Although not identical with Paul's nuclear conflict, this group focal conflict touched it closely. The disturbing motive was related to Paul's unsatisfied wish to be close to his mother. The group reactive motive touched on Paul's fear of rejection and abandonment. Whether or not Paul overtly participated in the generation of this group focal conflict, one can assume that he participated affectively. In effect, he was reliving, in another derived form, the wishes and fears originally experienced with reference to his mother.

Proposition 24	*Successive group focal conflicts constitute a threat to the individual to the extent that they expose him to crucial personal conflicts.*

When confronted with a threat, the individual attempts to protect himself. His behavior is directed to rendering the situation viable by transforming an intolerable situation to a rewarding, possible, or tolerable situation. The term "viable" thus refers to group conditions under which the individual can continue to exist. A range of group conditions is implied, from those which are maximally rewarding to those which, although uncomfortable or threatening to some degree, are at least tolerable. In this view, each patient's behavior can be understood as being motivated by a wish to establish what would be a viable group for him. We do not mean to imply that his efforts are conscious. Rather, the individual experiences threat without necessarily being aware of the source of his anxiety. His behavioral response is an automatic effort to avoid or allay anxiety. Thus the concept of "viability" is a construct which accounts for the individual's behavior in response to threatening group conditions.

The individual's first efforts to render the situation viable are likely to consist of attempts to institute relevant habitual personal solutions. Such solutions have been useful to him in the past. When analogous anxiety-provoking situations arise in the group, he is likely to reach for his repertory of past solutions. Past solutions are not invoked indiscriminately. Rather, the individual will seek to establish the habitual solutions which are appropriate to the current situation. For example, in response to the situation in which Paul found himself, one might expect him to try to be helpful to others or to engage someone in an argument. He might try to tell his fictional life history in an effort to demonstrate that he is worthy of acceptance.

Attempts to institute personal habitual solutions in the group can succeed only under certain group conditions, for to put a habitual solution into operation requires the cooperation or at least the permission of the others in the group. For example, in order for Paul to establish the pattern of helpfulness, members of the group would have to be willing to be helped. Even if not actively supported, his efforts to help others would at least have to meet with a neutral, not a punitive, response. In almost all instances, individual solutions have an interpersonal dimension which require a response if maximum success is to be achieved. Even such an individual solution as denial (which may be regarded as an intrapsychic phenomenon) has maximum probability of success if the individual attempting to utilize denial can get the other patients in the group to cooperate. For example, a patient who is faced with erupting sexual feelings and has utilized denial as a device for coping has greater likelihood of success in avoiding anxiety if he can get the others to avoid talking about or showing such feelings. It is much more difficult for him to maintain this solution if a prevailing group solution permits sexuality to be raised directly.

In general, a patient is most likely to be successful in instituting and maintaining a habitual personal solution in the group if this personal solution coincides with, supports, or is built into a prevailing group solution. For example, a group may cooperate with a patient who wants to institute the individual solution of dominating the group with personal ruminations because such behavior fits in with the solution "get one person to talk so that no one else will have to expose himself." Or a patient may succeed in establishing himself as the respected expert in the group because the group finds it useful to deal with disappointed or angry feelings about the therapist by finding a substitute therapist in the group. Or, patients may cooperate with an individual solution of argumentation if an argument fits in with such a solution as "express disagreement in intellectual terms." Conditions under which a group solution coincides with the personal goal of some individual patient are not likely to persist, however, for the group situation is continually changing. The group which has tolerated lengthy personal rumination may become restive as this pattern (which the individual might wish to continue indefinitely) generates a new focal conflict which has to do, perhaps, with angry feelings at having been deprived of the therapist's attention. Or the group which has cooperated for a time in maintaining an argument may find itself confronted with intensified anxieties about the potential destructive effect of anger toward peers and may try to find an alternate solution, even though one very argumentative individual might prefer to continue.

Sometimes, the prevailing group solution precludes the expression of a personal solution. For example, a patient for whom a personal solution involves being the center of attention would find this impossible in a group which established the group solution "all be alike." At other times, the group solutions are irrelevant to individual solutions. They neither actively support them nor actively interfere with them. In such a case, the individual is free to institute such personal solutions.

In Paul's case, the solution "all be alike," which emerged for the group, made it difficult for him to tell a fictionalized life story—or, indeed, for telling his true life story. Either tale would set him apart as someone special and would be likely to elicit the rejection which Paul was so anxious to avoid. Paul did not, in fact, tell the group anything about his background at this time. However, the group solution neither specifically supported nor specifically interfered with certain other of Paul's personal solutions. For example, for Paul to engage in intellectual argumentation or to help others was irrelevant to the group solution. He was free to do both, and did so, establishing the role of friendly arguer and breaker of silences.

Because the individual cannot consistently operate on the basis of habitual personal solutions, there are many occasions when he must find some other route to establishing viable conditions in the group. He might try to influence the group toward some state of alternate safety for him. Often, such a state fails to provide maximum rewards but still constitutes a tolerable environment. The individual settles for a compromise which is short of his preferred pattern yet provides some protection against anxiety. Or, his efforts to render the situation viable might not take the form of implicit attempts to influence the course of the group. Instead, the individual might try to protect himself against the onslaughts of the group by dissociating himself from the group, daydreaming, or resorting to temporary absence.

Proposition 25

When the individual experiences threat from a group focal conflict, he attempts to relieve his anxiety by rendering the group environment viable. He seeks a change in the current situation so that he will cease to experience anxiety.

(1) *His initial efforts consist of attempts to institute relevant habitual personal solutions.*

(2) *Such attempts are likely to be unsuccessful or only temporarily successful, for habitual solutions can be established only when they are compatible with or support a currently operative group solution.*

(3) *If he is unable to render the group viable by instituting an appropriate habitual personal solution, the individual will resort to:* (*a*) *efforts to influence the group solution toward conditions which, if not rewarding, do ameliorate the threat posed by the current group focal conflict; or* (*b*) *efforts to insulate himself from threatening aspects of the group focal conflict.*

The manner in which the individual expresses his desire to render the group viable depends not only on his personal characteristics, but also on the group conditions with which he is confronted. Some group conditions are, of course, more threatening than others. A patient might find his anxiety mounting when angry feelings seem about to erupt and diminishing when others reach out to him for greater intimacy. Another patient might find very different group conditions maximally threatening. Motivation to render a group viable is most intense when the group conditions lead the individual to experience maximum threat. A patient is likely to feel highly threatened when the solution prevailing does not provide a means for containing his anxiety. The group solution may allow greater individual expression of the disturbing motive than the individual can tolerate, or the prevailing solution or lack of solution may lead the individual to experience the reactive motive in a more direct or intense form than he finds tolerable. In either case, one would expect anxiety to be high and the patient to be highly motivated to render the group situation viable. A patient is also likely to feel highly threatened when the group is moving toward or operating on a solution which makes it impossible for some vital personal solution to operate. Here the associated group focal conflict is not necessarily closely related to the individual's nuclear conflicts. What is threatening is not a currently experienced conflict, but the threat to a personal solution. Under such circumstances, the individual experiences acute anxiety and again is highly motivated to render the group viable. He is literally forced to protect himself against mounting and potentially intolerable anxiety.

These acutely threatening group conditions can be differentiated from others which, although not positively rewarding, are not an acute threat to the individual. For example, a group may be moving toward a solution which fails to gratify some wish of the patient's but does not actually threaten an essential personal solution. Although the patient may feel vaguely uncomfortable, he can continue to exist in this milieu. His anxiety, though aroused to some extent, has not reached an intolerable level. Under such circumstances, the individual will make less persistent efforts to change the situation.

Proposition 26

The individual experiences maximum threat and, therefore, most intense motivation to render the situation viable when (1) *the prevailing group solution does not relieve the anxiety which the individual experiences through his participation in the current group focal conflict or when* (2) *the group solution makes it impossible for some habitual personal solution to operate.*

Each of the illustrations in previous chapters could be examined from the point of view of each patient's experience in the group and his efforts to deal with threat. For purposes of illustration, we will consider the inpatient group in which the patients struggled with the issue of revealing "bad" impulses and in which Arnold figured prominently as a deviant member (see Chapters 3 and 5). Three patients in this group—Arnold, Casimir, and John—displayed heightened anxiety at different points and attempted to deal with their anxiety through efforts to render the group viable.

In the first session, Arnold was confronted with a group situation which posed a considerable threat to him. The patients were moving toward establishing a solution which required shared agreement that no one was perfect and that all should tolerate one another's faults. If Arnold had entered into an implicit agreement with the others that he, too, was imperfect, he would have violated a long-standing personal solution. During later discussions, Arnold discussed experiences with an exacting and punitive father who had led him to feel that he must not make mistakes. He tried to present himself as strong and needed to regard himself as perfect. Had the group established its initial solution, the interpersonal setting would have become intolerable for Arnold. From his point of view, the group would no longer be viable. His behavior, then, could be understood as motivated by the need to protect himself from anxiety through rendering the group a viable interpersonal setting. His efforts were successful—the group eventually modified the initial solution in a way which was acceptable to themselves and to Arnold.

Arnold protected himself by direct protest. That this effort was successful was not so much due to the effort itself as to its relationship to the group situation. It was necessary to the general well-being of the group to maintain the solution which was almost consolidated at the time that Arnold interfered. This solution, if instituted, could have allayed fears of criticism from one another and, at the same time, allowed "faults" to be revealed. When Arnold challenged this solution, the others tried to change him and then to deny his protest by pretending that it was not serious. But Arnold could not respond to these efforts. Finally, the other patients were forced, in order to protect themselves from anxiety, to revise the solution in a way which Arnold could accept. It was because of this group necessity that Arnold succeeded in influencing the group toward a state which was tolerable to him.

During the second and third sessions of this group, a focal conflict emerged in which angry and destructive impulses were held in check by fears of punishment from the therapists and fears of overwhelming guilt feelings. During the third session, primitive feelings of guilt and fear of punishment were much in evidence. Tension accumulated until everyone appeared acutely uncomfortable. It was this situation which proved particularly threatening to John, who was emerging from an acute schizophrenic episode. When tension was at its height, John commented, "No one is going to make us go to the gas chamber" and, a few minutes later, walked out of the room.

From information which John later revealed to the group, it became known that, while still in an acutely psychotic state, he believed that he had murdered an adolescent girl and was in danger of being caught and executed for this crime. At this point, John was emerging from the psychotic condition and half-realized that he had not committed this act, but he was still very much preoccupied with the fantasy. Still later, John talked about early experiences with his grandmother, with which he associated strong feelings of guilt. These data suggest the reasons that John could not tolerate a group situation marked by guilty feelings and the expectation of punishment. At this point, the group constituted an overwhelming threat. He dealt with this threat by removing himself from the situation. John's efforts to reduce anxiety did not take the form of trying to influence or change the group situation. Instead, he resorted to physical flight to protect himself from what had become a non-viable group situation.

During the fifth session, a focal conflict prevailed in which angry feelings were held in check by fears of loss of control and punishment by the therapists. A solution was achieved in which the patients assured themselves that they could count on the therapists' strength to protect rather than punish them. This solution enabled some of the patients to talk more directly about angry impulses, and a conversation developed in which patients shared experiences about fights with their fathers. Casimir said that his father had beaten him but that it hadn't bothered him. As the others continued to talk, Casimir said that people have to "will" themselves to forget childhood incidents. When the conversation continued in the same vein, Casimir angrily protested, "Maybe your parents don't know any better. Would you hold a grudge against a blind man?" During the last few minutes of the session, Casimir withdrew from active participation while the others continued to discuss angry feelings.

What proved intolerable to Casimir was an upsurge in the strength of a disturbing motive involving angry feelings. The other patients, by virtue of a new group solution, were able to discuss angry feelings toward fathers. But Casimir was unable to do this. For him, the interpersonal setting had become exceedingly threatening. His first effort to cope with this threat involved denying that he shared the feelings of the others. In other words, he tried to render the group situation viable by psychologically dissociating himself from the group. Then he tried to actively influence the course of events by suggesting that the others should "will" themselves to forget incidents that might elicit rage. When this effort was ignored, he erupted in an even more direct effort to influence the others by shaming them. In this effort, Casimir also placed himself outside the group by indicating that he could not sanction such feelings in himself or in others. Finally, he withdrew from the discussion entirely.

In each of these instances, an aspect of the group focal conflict posed a specific threat to one of the patients. Each of the patients displayed behavior directed toward rendering the group viable—John by insulating himself, Arnold and Casimir by attempting to influence the group situation. Arnold was successful in this attempt; Casimir was not. Why? The crucial factor which determines whether a specific patient's behavior will influence the group does not depend on intensity of motivation, persistence of effort, or conscious intent, but rather on the state of the group at the time that the attempt to influence is made. Any comment, of course, is made at some point in time, when the group is in a particular equilibrium in relation to the current focal conflict. Perhaps the disturbing and reactive motives are just beginning to emerge, perhaps the reactive motive is in ascendance, perhaps many alternate solutions are being proposed but none has taken hold, or perhaps a particular solution is well established and generally supported by the patients.

Arnold's and Casimir's efforts to influence the group were introduced at quite different points in the group's movement. Arnold made his comments at a point when the group was about to consolidate a group solution. The group was bent on establishing this solution and could do so only if there was at least implicit unanimity. By his protest, Arnold effectively interfered with the establishment of the solution and forced the group to turn its attention to him. In contrast, Casimir failed in his attempts to get the others to stop discussing angry feelings. But Casimir's efforts came at a different point, after the group had constructed a solution which permitted the partial satisfaction of the disturbing motive without undue anxiety. Casimir did not actively participate in constructing this solution, nor did he actively challenge it. But at a point when the solution was already established, he attempted to gain the group's support for a different solution which would have permitted very little gratification of the disturbing motive. From the point of view of the group, this was a less satisfying solution because it would impose more restrictions on the expression of the disturbing motive than were necessary to manage anxiety. Thus, Casimir's efforts had little chance for success. He was a nuisance rather than a threat to the other patients, and they responded by ignoring his efforts.

As this suggests, we do not associate success in influencing the group with interpersonal skills or leadership traits. A person who, in the ordinary sense of the word, had no leadership skills might be highly influential under the appropriate group conditions. One does not expect any patient to be continually influential. Rather, a patient may have a significant impact on group events at one point and little or no impact at another time. And, during a particular session, certain patients are likely to have a greater impact than others. This differential impact occurs because the ability to influence is not a character trait, but a product of the constraints and opportunities of the immediate group milieu.

In an actual group situation, it is not precisely accurate to think in terms of one patient's influencing all the others. Rather, every comment will push the group in one direction or another and change, to some degree, the balance of forces in the group. As this occurs, each patient is motivated to lend support, protect, reinforce, or counteract the others' attempts to be influential. The attempts of any one patient occur in the context of all the others' attempts. The group is likely to include six or more persons, all diverse and all motivated to steer the group toward interpersonal conditions which are personally viable. Under these conditions, the eventual direction of the group is a compromise among the alternatives introduced by various patients. This process can be most easily seen during a period in which the patients are struggling to achieve a resolution to a current group focal conflict. The eventual solution may be related to, but not identical with, the preferred direction introduced by a patient. Such a solution is unlikely to suit any patient perfectly, yet it represents a combination of individual efforts and can usually be accepted by everyone.

Proposition 27

Each patient plays a part in influencing the interpersonal milieu. He is more influential at some points than at others. His success in influencing the group focal conflict or the group solution is greatest during the period prior to the establishment of a successful solution. Attempts to block solutions are likely to be more successful than are attempts to establish alternate solutions.

This discussion of the patient's experience in the group has been from an external point of view and has focused on his motivation, his behavior, and the mutual impact of group and individual. One can also consider the patient in the group from an internal point of view, focusing on how the patient experiences and conceptualizes the group situation. Up to this point, our major source of data has been the observation of group sessions. This source of data is insufficient for understanding the group experience from the patient's perspective. Although a patient may directly reveal some of his feelings and thoughts to the group, many remain unexpressed. What we shall say about the patient's experience and conceptualization of group events is based on a stimulated recall study of patients' perceptions in brief episodes of group therapy,[8] a case study in which a patient's spontaneous comments about his group experience were recorded as they were reported to his individual therapist, and a series of interviews with patients at the point of a group's termination.

The most striking feature of the data was the broad range and highly personal character of the patients' perceptions. When five patients were interviewed at the termination of an eighteen-month group experience, the events that they regarded as significant varied widely. In the stimulated recall study, where short taped episodes were played back to the patients individually, a broad range of reactions was again elicited. Feelings of satisfaction and tension, attitudes toward other group members, and conceptualizations of what was happening in the group were unique to each person. In general, feelings of satisfaction and tension varied, depending on the specific manner in which the continually shifting balance of forces in the group situation affected the patient. Attitudes toward other members were related to whether the member facilitated or blocked conditions regarded as personally viable. Each patient produced some conceptualization of the situation. Often, this took the form of judgments of whether the group was good, opinions about other patients (how someone was failing to cooperate, an analysis of individual problems or confusions), or accounts of personal motivations in the group (what I was really trying to do; how I was misunderstood by others). These perceptions and conceptualizations had a solutional quality; they helped each patient cope with the group situation as it affected him.

The patient's conceptualizations rarely touched group-level aspects of the situation and never included formulations of the sort which we have presented in the first six chapters. From the patient's point of view, then, the kind of group we have described does not exist. The fact that patients do not organize their experience in terms of group-level processes is understandable, for we assume that the group focal conflict exists outside the patients' awareness. The patients collaborate in the generation of successive focal conflicts and solutions without being aware that their individual reactions and contributions constitute part of a collaborative process. Even apart from this, they are rarely accustomed to thinking in terms of group processes; this approach lies outside their experience. Finally, the characteristics of the group as a whole can be grasped only by someone who views the group from a perspective different from that of the patients. To the extent that the therapist stands outside the focal conflict yet empathizes with the affect which is involved, he is in a position to be aware of group-level phenomena. In contrast, the patient stands inside the conflict as one, but only one, contributor to the over-all pattern. From this perspective he is not in a position to see or experience the group except from his own point of view.

Proposition 28	*Each patient experiences and conceptualizes the group situation in a highly personal way.* (1) *Feelings of anxiety and satisfaction vary, depending on the manner in which the shifting balance of forces within the group affects the individual's own concerns.* (2) *Attitudes toward other patients shift, depending on whether they facilitate or block conditions regarded by the individual as personally viable.* (3) *The group is conceptualized in terms which help the patient cope with anxieties and threats generated by the current group situation.*

Notes

[1] Thomas French, *The Integration of Behavior,* Vols. I and II.

[2] The material about Paul is adapted from an earlier article: Roy M. Whitman, Morton A. Lieberman, and Dorothy Stock, "Individual and Group Focal Conflicts," *International Journal of Group Psychotherapy,* 10 (1960), 259–286. The inpatient group to which Paul belonged has been described in Chapters 2 and 5. In this chapter, the group is discussed from the point of view of the personal experience of one member.

[3] We do not mean to imply that this nuclear conflict and the derived focal conflicts are Paul's whole story. For example, a nuclear conflict in which the disturbing motive involved anger at his mother was also important. Certain solutions may be relevant to several nuclear conflicts; Paul's pattern of forming relationships with degraded women can also be understood as a way of coping with angry feelings toward women. To describe a patient more completely, one would have to think in terms of a network of related nuclear conflicts and solutions and their derivatives. We have singled out only one such pattern for illustrative purposes.

[4] Terms similar to those previously applied to the group are now being applied to the individual. The following comparisons may be noted. (1) The term "focal conflict," when applied either to an individual or to a group, refers to a conflict experienced in a current interpersonal setting. When applied to a group, the term refers to a covert, shared conflict. When applied to an individual, the term refers to a personal conflict. (2) The term "nuclear conflict" is appropriate to the indi-

vidual but not to the group because of differences in the manner in which the focal conflict is generated. The individual focal conflict is a current expression of a prototypic nuclear conflict which has been experienced many times in a variety of settings. In contrast, the group focal conflict has no such history and is generated in the current group interaction. (3) The concept of "solution" has a similar function for the individual and for the group. For the individual, it is a defense against or a means of coping with the focal conflict. For the group, restrictive solutions relieve the anxiety associated with the group focal conflict, whereas enabling solutions actually solve the conflict—they have a goal-gratification potential. In the group, the solution is the product of implicit collaboration among all its members. For the individual, the solution is a product of his own making.

[5] Henry Ezriel, "The Role of Transference in Psycho-analytic and Other Approaches to Group Treatment," pp. 101–116.

[6] *Ibid.,* 106–107. Footnote defining "adequate" omitted.

[7] *Ibid.,* 107.

[8] Dorothy Stock and Roy M. Whitman, "Patients' and Therapist's Apperceptions of an Episode in Group Therapy," *Human Relations,* 10 (1957), 367–383.

8

The Therapeutic Process

The purpose of the therapy group is to establish conditions under which each patient can change. Hopefully, each patient can achieve a less painful existence, learn new behavior, and learn to think of himself and others in new terms. In short, he may be helped to discard old, maladaptive ways of thinking, behaving, and dealing with others and make new, more adaptive patterns a part of his way of life. It is a basic assumption of all psychotherapy that this therapeutic change can occur in an interpersonal setting. Individual therapy assumes that the special two-person relationship of therapist and patient can provide the basis for positive personal change. Group therapy assumes that the group situation, in which one or two people are therapists and the others are patients, can provide a setting for desirable personal change.

When the patient enters a therapy group, his state can be described in terms of some pathological process, and a therapeutic goal can be set for him. The goal and the pathological condition are, of course, linked; one implies the other. We view the person who enters therapy as handicapped by habitual maladaptive patterns of perception and behavior which prevent him from gaining the satisfactions he desires or require him to pay an inordinately high price for them. The therapeutic goal, then, is to establish conditions under which these maladaptive patterns of perception and behavior can be revised.[1] A similar view of the pathological process and the goal of therapy has been presented by Jerome Frank and Eduard Ascher:

> With improved understanding of the dynamics of human behavior, there has developed a greater appreciation of the importance of difficulties in interpersonal relationships as both expressions and sources of distorted attitudes, which may lead to the production of neurotic or psychotic symptoms. These may assume such proportions as seriously to interfere with an individual's functioning and prevent him from fully utilizing his assets. The goal of dynamically oriented psychotherapy is modification of the individual's noxious attitudes, thereby liberating those forces that enable him to carry on in his daily tasks and have an optimally low degree of disturbance to others and of anxiety within himself.[2]

In referring to the goals of psychotherapy, Foulkes has said, "Group analysis has not as its aim adjustment and socialization. It wishes to help human beings to find themselves and to live their own lives as well as they may be able to do. Moreover, they should do so without being inhibited, limited or disturbed by unnecessary difficulties or even, as happens only too often, by tendencies to do harm to themselves."[3] In all of these views, the patient is seen as being handicapped by difficulties in interpersonal relationships, by distorted attitudes, by painful feelings, by a personally disadvantageous style of life, or by maladaptive interpersonal patterns. Psychotherapy is directed to the revision of these attitudes and behaviors.

To understand the processes whereby the individual moves from predominantly maladaptive interpersonal modes to more adaptive and appropriate patterns, it is necessary to consider a number of intervening processes and experiences. We assume that the patient maintains a maladaptive pattern because it is functional—in fact, because he implicitly assumes that to give it up would lead to profoundly disastrous consequences. The pattern, maladaptive as it is, protects him from anxiety by dealing with underlying unconscious conflicts. Such conflicts involve impulses whose expression—and, sometimes, whose very recognition—is regarded as dangerous. In order to be effective, the therapeutic process must permit the patient to test out whether the habitual, maladaptive patterns are indeed as vital to him as he has unconsciously supposed; to assess whether preferable alternatives are available; and to differentiate the real from the fantasied dangers involved in recognizing or expressing his impulses. For the neurotic patient, the therapeutic process involves the experience that the feared consequences do not occur. His fears prove to be exaggerated, his impulses not so dangerous or uncontrollable as he had feared, and his habitual pattern not so necessary as he had assumed. This experience is sometimes, but not always, accompanied by insight into his dilemma: the character of his maladaptive pattern, the price he pays for maintaining it, the nature of the underlying conflict, and the manner in which both conflict and maladaptive pattern are rooted in past experience. For many patients, these two processes support one another, but the emotional experience appears to be primary. Insight without the affective accompaniments may be a sterile affair; the emotional experience without full cognitive understanding can, on the other hand, often lead to therapeutic change.

These processes may, of course, be described in other language. But whatever the language and emphasis, similar concepts appear in most theories of therapeutic change. In focal-conflict terms, the steps required for therapeutic change can be summarized as follows:

Proposition 29

In order for a habitual maladaptive solution to change, (1) *the patient must experience in the therapeutic setting personal focal conflicts relevant to core nuclear conflicts;* (2) *he must not cope successfully with the anxiety generated by these experiences by consistently using his past maladaptive solutions;* (3) *in consequence, he must experience, not disaster, but the new learning that these habitual solutions are not necessary to his existence.*

We believe that such a process must occur no matter what the therapeutic setting. However, the group and the two-person therapeutic settings are distinct, and the conditions under which a therapeutic experience can occur are quite different for the two situations. A primary question, then, is the specific manner in which the therapeutic experience occurs in the group context.

The eliciting function of the group was discussed in the preceding chapter. It was pointed out that, as a result of the manner in which the individual contributes to and participates in successive group focal conflicts, he will experience a range of conflicts relevant to his core problems. Unless the patient is consistently silent, he will play some active part in influencing which conflicts become focal for the group. Even if he is passive, influencing the course of group events only by failing to interfere with them, the focal conflicts which arise are likely to touch his own concerns in some way. However, it is at least theoretically possible for a patient to undergo an entire group experience without being exposed to certain crucial conflict areas. This could occur if the group culture were dominated by restrictive solutions. For example, a group which maintained solutions which dealt restrictively with sexual conflicts would literally insulate the patients from experiencing conflicts or exploring issues in this area. Perhaps such blatant avoidance of an important area is unlikely to occur in any reasonably well-conducted therapy group. However, there are many more subtle ways in which the group culture may preclude potentially useful experiences. For example, a therapist might intentionally or unintentionally cooperate with the patients in maintaining a solution in which he is regarded as an expert and the only reliable source of information. Such a solution could cut off information otherwise available in the form of interpretations and feedback supplied by peers. More important, such a solution could close certain vital areas to exploration. For example, it might make the patients unwilling to risk recognizing or exploring angry feelings toward the therapist. Thus, a potentially significant area—anger towards authority figures—would remain inaccessible to experience and examination.

In contrast, if the culture which develops in the group permits a wide range of issues and situations to emerge, the patient is likely to be exposed to group focal conflicts in personally significant areas. Such issues typically occur many times during the life of the group, enabling the patient to experience and re-experience their impact. The critical eliciting function of the group culture can be summarized as follows:

Proposition 30	*The individual is most likely to experience the full range of relevant personal conflicts if the group culture is dominated by enabling rather than restrictive solutions.*

When a patient experiences crucial personal focal conflicts in the group setting, he is likely to attempt to institute relevant habitual personal solutions. Such attempts, as we pointed out in the previous chapter, generally fail, and the patient experiences considerable anxiety. Thus the first two steps in the therapeutic process—the eliciting of crucial personal conflicts and the failure to institute personal habitual solutions—occur almost as a matter of course, provided that certain basic conditions are maintained in the group. These two steps are, however, not sufficient, for the neurotic has already spent a lifetime in the futile re-experiencing of conflict. The fact that he is unable to use his habitual solutions in the group might be expected to lead only to massive anxiety and not to constructive personal change.

However, although the group situation poses a threat to the patient, it also provides him with important guarantees of safety. This safety lies in the solutions which develop in response to successive group focal conflicts. In order to cope with the anxiety involved in successive group conflicts, the patients collaborate to establish and maintain appropriate group solutions; they establish a culture. Although no single patient is likely to succeed in establishing in the group exactly the conditions which he regards as ideal, the group solutions which emerge out of the interaction will cope, in some way, with the associated group focal conflicts. From the point of view of the individual, these group solutions are collective, unanimous guarantees that certain kinds of occurrences will or will not happen in the group. For example, there may be guarantees that competition will not get out of control because the patients have implicitly agreed to take turns; guarantees that sexual interests will not elicit punishment because these interests will be discussed only in symbolic terms; guarantees that hostile impulses will not lead to general destructiveness because the therapist can be relied on to protect the patients from their own and one another's hostile acts; guarantees that no one will be ridiculed for his weaknesses because everyone agrees that weaknesses are universal. The particular solutions which develop are, of course, specific to each group, but whatever their character, their function is the same. From the point of view of the group process, they cope with the anxieties involved in the group focal conflict. From the point of view of the individual, they provide guarantees against certain dangers. We have made a distinction between restrictive and enabling solutions; with reference to safety, this is an irrelevant distinction. No matter what its character, the solution can operate as a guarantee of safety to the individual. Safety results from the unanimity of the group solution.[4] Each of the potentially threatening persons in the group environment has agreed to behave in some way which protects the individual. The group solution persists. It is a guarantee that protection will be effective not only for the moment, but that it will continue. Such guarantees develop in response to the shared fears of the group members. They are guarantees which emerge out of the necessities of the group process.

This is a kind of safety which is not available to the patient in his day-to-day life, for the group is a closed system. Once a solution is established in the group, it will be retained until the group conditions themselves change in a way which allows for an associated modification in the solution. Once a solution is established, it is binding on all members, so that, for example, a guarantee against ridicule is effective for all members rather than just some. The outside world, in contrast, is an open system. The individual may feel safe with certain individuals whom he encounters and unsafe with others. In the outside world, the individual encounters a wide range of situations which offer varying guarantees.

It is important to underline the combination of circumstances in the group which create the conditions essential for the therapeutic experience. In the group, the individual is exposed to considerable threat in areas related to his neurosis, and he cannot, in each instance, utilize old patterns of behavior to avoid this threat. Yet the new environment offers new guarantees of a safety which is not contingent on the utilization of the patient's habitual maladaptive solutions. This new safety is not the safety which the patient prefers, but it is one he can use.

Proposition 31

The group culture provides the patient with a special form of safety which guarantees that certain damaging or disastrous results will not occur when he relinquishes the personal habitual solutions heretofore regarded as essential to his existence. Under these special conditions of safety, the patient may take steps to test the necessity for maintaining his old maladaptive solutions.

These circumstances make it possible for the individual to undergo, in the group setting, experiences which are discontinuous with those in the outside world. The manner in which the group impinges on the individual to facilitate a therapeutic experience varies. Some illustrations follow.

A Group Solution Offering Safety

Paul belonged to a group in which an important and persistent group solution was that all the patients were alike. The initial solution was restrictive in character. Under the shared agreement that all were alike, references to individual differences were suppressed. Bids to be different, to gain special attention, or to reveal unique features of one's life history were received with disapproval. During this period, Paul remained silent about his background. He neither revealed to the others his experiences in the orphanage, nor did he tell them about his fantasied background. As the sessions continued, the original group solution was gradually modified. Rather than insist that everyone was alike, the patients agreed that everyone was *basically* alike. Under this new solution, many superficial differences were recognized and accepted, but the patients underlined such basic similarities as a universal wish for love and affection. This new situation was relevant to Paul in two ways: first, the modified group solution recognized Paul's still concealed wish for love and affection as an acceptable and universal human desire; second, the modified group solution carried the implicit promise that Paul's unusual background would probably be accepted by the group as a superficial but not a basic difference. This constituted a new source of safety which had not been available to Paul. After the establishment of the modified group solution, Paul began, gradually and, at first, very obliquely, to discuss his true background. Eventually, he revealed his fantasy and was able to explore some of his feelings about both background and fantasy. This process took many sessions. At first, he mentioned briefly and almost inaudibly that he knew about institutions because of his past. Apparently, he had confided his secret to one of his fellow members, since, in one session, he mentioned cryptically, "Mike knows what I mean." Still later, he maneuvered Mike into telling the group that life in an orphanage had been a part of Paul's past. Three or four sessions later, Paul told the group that he had always been afraid to mention his background because people were critical of orphans. Thus Paul gradually tested the feasibility of giving up his habitual solution of presenting a fantasied life history. For the first time, he was putting his fears of rejection to the test. At each step, he found acceptance, respect, and interest, rather than the rejection he feared. Each step took him a little farther, though there were retreats, when his fears re-emerged. When this happened, he was prone to suggest that the group deal with trivial matters ("let's play cards") or even cancel sessions. Yet the process of testing continued. It was not until the twenty-first session of the group that he revealed his background in detail. At that point, he seemed to feel relieved of his loneliness and disillusionment. A therapeutic emotional experience had occurred for Paul: he had given up an important habitual solution and found that doing so did not produce the feared consequences. This experience could take place because a group solution became established which, in effect, guaranteed that the feared result would not occur.

A Group Solution Interfering with a Maladaptive Pattern

On entering group therapy, Alex presented himself as an expert who could draw upon his superior knowledge to help and advise others. This pattern was a habitual one, and, for a considerable period, the other patients collaborated with Alex in instituting his preferred mode of interacting. They were willing to do so because Alex's pattern provided a solution to a group focal conflict and thus was useful to the group as a whole. The relevant focal conflict involved anger toward the therapists for not fulfilling the role of offering advice to the patients versus a reactive fear of rejection by the therapists. Alex, in effect, offered himself as a substitute therapist, doing all the things that the others felt that the therapists ought to be doing but were not. By accepting Alex as a substitute advice-giver, the patients solved their dilemma and avoided the risk of rejection from the therapists. It was for this reason that the other patients were willing to collaborate with Alex in maintaining his preferred pattern of behavior.

However, as the group proceeded, alternative solutions for coping with the original focal conflict were established, and the group no longer depended on the solution which involved Alex's functioning as a substitute therapist. His continuing to do so stimulated intense competitive feelings, since Alex, in behaving as he did, created a special, prestigeful role for himself. As the group became involved in a sibling rivalry issue, Alex's behavior became intolerable; it was met with indirect attacks and, when these were unsuccessful, by more direct pressure. Finally, the others told Alex directly that they did not like what he was doing and would no longer permit him to behave this way in the group. After this, they pointed to his behavior whenever it occurred, thus effectively stopping it. For Alex, this was a dramatic change of events. Initially, his habitual solution had been supported and encouraged; now it was punished and repeatedly prevented from finding expression. When the group conditions forced Alex to abandon this solution, his feelings of extreme depression and worthlessness emerged for the first time. At first, he expressed these non-verbally by lying on the floor. In the sessions which followed, he began to reveal some of his long-standing private fantasies about being totally unworthy. Other fantasies followed about being god-like and special. It began to be clear that Alex had to convince himself and others of his superiority in order to prevent his feelings of unworthiness from emerging, for he unconsciously feared that they would be overwhelming. It was only when the group situation forced the abandonment of the habitual solution that these feelings could emerge and be tested. At this point, it became possible for Alex to learn that the underlying feelings of worthlessness were not, in fact, overwhelming and that the habitual solution of presenting himself as superior was not so necessary as he had supposed. This, in turn, opened the way for further explorations of his sense of unworthiness, so that it, too, could be examined for real and unreal elements.

A Group Solution Exposing Avoided Feelings

Marian, an adolescent girl, suppressed her Oedipal feelings by affectively isolating herself from her parents. In her eyes, they were neuter, ineffectual people for whom she felt mild affection. Marian maintained similar feelings about the group therapists and, for a long time, was supported in this by a group solution which considered therapists as people who, by virtue of their professional role, were not allowed to have feelings about the patients and about whom it was appropriate to have only vague positive feelings. This group experienced a series of focal conflicts which involved sexual feelings directed toward the therapists. The original group solution was gradually modified in a manner which permitted the direct expression of sexual feelings and fantasies about the therapists. Marian fought to maintain the earlier, more suppressive solution and, as the others showed a readiness to shift, became a deviant in the group. She expressed her feelings succinctly in a comment to the therapists: "I liked it better when you weren't people." In spite of her efforts, the therapists had become people, and Marian was led to experience feelings which she had previously considered exceedingly dangerous. This process, summarized so briefly here, took almost a year. As with Paul, the therapeutic experience was actually a series of experiences in which we have referred only to the culminating one. Prior to this, many tests occurred in which Marian expressed her feelings in more indirect ways or observed that others could express such supposedly dangerous feelings directly without eliciting disastrous consequences.

Common to each of these situations was the fact that important habitual solutions were given up and that the catastrophic consequences which the patients had unconsciously feared did not occur. The impact of the group was somewhat different in each case: the group guaranteed safety so that the habitual individual solution could be given up (Paul), or the group interfered drastically with the individual solution, punishing its expression and forcing its abandonment (Alex), or a shift in the group solution exposed the individual to the disturbing impulse (Marian).

Insight appears to play a varying role in the therapeutic process. Some patients undergo experiences which lead to the revision of a maladaptive pattern without understanding the character of the experience, the meaning of the maladaptive behavior with reference to underlying conflicts, or even the fact that change has occurred. Perhaps such a patient experiences some sense of increased freedom or notices that he has begun to do things he had been afraid to do. But he may have arrived at this point without awareness of what he had feared or what impulses had been involved in this fear. For other patients, insight seems to be an integral part of the therapeutic experience. For them, it appears that cognitive mastery at each step is necessary for successive risk-taking to occur. For still others, insight occurs after the patient changes a maladaptive pattern. Once the risks have been taken and the less-than-disastrous consequences have been experienced, the patient may conceptualize his experience. For such patients, insight may be an important part of the generalization process—the capacity to take similar risks outside the therapeutic situation itself. In our illustrations, the degree of insight which accompanied the therapeutic experience varied. Alex displayed little indication that he was aware of the source or implications of his behavior or even that he noticed that his behavior had changed. Paul indicated somewhat greater awareness. He realized that he had always been afraid to tell anyone about his true background because he expected to be rejected, but he did not appear to connect his fears of rejection with the original rejection by his mother, nor did he seem to understand other aspects of the underlying conflict. Marian, in contrast to Alex and Paul, seemed to need to understand her feelings and reactions as she moved through the group experiences. The experience of recognizing her sexual feelings was accompanied by a conscious attempt to relate her feelings about the therapists to her feelings about her parents and her current behavior and feelings to the past.

Insight cannot occur unless new information about his feelings, behavior, and relationships becomes available to the patient and unless he is prepared to utilize this information. A new perspective on himself and his relation to others is required. The information necessary to a new perspective is made available in the group setting through others' statements about the meaning of his behavior and experiences (interpretation), through reports of others' reactions to his behavior (feedback), through self-observation, and through observation of others.

It is a special feature of the group that an interpretation, in order to be useful to the patient, need not be directed specifically to him. During a period in which a particular focal conflict is emerging and being dealt with, various patients will introduce experiences, report feelings, display behavior, and make comments which are relevant to the current focal-conflict issue. To the extent that the group focal conflict is relevant to an individual's personal concerns, some of this material will constitute useful information for him. For example, in an inpatient group (see Chapter 4), a focal conflict developed concerning angry, hostile impulses versus fears of losing control over such impulses and becoming destructive. During this episode, one patient commented: "We lose our tempers a hundred times a day; it doesn't make killers out of us." This comment was not specifically directed toward anyone. The patient was probably trying to reassure himself that he need not fear his own anger, since it need not be put into action. However, his comment was made at a point when others shared closely related concerns about the catastrophic consequences of angry feelings. Under these circumstances, such a comment was relevant to many of the other patients. It pointed out the distinction between feelings and action, it differentiated a moderate from a massive expression of anger, and it put verbal labels on an important issue. Thus, comments which are not directed toward a specific patient, but are generated out of a shared concern, can be a potential source of useful information to various patients in the group.

It is not uncommon for patients to provide one another with information by specifically directed interpretations. One patient will say to another, "Maybe you feel that way because . . ." or, "You got mad at Pete last week for the same reason" or, "You seem to feel the same way about Marshall that you do about your brother." Interpretations offered to specific patients occur under a variety of group conditions, and these group conditions influence the relevance, accuracy, and utility of the interpretation. For example, interpretations are often directed to a patient who occupies a deviant position in the group in an effort to deal with his deviation. Interpretations offered to a patient under these conditions are not always useful. An example occurred in an inpatient group, when interpretations were offered to a patient, Max, in an effort to cope with his deviation. This group was constructing a solution which required unanimous commitment to the potential usefulness of the therapy group. Max could not endorse this solution and, thus, became a deviant in the group. The other patients first tried to get Max to change his mind. When this failed, they attempted to interpret his deviant behavior. In this instance, the interpretations which the patients constructed to explain Max's behavior consisted of a shared fantasy which had no basis in real data. The patients assumed that Max was not willing to believe that something good could come from the group because he had been consistently deprived and disappointed in the past. Although there may have been some truth in this guess, the patients went on to construct elaborate detailed "evidence" for their interpretation, suggesting that Max had worn "hand-me-down" clothing when he was a child, had been unable to get a job when he was released from the Army, and so forth. They ignored Max's protests that some of these things had not actually occurred.[5] This incident was a dramatic illustration of the fact that interpretations offered to a patient may be based on no real data and may be of dubious accuracy and utility.

Often, interpretations occur as part of some group solution. For example, in order for such a solution as turn-taking to be put into operation, various patients must take turns at being the recipient of interpretations and suggestions from the others. Interpretations offered in such a context seem to vary in quality and usefulness. Some have a sterile, ritualistic quality although everyone pretends that something useful is going on. At other times, the information gleaned under such circumstances can be useful. This variable quality is understandable if one remembers that the point is to maintain turn-taking as a solution; the relevance or accuracy of the information is a secondary matter. A related solution occurs when the patients focus on the problems of one person as a means of protecting all the others from exposure. Under such circumstances, the group may discuss the problems and experiences of an individual patient at considerable length. Again, the usefulness to the patient is variable, for the primary object is not to offer useful interpretations or even to check one's suggestions against fact. Rather, the primary object is to keep the solution in operation. Even if some of the comments have been accurate and useful, the group solution may be maintained beyond the point where it is useful to the patient who is the target of the group's interpretive efforts.

Interpretations may be offered in the context of solutions which involve displacing feelings onto a single patient. Such interpretations are likely to be unusable, partly because they may be inaccurate or inapplicable to the patient to whom they are directed and, more importantly, because they are very likely to take on the quality of accusations. In scapegoating, angry feelings experienced toward one person are vented on another, often under the guise of helpfulness. In another form of displacement, generally shared feelings are treated as if they belong to only one person. Thus, a common feature of such a solution is the attack on a target-person, which really represents the patients' attack on their own unacceptable feelings. Under such circumstances, the "interpretation" may be correct, but it is offered in a destructive spirit. The recipient is likely to feel called upon to defend himself against the hostile intent, thus making it impossible for him to benefit from the information.

Useful interpretations are likely to occur when comparisons, comments, and reactions are offered freely in open group discussion of a particular issue. This kind of interaction can occur when enabling group solutions are in effect, and free exploration of the disturbing and the reactive motives is possible.

To summarize, when interpretations are vehicles for maintaining a restrictive solution, they may be unusable for various reasons. The interpretation may be inaccurate, inapplicable, or sterile or it is offered with such hostile accompaniments that the patient has no recourse but to defend himself against hearing what is being said. Under other group conditions, more consistently useful interpretations are likely to emerge. The patients often display a high degree of sensitivity to one another's feelings and concerns and point out quite significant features and relationships.[6]

Feedback is a source of information which is distinct from interpretation and is of special significance in group, as opposed to individual, therapy. By "feedback," we mean both the reactions which a patient's behavior elicits from others and their verbal reports of such reactions. Feedback may be expressed verbally or non-verbally through a gesture of disgust, an attitude of attentive listening, or some indication of restless boredom. Sometimes reactions are made explicit: "When you do that, I feel this." Whether verbal or non-verbal, implicit or explicit, the others' responses provide the patient with certain information about how others react to him. If the paradigm for an interpretation is "this is what you are doing" or "I think you do that because . . . ," the paradigm for feedback is "I feel this in response to your behavior or comments." Interpretations may be incorrect and subject to projection and other forms of distortion, but feedback is correct by definition. Feedback is always a true reaction—it may not be appropriate or typical of the reactions of others, but it is an accurate expression of the manner in which one person reacts to another. Feedback is most useful to a patient if it can be made explicit, for, the more explicit it is, the harder it is for the patient to ignore the information which is being offered to him.

Much of what has been said about the importance of context in determining the usefulness of an interpretation is applicable to feedback as well. For example, when a patient is the scapegoat of the group or when he permits the group to discuss his problems at length, he may elicit reactions of scorn, respect, or interest which have little to do with his behavior itself but a great deal to do with the function which his behavior performs for the group. Although feedback, by its nature, is accurate, it may be useless to the patient because he feels he must defend himself against the accompanying affect (e.g., scorn). Or the reaction may belong more to the group situation than to the patient himself and, thus, provide him with information which is of little personal relevance. Under optimal conditions, when the feedback is not functioning to maintain a restrictive solution, it can be an exceedingly significant source of information for the patient. If the patient can gain information about the impact of his behavior on others, he is in a position to assess characteristic interpersonal patterns in a way which is not otherwise possible.

Another source of the patient's information about himself is an examination of his own position in the current focal conflict. This kind of self-exploration can occur at any point during the group experience. Extended periods of self-exploration are most likely to occur during the operation of enabling solutions. Through noting his own reactions and comparing them with others', the patient may become aware of the special way in which he experiences the prevailing wish, he may come to recognize the specific character of his fears, and he may clarify his attitude toward a current group solution. For example, in an adolescent outpatient group, the patients operated for several sessions on a solution of turn-taking. At the point when the patients seemed ready to give up this solution, they explored the feelings that each of them had had about this pattern and the reasons it had seemed necessary. In the course of this discussion, one patient, Kenneth, realized that he had taken an active role in instituting and then maintaining this pattern and that he had felt anxious about its dissolution. Along with others, he speculated about why he had preferred to operate in this rather distant, intellectual manner. By means of this exploration, Kenneth gained new understanding of himself.

Sometimes the patient observes the others using a coping device which has not been a part of his personal repertory of solutions. Sometimes, the group moves toward a solution which does not correspond precisely to the solution preferred by the patient but is not maximally threatening to him. Under such circumstances, the patient may find that he is able to accept this new solution and gradually make it a part of his own repertory. This occurred for Lou, who habitually solved personal problems by refusing to acknowledge and examine them in psychological terms. He literally never thought about his own feelings and, therefore, remained baffled by certain symptoms. He entered therapy because of a work problem but could not understand why this problem had developed, since he felt that his life was satisfactory in every way and that he had no problems with parents, brothers, wife, or friends. During the time that Lou participated in a therapy group, group solutions gradually were established which allowed the relatively free exploration of one's own and others' feelings. With the others, Lou participated in the introspection which this solution permitted and learned how to examine his own feelings. He was able to do this with relative ease, since no strong barriers against self-examination appeared to have been established. It was almost as if he had never thought of it before. In this sense, the therapy group may sometimes perform a teaching function. The group provides the patient with a special kind of information: "this activity, which has never occurred to you, is possible and can be adopted."

Proposition 32

Information about himself, essential for the formation of insight, may become available to the patient through (1) *being exposed to information which is not directed to him but which is relevant to the group focal conflict in which he shares,* (2) *being the target of interpretations and feedback by other members of the group,* (3) *examining his own position in regard to the current group focal conflict, and* (4) *observing the positions which others take with regard to the group focal conflict and the consequences of these positions.*

Proposition 33

The utility of the information to the patient's development of insight depends on the group conditions under which the information is offered.
(1) *Under certain group solutions, information made available to the patient is likely to be sterile, irrelevant, or incorrect. Such solutions include turn-taking and interpretations of deviant behavior.*
(2) *Under certain group solutions, information made available to the patient fulfills the primary function of attack and leads the patient to defend himself against hearing or assimilating the information. Such solutions include scapegoating and displacing feelings to one patient.*
(3) *Under enabling group solutions, information made available to the patient is likely to be relevant and useful.*

So far, we have discussed processes associated with therapeutic gain and the gradual modification of maladaptive solutions. Ideally, a patient will affectively involve himself in the group, utilize the safety offered by the group culture, undergo experiences which enable him to test the consequences of abandoning habitual maladaptive solutions, and utilize the available information for building insight. But not all patients gain equally from their group-therapy experience, and it must be regarded as a failure for some.

Total failure can occur under several conditions: when a patient insulates himself from affective involvement in the group situation, when he consistently succeeds in maintaining a habitual maladaptive solution, or when he reacts to gross threat with a behavioral breakdown. Persistent success in maintaining a habitual personal solution is unlikely, for this can occur only when the group culture consistently supports the individual solution. The culture does not remain static, and, when the group solution shifts, the personal solution which it supports is usually undermined. Persistent success does, however, occasionally occur. For example, Melvin, a patient who belonged to the same group as Paul, succeeded in maintaining the maladaptive solution of being regarded as the "pet" of the group—disdained yet permitted a special status.

Group Conditions Supporting a Maladaptive Pattern

Melvin belonged to the inpatient group in which the following focal conflict developed during the first session: "wish to have a uniquely gratifying relationship with the therapist" versus "fear of destructive punishment from the therapist." The solution the group developed to cope with this focal conflict was "all be alike in a superficial way." Melvin participated actively during this session. He made frequent and insistent attempts to achieve special attention; for example, he told the others that he deserved a medal for having been in more therapy groups than anyone else. However, Melvin did not contribute to the establishment of the solution "all be alike" and, in subsequent sessions, showed by his behavior that he did not feel bound by it. He frequently told the others that he would do anything for his individual therapist and that there were things he would never reveal in the group. It was as if he felt that, if he could not achieve an exclusive relationship with the group therapists, he could at least point out that he enjoyed such a relationship with his individual therapist. He missed several consecutive sessions. As the sessions continued, the original solution "all be alike in a superficial way" was modified to "all be alike basically." The new solution allowed many individual differences to be expressed but maintained that all shared certain basic needs. Melvin began to complain about not having received the things he wanted. By such complaints, Melvin clearly demonstrated that he could accept neither the original group solution nor the later, modified solution; he continued to yearn for a special position in the group. These repeated complaints were challenges to the group solution and placed Melvin in a deviant position. The others eventually dealt with Melvin and the challenges he presented by regarding him as an exception—a whining child who was not bound by the same standards as were the other group members.

We assume that Melvin was unwilling to adhere to the group solution because to do so would have rendered the group situation unviable for him. The reason that a milieu in which he was not special would have been unrewarding for Melvin lay in his personal history. He was the youngest child in a large family and, as an adult, was the only child still living at home with his parents. He worked only occasionally at minor jobs and seemed content that his parents supported him. He was angrily alert to any possibility that his brother or sisters might gain some advantage over him in the family. With reference to the therapy group, a maximally rewarding, viable milieu for Melvin would have been one in which he could approximate the position he held in his family—that of the pampered baby. Melvin could accept neither the original nor the modified group solution. His behavior was a persistent threat to the group solution, and the group dealt with him by persistently regarding him as an exception. This became Melvin's permanent position in the group, and it satisfied both him and the other patients, but, at the same time, it supported a habitual maladaptive solution and insulated Melvin from potentially therapeutic experiences. A patient who succeeds in maintaining a habitual pattern in the group may feel comfortable, but he has insulated himself from affective involvement and from any possibility of therapeutic change.

A very different pathway to insulation occurs under almost opposite group conditions. Again, the group situation is a threatening one, and the patient attempts to institute habitual personal solutions. This time, however, the group conditions fail to support the individual and his route to anxiety-reduction. In addition, the patient is unable to utilize the safety provided by the group culture. Somehow the guarantees provided by the solutions which emerge in the group are not relevant to his concerns or are not sufficient to cope with his anxiety. Under such conditions, the patient may leave the group in order to reduce anxiety. He may resort to temporary absences, or he may drop out of the group permanently. John, the patient whose temporary flight from the group was described in the previous chapter, ran from the room when his fears became intolerable. More often than physical flight, psychological flight occurs. Psychological withdrawal renders the patient temporarily inaccessible to the group forces but also enables him to re-enter the group whenever it becomes psychologically possible for him to do so. In an inpatient group, one of the patients always brought a magazine or newspaper to the sessions. He kept this resource ready and occasionally retreated to reading, re-entering the conversation when the situation had shifted and become less threatening to him. A retreat into daydreaming is not an uncommon device. Temporary physical or psychological withdrawal is, of course, preferable to dropping out permanently. But, in either case, the device consists of insulation from affective involvement.

A third route to therapeutic failure occurs when a patient reacts to acute threat with a behavioral breakdown. In this instance, he does not leave the group, does not succeed in instituting habitual personal solutions, and does not utilize the safety provided by the group culture. Instead, he remains in the group but resorts to extreme measures in the attempt to render the group situation viable. He may institute solutions which are even more maladaptive than the ones he ordinarily utilizes. These solutions are likely to be specifically directed toward protecting him from his fears. In taking such a step, the patient has rendered the group situation minimally viable, but he has done so at great cost. He is likely to feel in a chronically precarious position, with the constant threat of gross, intolerable anxiety. Behaviorally, the breakdown of previous solutional modes and the introduction of disorganized, inadequate behavior occur.[7]

In the first two routes to therapeutic failure, two differing devices insulate the patient from affective forces in the group. The person who follows these routes remains untouched and unhelped. In the third route to therapeutic failure, the patient is seemingly unable to insulate himself from the emotional forces in the group. He remains vulnerable and is actually damaged. In considering therapeutic failures, one important question which remains unanswered is why some patients are unable to utilize the safety offered by the group culture.

The chronic non-participant is less likely than the active member to gain therapeutic benefit. Such a patient must be differentiated from the patient who insulates himself from the group through psychological withdrawal, for, although both patients may be silent, their experience differs. Therapeutic gains are impossible for the former; they are limited for the latter. It is often difficult to know, during the period in which a patient is silent, whether he is participating emotionally or whether he has withdrawn psychologically from the group. Evidence that the patient has been highly involved, though silent, may appear later. For example, in the group to which Paul belonged, he and several others were silent or almost silent during the emergence of the group focal conflict: "wish to have the exclusive attention of the therapist and destroy one's rivals" versus "fears of rejection and abandonment by the therapist." In the subsequent session, these previously inactive patients reported the following dreams. Alan told of a dream in which he had bowled a 300 game and nobody had paid any attention to him. Paul told of a dream in which a beautiful woman wanted to adopt and marry him and of a dream in which he owned a troupe of actors. Someone rushed up to tell him of an accident to the troupe, and he became frightened and asked for help. Jean told of a dream in which she had five husbands.

Each of the dreams was relevant to the group focal conflict but emphasized different aspects of it. Alan's dream emphasized a wish for special attention and failure to achieve it. Paul's dream focused on the wish for exclusive possession and involved both sexual and dependent elements. His second dream expressed a wish to destroy his rivals and anxiety about this wish. Jean's dream expressed her wish for attention and possession. Such dream material occurs because the patients have participated emotionally in the group focal-conflict situation. When the focal conflict or some aspect of it touches something of importance to the patient, it may be built into a dream. This eliciting function is independent of active participation and can occur for the silent patient as well as for the active one. Thus, the patient who participates silently shares an experience with the active patient—the eliciting of crucial personal concerns. But other vital aspects of the therapeutic process are only partially available to the silent patient. He, like the others, has access to information pertinent to his own conflicts and concerns. He can also, of course, observe the consequences of others' expressing certain feelings or abandoning certain maladaptive solutions. But direct interpretations and feedback are not often available or, if offered, are often inaccurate or unusable.[8] Furthermore, the core of the therapeutic experience—the actual testing in interpersonal behavior of the reality of his fears and the necessity of a maladaptive habitual pattern—is inaccessible to him. For these reasons, the consistently silent patient is less likely than the active patient to benefit from his group-therapy experience.

The conditions under which failure to benefit occurs can be summarized as follows:

Proposition 34

Failure to benefit from therapy occurs (1) *when a patient succeeds consistently in maintaining a habitual maladaptive solution in the group, thus remaining comfortable but affectively untouched by the situation;* (2) *when a patient resorts to physical or psychological flight, thus insulating himself from the affective forces in the group; or* (3) *when a patient reacts to threat with the breakdown of previously established solutions and the substitution of disorganized, inadequate behavior.*

Proposition 35

Therapeutic benefit is limited for the consistently silent patient. He can experience affect associated with crucial personal conflicts in the group, can observe the consequences of others' yielding maladaptive solutions similar to his own, and can achieve insight through being exposed to relevant group information. Direct interpretations and feedback are less available to him and less likely to be accurate or usable. He cannot directly experience the actual testing of the reality of his fears or the necessity for maintaining habitual maladaptive solutions.

Whenever one sees changes in a habitual maladaptive pattern, there is always the question of whether the change occurs only in the group context or whether the patient also puts this change into effect in other life situations. For example, one might wonder whether Paul gave up his fictitious life story only in the group but continued to present it in other settings. The supposition that the change was restricted to the group context might be supported by recognition that conditions specific to the therapeutic setting permitted the change to occur. For Paul, it was the culture of the group and, particularly, one element of that culture ("we are all alike basically") which guaranteed him sufficient safety to test the feasibility of giving up his habitual solution. Since similar conditions might not prevail outside the therapy group, would the patient be incautious enough to take the same risk? To cite another example, Alex gave up a pattern of displaying superior knowledge. The conditions which led him to give up this behavior were specific to the group. A group solution developed which was incompatible with Alex's individual pattern, and, in order to remain a member of the group, he had to stop expressing his superior attitude. One might suspect that this change represented no more than a temporary accommodation to the special circumstances of the group and that, when Alex found himself in other interpersonal settings, he would reinstate his habitual pattern.

Systematic evidence about the maintenance of a change outside the therapeutic setting is often unavailable. The patient sometimes reports outside experiences which indicate that the new pattern has become generalized. Occasionally a change occurs which, by its character, must occur in all life situations rather than merely one (e.g., a dramatic weight loss). At other times, indirect evidence is available. For example, Alex told the group that he no longer felt as "phony" as he had previously. One might assume that this change could have occurred only if the habitual solution of maintaining a superior attitude had yielded in situations other than the group session. Similarly, Marian maintained a more consistently attractive appearance, which could be regarded as a visible sign of the shift from the habitual solution which had prevented her from recognizing and accepting her own sexual impulses. These are, of course, indirect indications that changes often extend to the patient's outside life.

The question of what makes it possible for generalization to occur is an issue which we have not explored systematically, and, therefore, our remarks are tentative. The ambivalence with which the patient regards his habitual maladaptive solutions appears to be an important factor. We have suggested that the patient maintains a maladaptive solution not because he wants to, but because he feels that he must. The solution is maintained because it seems the least dangerous alternative. As a consequence of these mixed—and largely unconscious—attitudes, the patient holds tenaciously to his habitual maladaptive solutions, yet stands ready to abandon them whenever conditions permit. This is part of the context for the therapeutic experience. It suggests that, when the patient experiences the possibility of giving up the old solution—something which heretofore seemed impossible—he will probably be motivated to follow through. The follow-through seems to include an increased readiness to take risks in the outside world.

Patients sometimes undertake preparatory work for risk-taking in the outside world while they are still in the therapy group. For example, after Paul discovered that his fears of rejection because of his orphanage background were groundless, he used the group setting to speculate about the possible consequences of revealing his true background outside the group. At this point, his primary concern was no longer the initial fear that others would reject him because of his background. Rather, he was embarrassed and worried because he would have to admit having lied to old acquaintances. In this way, he anticipated the consequences of giving up his habitual solution in other settings and prepared himself to deal with such consequences. For Alex, too, the initial corrective experience was followed by further therapeutic work. After yielding his habitual solution of maintaining a superior attitude toward others and finding that the feared consequences did not occur, Alex explored the conflict further. Facing his feelings of unworthiness opened the way to examining the roots of these feelings and determining to what extent they were realistic.

We do not assume that, if the patient is able to change a habitual pattern in the group, he will automatically be able to do so in other situations. The group therapy setting is not simply a testing ground. To see it as such is to assume that the reality in the group is the same as that outside it. The group culture supports risk-taking; the patient understands that he cannot expect the same culture to operate outside. This somewhat contradicts the common view of the group as a "slice of life"—a society in miniature, comparable to the larger society outside. The latter view probably derives from comparisons with individual therapy, for the group does indeed include fellow patients who are not bound by the therapist's role and who are free to respond as "real" persons to the patient's behavior. But, although this makes the group setting more like the outside world in one respect, it does not make it a true microcosm. Unlike outside reality, the group culture includes specific and unique guarantees of safety which set the conditions for giving up old and acquiring new solutions. If the patient experiences the group as a representative slice of his life, devoid of the special group guarantees, then change cannot occur, and his group experience is a failure. In this sense, testing in a "real" situation does not occur in the group and is not a part of the therapeutic experience.

It should be emphasized that, for any given patient, the group experience is a varying one. Few patients are consistently silent, few patients are consistently successful in maintaining a habitual maladaptive solution, few patients display permanent breakdowns in behavior. The experiences we have been describing do not happen all at once or consistently, and some may never occur for a given patient. One of the contrasts between the group and the individual therapeutic situation is that the group setting exposes the individual to a more shifting, unstable environment. In the two-person setting, there are shifts, of course, but there are also accommodations between the patient and therapist which render the situation less fluid. In the group, relatively stable accommodations are less likely to occur because the six or eight members of the group are less likely to achieve an enduring, mutually satisfactory accommodation.

Because of the fluid situation, a wide range of experiences is likely to occur for the patient. At times, a patient feels comfortable and at ease in the group because he is succeeding in establishing a habitual interpersonal solution; at other times, he feels excessively anxious because the state of the group interferes with the establishment of a habitual solution; at other times, he is relatively anxiety-free because the group culture provides guarantees against certain fears. The patient may display behavior which fits in with habitual solutions, or, in response to the group forces, he may display behavior or experience feelings which seem to him alien and uncharacteristic. Sometimes, his anxiety may be so intense that he must defend himself by not allowing the experience to touch him. At times, he may be the central figure in the group; at times, an onlooker. From time to time, he may find that the feared consequences do not occur, thus slowly learning that the solutions which he has developed to deal with crucial conflicts are not so essential as he had supposed. He may acquire a variety of insights about his behavior and feelings. In short, the group-therapeutic situation may touch him in a multitude of ways. The patient brings into the group various behavioral patterns which are related to a number of associated conflicts. These are elicited at different times by different group conditions. Some may yield, and others may not. In the group, the patient undergoes a wide range of experiences with varied therapeutic import. Taken together, these constitute the therapeutic impact.

Notes

[1] This view of the pathological process and the therapeutic goal refers to nonpsychotic patients, for whom the problem is not the breakdown of previously adequate coping devices, but the rigid maintenance of maladaptive devices.

[2] J. D. Frank and Eduard Ascher, "Corrective Emotional Experiences in Group Therapy," p. 126.

[3] S. H. Foulkes, "Group Process and the Individual in the Therapeutic Group," p. 28.

[4] Locating the source of safety in the group culture suggests one important distinction that can be made between group and individual therapy. In the latter, safety is attributable to the therapist; in the group, the therapist plays a role in influencing the culture but is not the major source of guarantees.

[5] This patient is described in greater detail in a previous paper: Dorothy Stock, Roy M. Whitman, and Morton A. Lieberman, "The Deviant Member in Therapy Groups."

[6] It is a very important function of the therapist to be aware of the group context in which patients offer interpretations to one another. If the therapist is aware of the function which interpretations serve for the group, he is in a position to correct and modify them where necessary. Of course, this is easier to do when the interpretations are blatantly inappropriate or when their function is obvious. Sometimes inappropriate interpretations involve subtle rather than obvious distortions, and

these are harder to deal with. A therapist who encourages the mutual offering of interpretation as a way of life in the group may find himself spending inordinate amounts of time and energy in detecting and correcting errors; he may sometimes even create problems for the group by reproving patients for doing what they have been led to understand the therapist wants them to do.

[7] It may appear that we are suggesting that high or low levels of anxiety are associated with therapeutic failure and that moderate anxiety levels are associated with therapeutic success. But this approach oversimplifies matters. Anxiety which becomes overwhelming may render the patient temporarily inaccessible to therapy, but the associated experiences may be capitalized upon later. Very low levels of anxiety are associated with success in instituting a habitual personal solution, but they may also occur under conditions when a group is operating on an enabling solution. With reference to high anxiety, it is either the massive eruption of overwhelming anxiety or a chronically high level of anxiety which is non-therapeutic. With reference to low anxiety, it is the consistent low anxiety level due to persistent success in maintaining a habitual solution which is associated with lack of therapeutic progress. For any particular patient, a more typical experience is one in which anxiety level fluctuates, seldom leaving him in any of these states for long.

[8] This occurs partially because the silent patient displays little of himself for others to comment on. Even more important is the manner in which the silent patient may be built into group focal conflicts. For example, it is not unusual for a group to implicate a silent person in the reactive motive by assuming that his silence means disapproval. Or a silent person may become involved in a group solution when others assume that, if only he would talk, he would provide the answers to their dilemma. Under such circumstances, the patients may succeed in dealing with the silent person to their satisfaction, but they are unlikely to produce interpretations useful to him.

III

The Therapist's Contribution

9

Strategy, Position, and Power

The therapist's goal is to facilitate the therapeutic process for each patient in the group. With this end in mind, he brings particular individuals together into a group and makes certain over-all policy decisions about meeting time and place, frequency of sessions, and the general manner in which he plans to conduct the group. Once the sessions begin, he makes continual decisions about which aspects of the session are important to attend to and when and how to intervene.

The group therapist is likely to approach his task from either of two points of view. He may focus primarily on individual patients, proceeding much as he would in a two-person therapeutic situation, or he may focus primarily on the group processes. We shall explore the latter approach, in which the group processes are seen as having a critical effect on each person's therapeutic experience.

In order to clarify similarities and differences in these approaches, consider Bob, a patient in a newly formed therapy group. Let us assume that, as the group therapist gains experience with Bob, he comes to understand that one of Bob's central problems is the severe suppression of sexual impulses. For Bob to think of himself as an adult, sexual person or to experience heterosexual feelings is to court rejection and punitive retaliation. Bob does not seem to recognize this as a problem. He moralizes about the sexual behavior of others and explains his own abstinence and lack of experience in highly intellectual, philosophical terms. He tells the other group members that he has entered therapy because he feels anxious and is vaguely dissatisfied with his life. To himself, the therapist might summarize Bob's situation as a sexual conflict which involves some fear of the consequences of recognizing or expressing sexual feelings appropriate to an adult male. The therapist might perceive that Bob has dealt with this conflict by repressing sexual feelings, adopting a moralistic stance, and maintaining intellectual rationalizations. Let us assume that this sexual issue is a dominant motif in Bob's life and that the therapist slowly comes to understand the ramifications and expressions of this problem, as well as its probable roots in Bob's past. Along with hypotheses about the nature of Bob's problem, the therapist also develops ideas about what needs to happen to Bob if therapeutic progress is to take place. Perhaps he forms the conviction that therapeutic growth would occur if Bob came to understand that his problems concern anxiety about sexual impulses or if he came to realize that the retaliation he fears is not likely to occur. Or the therapist might decide that it would be a good thing if Bob experienced sexual feelings in a setting which did not elicit punitive retaliation, or he might feel that it would be beneficial if Bob experienced affect related to the core conflicts which led him to adopt such drastic defensive measures. When the therapist begins to think in these terms, he has proceeded to the point of formulating a general prescription. Now the issue is how to put this prescription into operation. What can the therapist do that will enable the patient to gain the experience or insight which the therapist feels are required in order for positive therapeutic change to take place?

It is at this point that the two therapeutic approaches diverge. The therapist who thinks in terms of directly dealing with each patient might try to help Bob by introducing interventions aimed at coping with his resistance to sexual exploration. Bob's defensive maneuvers would surely be elicited in the group, thus giving the therapist the opportunity to observe and interpret them. The therapist might point out to Bob certain characteristic defensive operations and suggest the reasons that Bob may have found it necessary to maintain them. Or the therapist might use the relationship which has developed between him and Bob in order to point out that the fears of retaliation which the patient experiences about the therapist actually belong to someone in his primary family. Such an interpretation might lead the patient to the recognition that the fears which keep him from experiencing sexual feelings are unrealistic. Or the therapist might use the positive relationship which he has developed with the patient in order to provide the support required for Bob to take what he regards as the dangerous step of exploring his sexual feelings. These and other operations might be introduced or considered by a therapist whose basic strategy is geared toward dealing with a patient's problems by interventions specifically directed toward the individual.

In general, a therapist who focuses directly and specifically on individual patients is likely to offer direct personal interpretations to the patient, probe into the history of the patient in order to clarify links between current and past situations, use dream material, encourage other patients to provide feedback and interpretations, and try to develop a relationship which provides sufficient support to explore anxiety-laden areas. A therapist following such an approach is likely to perceive the principal advantage of the group as its capacity to evoke the patterns which are the heart of the patient's neurosis. The group is helpful to the therapist primarily because it provides him with extensive information on which he can base interpretations. Secondly, the group is useful because it includes auxiliary therapists—the other patients—who can also offer interpretations and reactions to the patient. A therapist operating from this orientation is not likely to pay much attention to group forces unless they interfere with his therapeutic work.

A therapist whose approach focuses on the group processes might see Bob as sharing the group's inability to talk and think about a variety of human issues, be it sex, anger, or affection. This inability would be characteristic of Bob, yet supported by a restrictive group atmosphere. In focal-conflict terms, Bob's fears of rejection and retaliation are also experienced by the others and are dealt with by a group solution which may alleviate fears but also prevents free expression of the underlying issues. The therapist might direct his efforts to encouraging the modification of the group solution, substituting an enabling solution for the restrictive one. If he could accomplish this, a number of consequences would follow, making a therapeutic experience for Bob as well as for others more likely to occur. For example, under free group conditions, issues relating to sexuality are more likely to come to the forefront in an explicit manner. Bob would be exposed to affect in the forbidden area. He would have the opportunity to listen to the explorations and feelings of others and perhaps observe that others are able to admit to sexual feelings without eliciting punishment. Some of Bob's underlying fears might be brought out. If this occurs and if Bob has gained some sense of safety from the group culture, he might be able to experience the disconfirmation of his fears and examine them for their real or unreal character. He might reveal enough about himself so that it becomes possible for others in the group to make suggestions and interpretations and to offer feedback. In general, if the appropriate group cultural conditions evolve, Bob is certain to be confronted with experiences relevant to his underlying conflict, might be able to undergo a corrective emotional experience, and might be directly and indirectly exposed to information relevant to his own concerns.

In general, a therapist who emphasizes the group processes may encourage the development of a group culture which allows the patient to re-experience crucial conflicts in the group setting; he may attempt to influence the general anxiety level of the group so that the individual need not flee from the group nor psychologically insulate himself; he may encourage group conditions which provide a sense of mutual support and safety; he may direct his interventions toward freeing the group and widening the boundaries within which it operates; and he may at times point out to patients unique qualities of their own participation and feelings. A therapist with such an approach sees the group as an ever-changing context for the patient's behavior and the group forces as having a direct impact on the patient's therapeutic experience. The group's eliciting effect is perceived as important, but is regarded as merely the first of many ways in which the group forces may have an impact on the individual's therapeutic experience. The therapist with this orientation is likely to attend to the over-all characteristics of the group as they unfold, as well as to the manner in which each patient contributes to and is influenced by these processes. The individual is viewed in the context of the group.

These approaches have the same goal—promoting the growth of the patient. We emphasize this point because it has sometimes been assumed that to emphasize the group processes means that the therapist is interested in or is treating the group rather than the individual. To state matters as a choice between the individual and the group sets up a false issue. It implies that therapists disagree about goals and that the goal of some therapists is to treat the individual, whereas the goal of others is to treat the group. Actually, the distinction is between means. In one case, the therapist believes that the most appropriate strategy is one which deals directly and specifically with each patient in the group. In the other case, the therapist believes that attention to the group as a whole will create conditions which will facilitate therapeutic change in each patient. In both instances the therapist's goal has to do with the individual and not the group.[1]

Nor can the two approaches be differentiated on the basis of the target of the therapist's interventions. The therapist who emphasizes attention to the group will sometimes introduce interpretations directed to individuals; the therapist who concentrates on individual patients will at times attend—often implicitly, sometimes explicitly—to group phenomena. Apart from this, a comment directed to the group may nevertheless have significance for some patient; a comment directed to a specific individual will inevitably have an impact on the group process. For example, a therapist who invites a patient to report a dream is interacting not only with that patient but also may be stirring up competitive feelings in others, thereby rendering ineffective some previously established group solution for dealing with competitive feelings. A therapist who calls attention to the sexual feelings of one patient toward another may be interpreting a shared disturbing motive and thereby interfering with a group solution which involved denial of sexual feelings in the group. A particular intervention may refer to the group, an individual patient, several patients, an individual in relation to the group, subgroups, or any other element or combination of elements in this complex situation. It may be directed toward an individual, the whole group, or a portion of the group. It may take the form of interpretation, comment, reaction, or question. It may even take the form of a *failure* to intervene. Whatever its character, form, or target, however, an intervention is likely to have an impact on the group process. Thus, although the therapist may not think in terms of group forces and may not direct his comments to the whole group, he nevertheless cannot escape the fact that what he says or does not say affects the group process.

In order to understand the kind of influence which the therapist can deliberately exert on the group, it is necessary to understand the position from which he operates. His position in regard to the patients and the emotional forces of the group is not directly comparable to his position in a two-person therapeutic situation. Nor is it the same as that of the patients. Similarly, the therapist's power to influence the situation must be examined anew, for it is not analogous to the therapist's power in individual therapy nor to the patient's power in the group.

The therapist's position in the group permits him to view group events from a unique perspective. He is in emotional touch with the forces which operate in the group, but at the same time can stand aside and observe them in a way which is not ordinarily possible for the patients. This unique position makes it possible for the therapist to empathize with the patients' affective experience and yet be able to comment on rather than associate to the material which emerges. One of our basic theses is that powerful emotional forces emerge and significantly affect the behavior, feelings, and experience of the patients. A focal conflict which involves, for example, powerful competitive feelings versus nearly overwhelming guilt has an impact on each patient. None can escape its impact, though each has contributed to the shared group feeling in a different way and each reacts to it in his own unique way. A focal conflict which involves sexual feelings about one another versus fears of retaliation from the therapist is experienced and reacted to in some way by each person in the group. The therapist is also affected by these emotional forces but does not share in them in the same way that the patients do. In his own way, each patient shares in the wishes and fears that comprise the group focal conflict. Each patient wants the therapist for himself, feels angry, fears retaliation, worries about getting out of control, urgently wants the therapist to come to his rescue, reacts strongly to a deviant member, collaborates to maintain an apathetic mood, experiences relief when a successful solution is achieved, and so on. As such forces find expression in the group, the therapist can hardly expect to remain unaffected by them. Not only does he observe the apathy or panic or relief, but to some extent he experiences them. But, if he is able to maintain an appropriate therapeutic stance, he is not a part of them in the same way. He is touched by the emotional forces in the group but not gripped by them. He recognizes but does not participate in them. Under ordinary circumstances, the therapist does not share in the wish for special recognition in the group; he does not share the fear of retaliation.[2] It is the therapist's capacity to be affected by the emotional forces in the group which makes it possible for him to intuitively grasp the nature of the emotional events. And it is his capacity to stand aside from these emotional forces which makes it possible for him to control his interventions: to assess the prevailing group forces and guide his participation in terms of certain therapeutic goals.

Proposition 36	*The therapist views the group from a unique position. Though not usually participating in the generation or expression of the group focal conflict, he experiences the affect involved in it. Thus, he is in emotional touch yet stands outside the conflict and can observe its character and course.*

Assuming the therapist's awareness of the character of group events, an important issue is the extent to which the therapist, operating on this knowledge, can influence the course of group events. If the therapist has no power to influence the group, his awareness of the group processes is merely an intellectual exercise with no consequences for the patients' therapeutic experience. The therapist's power comes into play long before the first session of the group; in fact, it is then that his power is clearest, for it is the therapist alone who makes the important decisions about who is to be in the group (subject, of course, to the policies of his work setting and to the available patients). It is also up to the therapist to make decisions concerning the manner in which the group is to be structured and conducted.

The therapist's ability to influence the course of group events, by interventions and style of participation, is a more complex issue. The character and extent of the therapist's power in the group can be understood partly in terms of real power and partly in terms of imputed power. Because of his special training, experience, and perspective in the group, the therapist is in a position to see aspects of the group that the patients cannot see. He is likely to view the group in a broader perspective, noting relationships between current and past events. He is more likely to be aware of characteristics of the group as a whole, and he is in a better position to observe how individual patients participate in and contribute to the group processes. The special perspective of the therapist is as important as his special training and experience, for without this unique perspective, his special training and experience would be of little value. When the therapist participates in other kinds of group situations, such as a staff or committee meeting, his special training does not prevent him from participating in the group forces in ways similar to the patients' participation in the therapy group. But in the therapy group the therapist's unique perspective makes him the only person who can intervene from a position outside the group focal conflict.[3]

Another aspect of the therapist's influence in the group has its source in the fact that patients are likely to attribute special powers to the therapist and, therefore, are inclined to involve him in successive group focal conflicts and solutions in special ways. From the patients' point of view, the therapist is endowed with unique powers. In part, this endowment of special power is realistic. For example, the therapist has placed the patient in the group and presumably could also ask him to leave. He is unlikely to utilize his power punitively, but the patients may assume that he will. Another source of his imputed power is his status as an expert. Although the therapist does have special training and experience, patients are likely, especially during the early phases of the group, to endow him with omniscience and misunderstand the character of his expert knowledge. That is, the patients are likely to assume that, if only the therapist has sufficient data, he will be able to explain them to themselves or give them advice and that, once this is done, improvement will occur. They are likely to assume that the therapist can handle anything that comes up in the group as well as any problem of their own. Such expectations amount to a magical belief that the therapist can understand and fix everything. It is the patients' tendency to attribute such powers to the therapist that accounts for the way the therapist is often involved in the group focal conflicts. For example, the disturbing motive "wish to have a special relationship with the therapist" would be unlikely to develop were it not for the assumption that something special can be gained from the therapist, compared with the others. The reactive motive "fear of retaliation from the therapist" could not arise were it not for the assumption that the therapist possesses special powers that he may use destructively. The therapist is often perceived as a potential source for solutions. Frequently, the patients attempt to utilize the therapist to cope with particular focal conflicts. The patients assume that the therapist has the power to control the uncontrollable impulse, deal with the deviant patient, or explain each person and thus bypass the otherwise extended and painful path to therapeutic change.

When the therapist is the object of the wish or fear in a focal conflict or when he is the potential source of a solution, he is in a position to have a special impact on the group. For example, in a focal conflict in which the patients share a wish to have a special relationship with the therapist, any intervention which pays special attention to a particular patient may have a more than ordinary degree of influence on the others. In a focal conflict in which the reactive motive involves fear of retaliation from the therapist, any interpretation on the part of the therapist may be perceived as a negative judgment and intensify the reactive fears. If the therapist introduces an interpretation to an individual patient at a time when the group is operating on a solution which involves perceiving the therapist as an expert, he may find the patient taking the therapist's comments very seriously, for to do so is to contribute to the maintenance of the group solution. If the group is pushing toward a solution the success of which requires the active collaboration of the therapist, withholding such collaboration will have a potent blocking effect in the group. When the latter occurs, the therapist is in the position of a deviant and is exerting the influence of a deviant. This source and character of influence corresponds exactly to that exerted by a patient when he is in a deviant position. That is, if a solution cannot be established without the cooperation of some patient and that patient withholds his cooperation, he is in a position of power. Whether the deviant is a patient or the therapist makes no difference, for the degree and source of influence are the same. In general, we have observed that the therapist's influence on the course of group events is, in many cases, no different from that of the patients. Both may influence the group by blocking an emerging group solution, both may make a comment which increases the reactive fears or the intensity of the wish, both may introduce a comment which leads to the modification of the group culture. Just as the patients sometimes succeed and sometimes fail in their attempts to influence, so does the therapist.

Sometimes the patients respond to the therapist's comments exactly as he intended; at other times, the group feels like a stubborn mass, and no efforts on his part can move it from its current state. Success or failure in influencing the group depends, as is the case for patients, on the state of the group forces when the intervention is made. The principles which govern the degree and character of the therapist's influence on the group focal conflict are the same as the principles which govern the influence of other participants in the group.

Yet, even casual observation reveals that on the whole the therapist does exert greater influence on the course of the group than does any patient.[4] This apparent contradiction is resolved if one keeps in mind that the therapist is more likely than a patient to be an object of shared wishes and fears and more likely to be perceived as a source of solutions, because special powers are more often attributed to the therapist than to a patient. Under such conditions, the therapist's interventions have a special impact because of their relevance to the group forces. It is in this sense that the therapist "counts more" in the group and is more often in a position to influence the situation than are the patients. In this sense, attributed power is translated into actual power to influence the processes of the group.

Proposition 37

The therapist's power to influence the group derives from (1) the unique position from which he views the group focal conflict and which permits him to intervene on the basis of information unavailable to the patients and (2) from the frequency with which the patients impute to the therapist the power of gratification,

> *threat, and magical solutions. On this basis, the therapist becomes an object of impulses involved in the group focal conflict and a source of solutions. On such occasions, the therapist is in a position of special influence in the group.*

The extent and character of the therapist's power in the group situation has to be understood in its own terms, distinct from the extent and character of his power in a two-person therapeutic relationship. In individual therapy, the extent, if not the character, of the therapist's influence is taken for granted. It is generally recognized that with only two people present, both play a significant though different role in affecting the character and course of the therapeutic situation. Questions about the influence of the therapist are not so likely to focus on the extent of his influence, but on its character and source. In the multiple-person situation of the group, the issue of how much influence the therapist can exert becomes more critical, for he is only one of a number of people whose participation has an impact on the course of group events. In the group, no individual has as much consistent influence on the character of the situation as either the patient or the therapist in the two-person relationship. As we have just suggested, certain real powers and consequences of imputed powers put the therapist in a position of special influence in the group. But in quantitative terms, the extent of his influence is never so great as that which can be exerted by a therapist in individual therapy. He is confronted with a control and influence problem which radically differs from that which faces the individual therapist.

A therapist who undertakes a therapy group is confronted with pressures and requirements which are unique to the group situation. These are such that he cannot realistically expect to avoid making errors from time to time. Therapeutic error can occur because the therapist has failed to understand the character of the group situation or the meaning of an individual's behavior in the context of the group. Such errors are errors of understanding. The therapist has failed to be sufficiently in touch with everything that is happening and thus misses significant aspects of the situation. In so complex a situation, such errors are inevitable. Other errors can more properly be regarded as counter-transference errors. In focal-conflict terms, counter transference can be described as occurring when the therapist loses or temporarily abandons the perspective appropriate to his role and participates from within the group focal conflict. Rather than operate on appropriate therapeutic goals, the therapist is driven by attempts to establish group conditions which are personally viable. The specific point at which a therapist is most vulnerable to the group forces and most likely to lose appropriate perspective will, of course, vary from person to person. That is, the particular ways in which the therapist may participate in a group focal conflict and the particular situations under which he is motivated to move the group in directions which are viable to him rather than useful to the group will depend on the therapist's personality and the way it interacts with the group forces.

It is often difficult to differentiate errors which have their source in counter-transference reactions from errors which have their source in faulty understanding of the group situation. One might take the position that all errors can be regarded as counter-transference errors, since a failure in understanding is inevitably attributable to some counter-transference reaction. However, this view assumes that the therapist is equipped with superb and unfailing intellect and sensitivity. Any human being who decides to conduct a therapy group will certainly make errors of understanding from time to time, entirely apart from his possible affective involvement in the group forces. It is often a matter of definition and choice to decide whether a particular error is based on faulty understanding or on counter-transference. For example, a common therapeutic error during the early group sessions is impatience with the group for operating on restrictive solutions and premature efforts to widen the group's boundaries. Such efforts may unduly increase the anxiety in the group and interfere with the necessary development of conditions of safety. Often it is appropriate for the therapist to accept the operation of restrictive solutions during the early period and wait until later to encourage shifts toward enabling solutions. It is very difficult to say whether this error is rooted in counter-transference reactions or whether the therapist has simply misjudged the group situation. For different therapists it could be one or the other or both. It seems preferable to view errors on a scale ranging from misunderstanding to loss of appropriate therapist perspective.[5]

It would not be useful to discuss the multitude of qualities of the therapist's personality which might lead to his losing appropriate therapeutic perspective and becoming involved in the group focal conflict. Counter-transference involvements vary from therapist to therapist. However, it does seem useful to mention certain aspects of the group situation which may present particular challenges to the therapist.

There are times when the therapist operates under special pressures because of the manner in which he is built into the group focal conflict. The therapist may become the object of pressures from the patients, who perceive him as a potential savior, punisher, or source of gratification. He may be built into the disturbing motive by being the object of hostile, sexual, or succorant drives; he may be built into the reactive motive by being perceived as the source of punishment, envy, or retaliation. He may be built into the solution by being pressed to share his supposed omniscience with the group. Whenever anything of this sort happens, the therapist may feel great pressure because of the unanimity of the patients' feelings toward him. The group as a collective body is perceiving him in a particular way or is pressing him to behave in a particular way. If these pressures coincide with vulnerabilities in his own personality, he may find it especially difficult to maintain a proper perspective.

The therapist may feel vulnerable and threatened because of the character of his influence and control in the group situation. As we have pointed out, the amount and kind of influence and control which the therapist has in the group are radically different from the influence he can exert in the two-person therapeutic situation. Because the therapist may be accustomed to a two-person situation or is making inappropriate analogies from the one situation to the other, he may expect to have more impact or a different kind of impact on the group situation than is really possible. For example, he may feel that he ought to be able to establish enabling solutions at the start; he may feel that in every case he ought to be able to prevent patients from experiencing undue anxiety; he may feel he ought to be able to exploit all the personal material which the patients reveal. This last point is very much related to another possible source of pressure. In the two-person therapeutic situation, the therapist is dealing with only one person and can pursue the material being introduced by his patient in any manner he wishes. He may assume that the therapeutic tactics appropriate to individual therapy are also appropriate to the group or should be modified as little as possible. If he makes this assumption, the therapist will be confronted with continual frustration, for, in the group setting, individual patients are continually presenting data about themselves which cannot be pursued on a one-to-one basis. If the therapist assumes that this is the only road to therapeutic improvement, he operates at a decided disadvantage. Logically, he is forced to the conclusion that he must fail and that he is offering second-rate treatment to the individual.

The therapist may perceive the group situation as one in which he is the primary source of interpretations and the security that the patients need in order to express themselves and explore their concerns freely. If so, he is again certain to experience failure and frustration. As we have suggested throughout, the individual therapeutic situation is an inappropriate model for the group. If crucial differences between the individual and the group-therapeutic situation are not recognized, the therapist will not recognize that his role and task cannot be the same in both situations. In our view, the therapist has a significant role in the group, but it is not the same as his role in individual therapy. In the group, the therapist's primary task is that of influencing the interpersonal conditions under which the therapeutic experience occurs and of exploiting the group situation appropriately for the benefit of each patient. In this view, the therapist's role is conceptualized, in large part, as that of influencing the group situation. Some of the functions which belong primarily to the therapist in the individual-therapeutic situation will, in the group-therapeutic situation, be assumed by the patients. What remains the unique province of the group therapist is attention to the group forces, for this is essential to the movement of the group and cannot readily be undertaken by the patients. We perceive this not only as the unique role of the therapist, but also as one which makes a crucial difference in each patient's therapeutic experience.

Notes

[1] To suggest that "the individual versus the group" is a false issue does not imply that the therapist is never faced with choices in strategy which take on the character of a choice between an individual and some aspect of the group. For example, the therapist may avoid interpreting some specific point to a patient because of a potentially negative effect on the group process, or he may be careful about the manner in which he refers to a group issue because of its meaning for a particular patient. This choice is the same that is faced by a therapist whose individual patient is presenting him with complex material which could be exploited in several directions. The group therapist who does not think in terms of total group aspects of the situation is continually faced with decisions about which patient to concentrate upon. These are all choices in strategy which face any therapist no matter what his theoretical orientation or whether he is dealing with an individual or a group.

[2] There are times when such sharing does occur and the therapist gets caught up in the wishes and fears of the group. When this happens, one is inclined to say that the therapist has lost his perspective or that he is experiencing counter-transference feelings. This is discussed more fully later in the chapter.

[3] With reference to individual patients, the therapist is not the only person in the group who stands in an observer's role. Thus he shares with patients the function of commenting on and offering interpretations about *individual* behavior and processes.

[4] Short-term exceptions occur, as when a deviant patient dominates a session

or when the experience of one individual has a potent effect on the character of the entire group focal conflict. Over an extended period of time, however, the therapist is more influential.

[5] Loeser and Bry have emphasized that it is difficult to differentiate counter-transference and non-counter-transference factors. They say, "As we explored the subject further, testing, observing and collecting data, it became increasingly clear to us that the data being accumulated dealt with the total impact of the therapist upon the group and that any attempt to restrict our interest to one aspect of the problem would be difficult. Our study would indicate that there is no sharp demarkation between countertransference and non countertransference factors, that they merge by gradation over a wide scale." (Lewis H. Loeser and Thea Bry, "The Position of the Group Therapist in Transference and Countertransference: an Experimental Study," *International Journal of Group Psychotherapy,* 3 [1953], p. 389.) They suggest that it is more appropriate to think in terms of the therapist's position in the group rather than in terms of counter-transference. Ross and Brissenden have followed the same line of thought. See Donald W. Ross and Arik Brissenden, "Some Observations on the Emotional Position of the Group Psychotherapist," *The Psychiatric Quarterly,* 35 (1961), 516–522.

10

General Policy

The therapist's efforts to make the group an effective milieu begin before the patients convene for the first session. He must make prior decisions about the composition of the group and certain matters of policy.

Decisions about the composition of a therapy group have enduring consequences for the quality and characteristics of the therapeutic experience. We have found that homogeneity in certain features and heterogeneity in others produce an optimal composition. Homogeneity is preferable with reference to the vulnerability of the patients. A wide range in degree of vulnerability poses serious problems for the group. We use the term "vulnerability" to refer to the adequacy of a patient's habitual solutions and especially his capacity for tolerating anxiety.[1] When patients who differ widely in degree of vulnerability are brought together into a group, group solutions emerge which are either highly threatening to the more vulnerable patients or excessively and unnecessarily restrictive from the point of view of the others. This occurs because of the manner in which the vulnerable patient experiences and expresses the group focal conflict and because of the manner in which the group solutions are built from the interaction of the patients. A highly vulnerable individual is likely to experience and, at times, express the focal conflict facing the group in intense and primitive terms. For example, when the group is faced with an issue involving the fear of punishment from the therapist, the highly vulnerable patient may experience this as a primitive fear of literal destruction. Imagery may involve the electric chair, the collapse of the building, and so forth. He is likely to feel defenseless in the face of such fears and have inadequate means for mitigating them. Other less vulnerable patients may experience equally intense and primitive fears at peak periods of anxiety in the group, but are better able to cope with and mitigate their fears. The focal conflicts which develop in a therapy group are generated from the patients' interactions and are the product of each person's wishes and fears. Not all patients contribute to the emerging focal conflict in the same way, nor do they experience it with the same intensity. The associated solutions which emerge are the product of the varied individual contributions. Not everyone contributes to the group solution in the same way or to the same degree. A group solution which becomes generally established is a compromise, the product of everyone's efforts to render the group viable. As a compromise, the group solution rarely represents the ideal solution for any individual. Consequently, different patients are exposed to various degrees of anxiety under any given group solution. The group solution which is finally established usually provides sufficient safety for each patient to tolerate the level of anxiety that the situation arouses in him. Consider, though, what is likely to happen in a group composed of patients who have a very broad range of vulnerability. Often, the kind of group solution which would be appropriate for the less vulnerable patients does not provide sufficient protection for the more vulnerable patient. If a solution is constructed which encompasses the needs of the highly vulnerable patient, a more restrictive therapeutic milieu than is necessary for the others may result. If, on the other hand, the group constructs a solution which is viable for the less vulnerable members, the vulnerable individual finds himself in a situation which lacks viability for him. In such a situation, the group may be faced with a chronic deviant. The highly vulnerable individual, who has not been able to establish himself in a tolerable environment, may physically flee the group, or he may display disorganized behavior, creating problems for the other patients; at the very least, he will experience anxiety sufficient to prevent him from utilizing the situation therapeutically. As this suggests, the best composition is one which avoids marked extremes in the degree of vulnerability.

The distribution of age, sex, and race is less important because the problems generated can be dealt with more readily. A group of young adults and one much older person might construct solutions in which the older person is cast in the role of a wise senior citizen. Such a solution might be disadvantageous to all, for the older patient is locked into a solution which excludes potentially useful therapeutic experiences and the younger ones maintain a restrictive solution which deprives them of the opportunity of exploring directly the associated wishes and fears. Similarly, in a male group that includes one woman, there is the likelihood that the woman will be utilized in a stereotyped way in solutions. Here again, such a solution is likely to have a non-therapeutic effect. In general, a group in which one or two patients are in some obvious minority status generates certain kinds of anti-therapeutic solutions. However, unlike the problems which emerge when a group is composed of individuals with a wide range of vulnerability, these are problems which can be worked out in the group so that the potential disadvantages can be overcome.

Maximum heterogeneity in the patients' position on specific conflict areas appears to be desirable. For example, one would not expect marked therapeutic benefit to occur in a group whose members all experienced major conflicts about hostile affect and all dealt with these conflicts through denial. Nor would one expect maximum benefit in a group in which all the patients were characterized by a marked conflict in the area of dependency and so assumed reciprocal stances (for example, bossiness and deference). On the other hand, a group in which the patients experienced marked conflicts in the same area but dealt with their conflicts in a variety of ways might work better. Better still would be a group composed of individuals with dominant conflicts in a number of areas and a variety of coping mechanisms. In focal-conflict terms, such heterogeneity would be described as widely varied positions with respect to specific focal conflicts. There is no consensus about the kind of group which is viable. Such a composition is desirable because it provides guarantees against the *unyielding* establishment of restrictive solutions. Where there is general agreement about the conditions which constitute viability, solutions are quickly established. And, if what is felt to be viable adds up to suppression, denial, choosing a scapegoat, or the like, the group solution will be restrictive. Such a therapy group includes no individuals who are likely to challenge restrictive solutions by attempting to gain greater gratification of the disturbing motive, by re-introducing reactive fears, or by challenging the solution. Under such conditions, the established restrictive solution will be difficult to modify. The patients will be inclined to establish and maintain group conditions which are comfortable for all but challenging to none. They remain unexposed to competing or challenging positions; thus, the opportunities for a corrective emotional experience are much reduced and the patients are likely to experience little except the successful reproduction of habitual maladaptive solutions.

Proposition 38

Groups that are heterogeneous with respect to degree of vulnerability are likely to develop solutions which generate excessive non-constructive anxiety for the more vulnerable patients or solutions which are unnecessarily restrictive from the point of view of the others. Groups that are homogeneous with reference to position on specific conflicts are likely to translate individual viability goals into an unyielding, predominantly restrictive group culture.

In addition to deciding how to compose the group, the therapist makes a number of policy decisions about the way to conduct the group and the stand he will take on certain issues. Such decisions stem from a complex base which includes matters of individual taste, distillations of clinical experience, therapeutic lore, and theoretical considerations. They are directed toward precluding events regarded as anti-therapeutic (outside contacts among patients) or toward ensuring others regarded as therapeutic (never divulging confidential material). Decisions include not only settling on a policy, but also on appropriate ways of putting the policy into operation. For example, the therapist may decide to verbally communicate a decision about policy. Just as the psychoanalyst may instruct his patient to associate freely, the group therapist may instruct his patients regarding ground rules concerning such matters as confidentiality. Or, the therapist may put his policies into operation by structuring the situation in accordance with them—for example, providing opportunities for the patients to see him privately or arranging for alternate sessions without the therapist. Or, he may work toward establishing group conditions which will allow the policy to emerge from the interaction of the patients.

The theoretical framework which we have presented suggests certain guidelines for decisions about establishing and implementing policy. To illustrate, four common matters of policy will be examined from a focal-conflict point of view: structuring during the early sessions, honoring confidences, outside contacts among patients, and contacts between the therapist and the individual patient.

Structuring during the Early Sessions

It has been our practice to allow a therapy group to develop with a minimum of structure. In practical terms, this means that the therapist suggests no agenda, topics, or procedures. Typically, the therapist might begin the first session with some general comment to the effect that the group situation is intended to be of use to the patients and that the discussion will focus on matters which they regard as important. An instructional set is implied in such a comment: the therapy group is presented as a serious enterprise with a goal which is geared to the needs of the patients and which utilizes procedures of open discussion. With this amount of structuring, the group begins. Consistent with this policy of minimal structuring, we avoid summaries at the close of sessions and are not likely to suggest that a current topic be continued in the next session nor remind patients at the beginning of a session of what has preceded it.

This decision is based on several theoretical considerations. During the formative phase, an initial group culture develops which renders the group a viable milieu. The solutions which comprise the initial culture provide the patients with a feeling of safety and encourage a sense of commitment. On the basis of the initial culture, the patients begin to feel that it will be safe to reveal themselves and to express their opinions and feelings with some frankness. The establishment of such a culture is the prime business of the therapy group during the early sessions. The initial culture develops in response to the patients' need to cope with the initial focal conflicts which emerge in the group. And, it is the patients' individual concerns which determine the initial group focal conflicts. In order to establish an initial group culture which is relevant to the patients' concerns, it is necessary to permit those concerns to emerge without interference.

The therapist who introduces structure by suggesting procedures, providing definitions, and offering reassurances probably does so in an attempt to find a short cut to establishing a feeling of safety in the group. The hope is to relieve the patients of experiencing painful fears about the potential dangers in the group situation. In effect, the therapist tries to establish a sense of safety in the group by establishing group solutions for the patients. This cannot be done, for it is impossible to establish group solutions by edict. The therapist cannot predict the exact nature of the concerns which will emerge in a particular group, nor can he predict the precise character of the solutions which will prove adequate to cope with the initial concerns. To be effective, a group solution must match the associated group focal conflict, and the latter will always vary in its exact character because of the unique composition of every group. At best, then, a therapist will be ineffective when he attempts to introduce a sense of safety into the group by edict. At worst, he will vitiate the emergence of the specific concerns that are most important to the patients. If this occurs, his attempts to create conditions of safety will actually have prevented such conditions from becoming established.

Honoring Confidences

Therapists agree that the maintenance of confidences is an important source of a sense of safety in the group. Without it, patients will feel that they must be guarded about what they reveal, for they will expect such revelations to lead to shame, ridicule, or criticism, not only from the other patients in the group but from persons outside the group. Disagreements among therapists are not likely to arise about the desirability of establishing standards of confidence, but about the means by which such standards can be achieved.

This issue is similar to the point discussed in the previous section. Should the therapist structure the situation by introducing a ground rule about confidences, or should he wait for agreements about confidences to emerge from the group interaction? The position presented previously is relevant here. To be effective, a group solution or standard must emerge in response to the felt needs of the group. The patients will adhere to a standard if it emerges in response to shared concerns and if it functions to alleviate the anxieties associated with those concerns. They are less likely to adhere to a standard which is introduced by edict. In addition to being less effective, an edict about confidences is also unnecessary. One can rely on the group processes to generate such standards, although the standard is not always explicit.

Invariably the early sessions will see the emergence of a group focal conflict in which a wish to reveal shameful or difficult material operates in conjunction with fears about potential criticism or ridicule. Solutions which are established in response to such focal conflicts often implicitly subsume standards about maintaining confidences. For example, variations of the solution "all admit we have problems and faults" involve the implicit agreement that patients will not take advantage of one another's vulnerabilities. During the establishment of such a solution, the patients sometimes warn one another of particular vulnerabilities. They may compare notes about how each feels about parents' or friends' knowing they are in group therapy or about how each feels about others' knowing about his problems. Once the solution is established, this guarantee of mutual protection includes the maintenance of confidences. In a group which follows this typical course, the issue of confidence may never explicitly arise. If it does, it is usually in response to a real, imagined, or potential breach in the implicit agreement. For example, in an adolescent group implicit standards about maintaining confidence became explicit when one of the patients felt she had had a narrow escape. On the way to a group-therapy session, this patient had passed a fellow patient, who was talking to a mutual acquaintance. She had been frightened that the fellow patient might mention that they were both on their way to a therapy session. During the session the first patient thanked the second for not mentioning this. This incident led to a more explicit definition of what the patients regarded as appropriate behavior about honoring confidences.

In general, it is our observation that the issue of confidence will be settled by the patients themselves at a time when the issue is meaningful and in a manner which is appropriate to the group. For the therapist to introduce standards or assurances about the maintenance of confidence is unnecessary and will be ineffective unless concomitant developments within the group establish such standards as a part of a group solution.[2]

Outside Contacts among Patients

Many therapists agree that outside contacts among patients work against the therapeutic process, especially if they develop into intense involvements or extend over a period of time. Such behavior is generally regarded as "acting out." The patients express feelings through behavior, thus rendering them inaccessible to the therapeutic process. In focal-conflict terms, such outside contacts are a device adopted by a few patients to establish mutually played out personal maladaptive solutions and/or as a solution to some group focal conflict. In either case, the behavior is a response to feelings generated in the group situation.

During the formative phase of an adolescent group, the patients met for coffee after each session. The therapists were not aware of this until the patients commented, in the group, that they seemed able to speak more freely during the coffee sessions than during the group meetings. They speculated that it was the presence of the therapists that made the difference and compared notes about fears of criticism from the therapists if they failed to be serious at all times. It appeared that the outside contacts functioned as a solution to a group focal conflict and provided a safe outlet for the expression of non-serious feelings. Such a solution is restrictive because it makes it impossible to explore or resolve the issue in the therapeutic setting. In this illustration, feelings the patients regarded as non-serious (and which the therapist might have regarded as important) were outlawed from the group. The solution was not maintained indefinitely and was brought up in the group when the focal conflict was no longer an issue.

Outside contacts between two patients can also constitute a restrictive solution for the group as a whole, as well as have special meaning for those patients. For example, under some circumstances, sexual contact between two patients can constitute a group solution. It is as if the group delegates sexual matters to two people and thereby makes it possible for the others to avoid confrontation with such feelings.

It has been our experience that no outside contacts persist indefinitely. If such behavior constitutes a restrictive group solution, it will be maintained as long as the associated group focal conflict remains unchanged. But the group focal conflict is inherently unstable, and the balance between the disturbing and the reactive motives shifts. As this occurs, the group conditions which required the maintenance of the solution are no longer present. It is at this point that the acting-out behavior can be brought up in the group session, discussed and abandoned.

Individual Therapeutic Contacts

Before the sessions begin, the therapist usually forms a policy about individual therapeutic contacts with the patients in the group. Two decisions are involved: whether to provide regularly scheduled individual sessions and, if not, how to respond to occasional requests for individual sessions.

If the therapist provides regular individual sessions, it is usually because he regards the group as an inadequate milieu for achieving the goals of therapy. He is likely to think of the group primarily as a stimulator—an affect-laden situation useful for eliciting important feelings, which, however, can best be thoroughly explored in a two-person situation. This view of the group differs from our own (Chapter 8). We see the group as the major vehicle for therapy and therefore do not offer routine individual contacts.

If the therapist chooses not to provide regular individual sessions, he must still decide how to respond to occasional requests for individual sessions. These arise in a variety of contexts. During a group session, a clamor sometimes arises, and each patient insists that he needs to talk to the therapist privately. This is most likely to occur during the early sessions and is likely to be an attempt to get the therapist to collaborate in a group solution. Usually, such a collective request indicates that an issue the patients regard as dangerous has come up. The request for individual sessions is an attempt to solve the related focal conflict by finding a private, presumably protected, channel for the expression of some feeling or problem, so that they need not fear the consequences. If the therapist accedes to such a request, he is cooperating in a restrictive solution, since he is allowing the patients to deal with crucial interpersonal issues through isolation. He may also be perpetuating what is likely to be an associated fear—that their feelings are so dangerous, so potentially explosive, that to express them in the group is to create an intolerably threatening situation. On several counts, then, the therapist may insist that the issue can be handled in the group.

When the request comes from an individual, the therapist must first assess the meaning of the request for the individual and for the group and then make his decision accordingly. If a patient requests an individual contact and he is supported in this by the other members of the group, it is likely that the patients are trying to get the therapist to collaborate in a restrictive group solution. Perhaps the group as a whole is attempting to get the therapist to deal privately with a deviant patient; perhaps the patient is regarded as a carrier of dangerous affect, and the others are, in effect, trying to expel him from the group. In such a case, the appropriate decision is to refuse to cooperate in the restrictive solution and to explore the issue with the patients in the group setting.

A request for an individual contact is often made because the patient feels that some issue which currently concerns him is too inflammatory to be dealt with in the presence of others. The therapist must avoid unduly cooperating with the patient in establishing such a pattern, for it may restrict the therapeutic usefulness of the group for the patient. If the request is made during a group session, it becomes a matter for group discussion, and often the issue can be explored so that the need dissipates by the end of the session. If the request is made between sessions, the therapist may agree to see the patient, utilizing the time to explore the issue and clarify the reasons that the patient felt he had to resort to a private meeting to resolve his inner conflicts. At this point, the patient can be helped to understand the reasons he felt the matter could not be brought up in the group.

Sometimes the request for an individual session stems from a motivation other than the fact that a patient is experiencing gross anxiety in the group situation. It may constitute an attempt on the part of a patient to establish himself as the therapist's favorite or as a special person in the group. In such an instance, the content of the problem which the patient presents is unimportant, functioning merely as a passport to special status. Under these circumstances, efforts to explore the issue in terms of content or to encourage the patient to discuss the matter in the group will fail because they are irrelevant. It is necessary to understand the issue from the point of view of the interaction. Once explored from this point of view, the effort would again be to enable the patient to bring the issue back to the group.

In general, the danger in acceding to requests for private contacts is the possibility of vitiating the critical therapeutic experience for the patient. That is, the private interviews provide the patient with a way of coping with conflict, but a way which increases his personal sense of comfort at the expense of isolating him from potentially therapeutic experiences in the group.

The range of policy matters just discussed is intended to be illustrative rather than comprehensive. In some instances, the primary issue involves deciding which of several policies is preferable; in others, the primary decision is how to put a desirable policy into operation. In examining policy decisions from a focal-conflict point of view, no new principles are involved. Relevant theory is contained in Propositions 29 through 35, which refer to the character of the therapeutic process in the group. If the policy is likely to enhance the therapeutic process, it ought to be adopted. More specifically, a desirable policy is one which encourages the establishment of enabling solutions, maintains conditions of safety in the group, and increases the probability that individual patients will experience relevant personal conflicts, be provided with relevant information, and utilize the group setting to test the feasibility of yielding maladaptive personal solutions and to examine the reality of underlying fears. Conversely, if the policy is likely to interfere with the therapeutic process, it ought not be adopted. An undesirable policy is one which allows the group to maintain restrictive solutions, preventing the individual from experiencing relevant personal conflicts, or insulates him from relevant information. On these grounds, policies which we regard as desirable include encouraging standards which ensure the maintenance of confidence, discouraging outside contacts among patients, introducing minimal initial structuring, and omitting regular individual contacts with the therapist.

In some matters of policy, the crucial decision concerns the best way of implementing the policy. The therapist feels that certain standards should be established in the group. Usually, the choice involves deciding whether to introduce an explicit rule. In focal-conflict terms, group standards are group solutions. In order for a standard or solution to be effective, it must emerge from the patients' interaction in response to shared and immediately experienced group focal conflicts (see Propositions 1 through 5 and 16 through 18). On these grounds, it is our opinion that standards about maintaining confidence and outside contacts among patients can best be established by permitting relevant solutions to emerge from group interaction. The alternative—a ruling or a guarantee introduced by the therapist—is likely to be ineffective unless supported by developments in the group. In the latter case, the ruling is gratuitous. The therapist also takes the risk of introducing a ruling at an irrelevant moment, when the group is not concerned with the issue, or he may push for a standard which is not specifically suited to the underlying concerns. Most important, the therapist who attempts to short-cut the group processes by introducing such edicts may vitiate the interactive processes which are the heart of the therapeutic experience.

Notes

[1] Note that vulnerability is not directly comparable to pathology. The crucial dimension in vulnerability is the defensive structure—in focal-conflict terms, the repertory of individual solutions—rather than the degree of pathology itself. In the groups we have studied, the individuals we would describe as highly vulnerable have been primarily patients in an acute psychotic state or, sometimes, neurotic patients with limited solutional resources.

[2] The position taken here should not be confused with permissiveness. The general position is that the therapist should not make an intervention which is unnecessary and likely to be ineffective and to curtail some useful experiences.

11

Influence through Participation

Once the group composition is established and the therapist has made his decisions about over-all policy, the sessions begin. From this point on, by far the most important source of the therapist's influence is the manner in which he participates in the group. The therapist who seeks to accomplish his psychotherapeutic goals through emphasizing and utilizing the group processes will direct his efforts toward and make decisions about three critical areas—the state of the group culture, the conditions of safety in the group, and the individual patient in relation to the group processes. These are the three focuses around which the therapist must work if he is to ensure a maximally useful therapeutic milieu and, hence, a useful therapeutic experience for each patient in the group.

Establishing and Maintaining an Appropriate Culture

The kind of culture a group establishes crucially affects the individual's therapeutic experience. If the culture is dominated by enabling solutions, a wide range of group focal conflicts will emerge, maximizing the possibility that each patient will experience crucial personal conflicts in the therapeutic setting. In contrast, if the group culture is marked by predominantly restrictive solutions, whole areas of experience, some specifically relevant to certain patients, will be ruled out. Certain restrictive group solutions are to be especially avoided, for they may have a damaging effect on some patients. If a group solution permits an individual to operate on a habitual maladaptive solution, the group culture is insulating that individual from potentially useful therapeutic experiences. If a group solution exposes an individual to gross threat, it may cause him to flee the group or to respond in some grossly maladaptive way. The culture of the group is also important in establishing conditions relevant to the development of insight. Under certain group cultural conditions, information about the patient or about personally relevant concerns is available, accurate, and usable. Under other group cultural conditions, such information is likely to be inaccurate, irrelevant, or unusable.

For these reasons, it is important for the therapist to utilize his influence to encourage the establishment and maintenance of a group culture in which enabling rather than restrictive solutions predominate. In pursuing this goal, a hazard to be avoided is the inadvertent support of a restrictive solution or interference with the establishment of an enabling solution. Such errors are most likely to occur when the therapist is out of touch with the meaning of group events, when he loses the perspective appropriate to his role, or both.

Inadvertent support of a restrictive solution is likely to occur when the therapist gains some personal gratification from seeing a particular solution maintained in the group: perhaps he, too, feels most comfortable when certain areas are avoided; perhaps he enjoys being perceived as an expert or a powerful force, as is required in some restrictive solutions; perhaps he permits a scapegoating solution to persist in order to avoid becoming the direct target of the patients' anger. Here, conditions which are personally viable for the therapist coincide with some restrictive group solution. If the therapist fails to interfere with the maintenance of such solutions, he is allowing non-therapeutic conditions to persist in the group. Therapist behavior which inadvertently interferes with the establishment of enabling solutions occurs under similar conditions. Often, such errors are errors of omission. The therapist fails to notice, and hence to support potential enabling solutions.

Establishing and Maintaining Conditions of Safety

A generally shared sense of safety is an essential condition for therapeutic progress. The group must provide the patient with a new source of safety which is not based on his usual source of safety—his habitual maladaptive solutions. This source of safety stems from the group solutions which the patients establish in response to successive group focal conflicts.

The task of encouraging the development of conditions of safety in the group is, in one sense, a simple one. Provided that the group has been appropriately composed, the processes of the group will work in the therapist's favor. The patients, as a group, are motivated to cope with successive group focal conflicts by instituting solutions which will relieve reactive fears. If the group is relatively homogeneous with reference to degree of vulnerability, the solutions which emerge can be expected to contribute to a sense of safety for each patient in the group; thus, the patients' goal coincides with the therapist's goal of encouraging conditions of safety.

However, although all successful solutions contribute to conditions of safety in the group, the therapist prefers to see the group operating on enabling rather than restrictive solutions. It is here that the patients and the therapist may find themselves in conflict. From the point of view of the patients, any successful solution will relieve anxiety. The therapist, however, who is motivated by additional goals, prefers that safety be achieved by enabling solutions rather than restrictive ones.[1] This points to a special consideration confronting the therapist—the relationship between the establishment of enabling solutions and the establishment of a sense of safety in the group. The therapist must constantly weigh his goal of instituting and maintaining enabling solutions against his goal of maintaining conditions of safety. There are times when it is necessary for the therapist to tolerate, temporarily, restrictive group solutions in order to prevent conditions of safety from deteriorating. To put this another way, there are times when it is appropriate for the therapist to cooperate in maintaining restrictive solutions, or at least to refrain from interfering with them, in order to avoid the emergence of overwhelming anxiety. This point is particularly important during the formative phase of the group, which is likely to be characterized by restrictive rather than enabling solutions. Although restrictive, such solutions constitute a primary source of safety for the patients. If the therapist is impatient and attempts to interfere with these restrictive solutions prematurely, he is likely to create a milieu characterized by gross and persistent anxiety. Even after the group is well established, it is unrealistic and even undesirable to expect the patients to operate exclusively on enabling solutions, for under enabling solutions meaningful exploration occurs. This exploration inevitably leads to new concerns and fears, necessitating the establishment of restrictive solutions. The restrictive solutions are safety valves and, although they may seem to be temporary regressions, they are vital for maintaining a sense of safety in the group environment and hence for continued therapeutic progress.

Encouraging Group Conditions which Benefit the Individual

Managing the group for individual benefit consists of several distinct tasks, each concerned with the individual in relation to the group forces. The individual is in danger of being harmed when the group processes allow him to maintain a habitual maladaptive solution which insulates him from potentially useful experiences or when the group situation elicits gross anxiety which leads him to flee or react with disruptive behavior. The task for the therapist is to prevent these potentially damaging conditions from arising.

A patient occasionally succeeds in establishing a habitual personal solution and maintaining this position through his group experience (Chapter 8). If this occurs, the patient may feel relatively comfortable but remains untouched and, therefore, unhelped by the group. One of the therapist's tasks is to forestall the permanent success of a patient's maintaining a habitual maladaptive solution in the group. Such success is tantamount to therapeutic failure. For the therapist, the most difficult aspect of this task is to recognize the maladaptive solution and to avoid the trap of feeling that it is the fault of the patient's pathology. If the therapist sees what is happening to the patient and understands it in terms of the interaction between the patient and the group forces, he may be in a position to interfere with the patient's success in maintaining this solution. We emphasize the need to prevent *permanent* success, for temporary success in instituting a habitual solution occurs with some frequency. The fluid group situation ordinarily interrupts such success, and it is only under special group conditions that a patient can indefinitely succeed in maintaining a habitual personal solution.

There are times when the group processes impinge on a patient in such a way that they elicit massive anxiety. An eruption of overwhelming anxiety may lead a patient to evoke such extreme protective measures as dropping out of the group, frequently being absent or late, repeatedly asking for individual interviews, or daydreaming during sessions. Thus, the patient may insulate himself from the group by physical or psychological means. Or, breakdown in behavior may occur in response to gross anxiety. A critical task for the therapist is to forestall such experiences by interfering with the group conditions which may cause them. Often, this requires interfering with group solutions that offer most of the patients considerable safety. The patient is in danger because he is playing a particular role in a group solution.

Although such a solution is a source of safety for most patients, it requires one patient to play a role which is threatening to him. Such roles occur in solutions which utilize one patient as the spokesman for some wish or some fear, those which locate feared impulses in one person and then make that person the object of attack, those which displace angry feelings to one person who becomes a safe substitute target, and those which encourage one person to expose himself in order to protect the others from exposure.

Under certain group circumstances, patients may direct toward one patient interpretations which are inaccurate, irrelevant, or communicated with a hostile intent that causes the patient to erect defenses against hearing the interpretations. This is especially likely to occur when the group is operating on such solutions as turn-taking or scapegoating or when the group is attempting to deal with a deviant patient by agreeing on an interpretation of his behavior (see Chapter 8). Here again, the therapist's task is to interfere not by contradicting the interpretations after they are made, but by forestalling the full development of such solutions.

There are times when the therapist sees an opportunity to capitalize on a current group focal conflict for the specific benefit of some one patient. He may wish to direct the attention of the patient to some aspect of the group situation, to point out the specific character of the patient's fears, to underline the potency of his wishes, to point out the unique way in which the patient wishes to cope with the current group focal conflict, or to point out the manner in which the patient's current position on the group focal conflict is related to his personal history. In short, there are times when the therapist feels that an individual is undergoing an experience or revealing personal material which could be beneficially exploited, interpreted, or underlined. We think that a great deal of caution is required in introducing individual interpretations. It is important for the therapist to be aware of the group context and of the potential effects of his comment. Apart from its impact on the individual, the intervention may also support a restrictive group solution, or it may be illuminating to others and move the group in a positive direction. If the therapist is aware of the potential effects, he can decide whether it is the right time for the comment he has in mind—whether it will really prove useful to the patient and whether he wishes to introduce the group conditions likely to follow his intervention. A further consideration is whether the interpretation is relevant to the patient's immediate affective experience. In any therapeutic situation, group or individual, interventions which are not related to an individual's current affective concerns have little impact. In the group, the meaningful emotional experience for each patient lies in the manner in which he contributes to, participates in, and reacts to the shared emotional forces. It follows that, if the therapist focuses on the individual, he should focus on that aspect of the individual's behavior which is relevant to the current group focal conflict. This is the crux of the emotional experience for the individual.

Any extended focus on the concerns of one person seems inappropriate. Such a focus amounts to individual therapy with an audience and does not utilize the special opportunities presented by the group. Furthermore, extended focus on one patient usually involves the support of a restrictive group solution. Other patients are likely to permit one person to monopolize the group only when such behavior serves a prevailing group solution. The central person is built into the solution as an object of displaced or projected feelings, or he fills up the time and protects the others from self-exposure. Unlike individual therapy, where focusing on one patient is, of course, the core procedure, the group offers other avenues to therapeutic gain.

If the therapist succeeds in these critical tasks, he will have maintained a therapeutic setting in which each patient experiences crucial personal conflicts, can avail himself of special sources of safety, can test the necessity for maintaining habitual maladaptive solutions, and can utilize a variety of sources of information for developing insight. Simultaneously, the therapist will have avoided or forestalled potentially non-therapeutic experiences for specific patients.

The therapist's tools for accomplishing these tasks are words; his comments have an immediate collective impact on the course of group events and on the experience of each patient in the group. Any intervention, no matter how brief, is many-faceted. An intervention may refer to the disturbing motive, the reactive motive, the solution, or to several of these. It may be directed to an individual patient or to the group as a whole; it may be introduced purposefully or intuitively; and it may take the form of an interpretation, a question, a comment, or a personal reaction. In our view, the critical features of an intervention are the aspect of the group process to which the words refer and the timing of these words. The form and target are less crucial.

All interventions, no matter what their form or target, have some impact on the group processes. Their particular impact depends a great deal on the timing of the intervention. The moment at which an intervention is made can be described in terms of the immediately prevailing balance of forces among the elements of the current conflict. Also, an intervention occurs at a specific point in the group's history;

the group continually operates on a different cultural base, for the body of successful solutions which forms its culture is always changing. Thus, a distinction can be made between the formative phase and the established phase. The major task of the psychotherapeutic group during the formative phase is the development of a group culture and the establishment of safety. Therapeutic interventions which block solutions during the formative phase usually magnify the anxiety of the group. A similar intervention after the culture has been established is not likely to increase the anxiety to the same extent, for then the group is operating under more stable conditions of safety. Hence, interventions appropriate to one phase are not appropriate to the other and may have different effects. Thus, in intervening, the therapist must keep in mind both the momentary situation and the general developmental stage of the group. The first refers to the exact balance of forces in the group focal conflict at the moment the intervention is made. The second refers to the broader development of the group, particularly the cultural base from which the group is operating.

To illustrate these points, we shall refer to the first illustration in Chapter 3 and examine some of the therapist's interventions. This session—the fourth of a schizophrenic group—was summarized in terms of the focal conflict "wish to be helped through revealing personal problems" versus "fear of being attacked, harmed, or made sicker through contact with other sick patients." At one point, the therapist said, "There is a lot of frightening stuff here. Should we expose ourselves?" In this intervention, the therapist is referring to both aspects of the focal conflict but emphasizing the reactive motive. He is pointing out that there is an impulse on the part of the patients to expose themselves (disturbing motive) but that, at the same time, the prospect of exposure is frightening (reactive motive). At another point, the therapist comments that talk can be both good and bad. Here again, he is referring to both aspects of the focal conflict, although in very general terms.

Later, the therapist made a comment which, on the surface, had no relevance to the group processes. During a period in which Bill had begun to dominate the discussion, the therapist asked Larry, "Is this what you meant by one person talking?" In order to understand the relevance of this question to the group processes, it is necessary to understand the context in which it was made. Earlier in the session, Larry had commented that so far only one patient, Bill, had revealed anything about himself. He was referring to the fact that, in a previous session, Bill had revealed a good deal about himself in a long psychotic monologue about his paranoid delusions. Just before the therapist's intervention, Bill had begun another monologue. From the point of view of the group processes, the therapist's intervention refers to a group solution which had previously been important in the group. The therapist's comment is an attempt to block the solution "deal with fears of exposure by getting one person to talk."[2]

The importance of timing is also demonstrated in this illustration. When the therapist said, "There is a lot of frightening stuff here. Should we expose ourselves?" the patients were attempting to cope with their anxieties about the group by introducing possible solutions. None of these could be established in the group. At this point, anxiety was high since efforts to render the group viable did not work. When the therapist introduced a comment which referred to reactive fears, he led the patients to focus on these fears. The intervention directed to Larry ("Is this what you meant by one person talking?") was introduced at an entirely different point in the session. Here, the group was moving toward the establishment of a group solution but had not yet firmly established it. The intervention was effective in blocking the solution.

Timing and referent are related. For example, suppose a therapist interprets for the patients the character of their shared wish at a point prior to the development of a successful solution. Such an intervention is likely to increase markedly the anxiety in the group, for the disturbing motive has been uncovered before any means for coping with recognition of the wish has been developed. The intervention may force the patients to resort to a more restrictive solution than might otherwise have been necessary. The same intervention at another time would have a different impact. For example, such an intervention might be made after the group had constructed a successful restrictive solution. At such a time, the intervention might be ignored in order to avoid reopening the "solved" focal conflict, but it would be unlikely to raise the general anxiety level. Or the same intervention might be introduced after the group had constructed a successful enabling solution. At such a time, the patients would be more likely to accept and build on the interpretation, for a solution has emerged which enables the patients to feel safe in dealing with the impulse.

The effect of an intervention directed to the group solution also depends on timing. If the therapist attempts to block a solution when it is still emerging, he is likely to be successful. However, if the therapist attempts to block or challenge a solution after it has been established, he is likely to be unsuccessful, for he has placed himself in the position of a deviant and will experience all the consequences and effects. Under such circumstances, it is more effective to focus on the reactive motive rather than on the solution. If the patients become convinced that their fears are unreal or exaggerated, conditions under which the solution can be surrendered have been established.

From the point of view of the potential impact on group-level interaction, the target of the intervention is immaterial. That is, an intervention may be directed to an individual patient, to some segment of the group, or to the whole group and still be related to the focal-conflict pattern. We do not mean to imply that the target of the intervention is irrelevant. There may be very cogent reasons for a therapist to focus on one patient at one point and on the whole group at another point. At some point, he may prefer to direct a comment to one person because of the special meaning the comment has for that person. A tendency to focus on the group or the individual may dominate a therapist's style and will influence the manner in which he "trains" the patients to attend to certain aspects of the situation. Our point is that, from the point of view of the impact on the focal-conflict pattern and of the influence on group events, the target of the intervention is not the critical factor. Form, too, is a less crucial factor. From the point of view of an intervention's impact on the group processes, form is irrelevant.

Finally, it might be mentioned that not all interventions are made with the deliberate aim of influencing the course of the group. Often a comment is so complex that one cannot imagine a therapist's being aware of all its implications at the moment he made it. (This was certainly true of the question, "Is this what you meant by one person talking?") It is preferable for the therapist to be as aware as possible of the character of the group forces and the probable impact of his comments on the situation, but, in practice, the therapist often relies on partially formed hypotheses and an intuitive grasp of the group forces. Failure to appreciate the group forces does not inevitably interfere with sound therapeutic interventions (see fifth illustration). However, we believe that the therapist can more easily avoid serious errors if he bases his interventions on an understanding of group forces (see eighth illustration).

We have offered no propositions in this chapter, for we are dealing with the application of all the propositions presented previously. In general, the therapist is concerned with facilitating the therapeutic process (Propositions 29 through 32, Chapter 8). In so doing, he must take into account the character of the group processes (Propositions 1 through 23, Chapters 1–6), the experience and motivation of each patient in the group (Propositions 23 through 28, Chapter 7), and the group conditions under which individual patients may be harmed (Propositions 33 through 35, Chapter 8). In attempting to influence and exploit the therapeutic situation, he must be aware of the likely impact of his interventions on the group events and on the patient's experience. The therapist's impact on the group is a special case of the impact of any person (Propositions 8 through 10, Chapter 3) but must be understood in terms of his position and power in the group (Propositions 36 and 37, Chapter 9).

We have discussed the related tasks of the therapist and his tactical considerations in performing these tasks. In a particular situation, certain tasks are in the forefront, and specific tactical considerations are crucial. The following series of group episodes will illustrate these points.[3]

First Illustration: Interfering with a Restrictive Solution by Introducing an Interpretation

> In an outpatient adolescent group, the prevailing focal conflict involved sexual feelings about one another versus fear of a retaliative response on the part of the therapist. The patients operated on a series of restrictive solutions. Toward the close of the session, the patients made fun of their sexual interests. This was a group solution which involved not taking one's feelings seriously. A giddy interchange developed in which the patients joked about "phallic symbols." At the height of a rather hysterical period, the therapist said, "Now that we have dealt with this by reducing it to an absurdity, . . ." The giddiness immediately subsided. One of the boys asked, "Yeah, why do we have to make it absurd?" and the discussion turned to speculations about why it had been necessary for them to make a joke of sexual matters.

This intervention effectively interfered with the restrictive group solution "make fun of sexual interests." The intervention was an interpretation of group events: the therapist pointed to the solution (reducing it to an absurdity) and also hinted at the fact that the solution was functional to the group ("now that we have dealt with this . . ."). A crucial factor in the success of this intervention was its timing. The restrictive solution on which the group was operating involved giddiness which was approaching loss of control. To the extent that the potential loss of control was beginning to introduce new fears, the patients may have been ready to respond to any opportunity to shift from their joking. The therapist's interpretation offered such an opportunity. One might ask whether the fact that the comment was an interpretation was as important as the fact that the comment provided a model for a new mode of interacting—sober examination rather than wild joking.

Second Illustration: Interfering with a Restrictive Solution by Exposing the Disturbing Motive

In an inpatient adolescent group, one of the girls was absent, and another patient informed the group that Harriet was absent because her mother was seriously ill. This information was delivered casually, and no one commented on it. The patients talked about movies, and all seemed very enthusiastic. One of the boys was extensively teased because he had not heard of a current film. After an uneasy silence, a long argument about reading newspapers developed. One of the girls said that she didn't read newspapers because she didn't like to be bothered with depressing things. A boy answered that that was hiding from real life. The therapist asked, "Has anyone had Harriet on his mind?" One of the girls replied, "Not really, have you?" The therapist said that she had been thinking of Harriet and what a tough spot she was in. In response to another question, the therapist said she had been thinking about how she might feel if she were in the same situation. One of the boys began to talk about the serious illness of his father, something he had not mentioned until this point. There followed a general discussion which touched on feelings of love, dependency, guilt, and anger toward parents. One of the girls described with great feeling her terror about losing her mother when her mother had been ill several years previously.

In this episode, the news about Harriet's mother's illness apparently stirred up feelings which seemed too dangerous or painful to discuss. A series of restrictive solutions which involved avoidance and denial of depression was instituted. Specific devices included dwelling on pleasurable activities, diverting one another by joking among themselves, and attempting to establish a solution in which there was general agreement to ignore depressing facts. The therapist's first intervention was a question directed to the whole group and calling attention to the ignored event. In the following interventions, the therapist shared a personal reaction with the patients. With reference to the group focal conflict, the comments referred to the disturbing motive. They indicated the therapist's personal recognition of depressed feelings and her readiness to talk about them. The effectiveness of this intervention in changing the character of the discussion can be attributed to two factors. First, the therapist indicated to the patients that she felt it was permissible, not dangerous, to discuss depressed feelings. Thus, the therapist indicated that she did not regard the restrictive solution as necessary. Second, the comment was introduced when one of the patients had indirectly indicated a readiness to yield the restrictive solution.

This episode illustrates the fact that a group therapist often relies partly on specific hypotheses about the meaning of the group material and partly on an unrecognized responsiveness to the group situation. In reporting her thoughts, the therapist afterward said that, during the long discussions about movies and newspaper reading, she developed the hypothesis that the patients were avoiding the feelings aroused by the news of a parent's illness. For a long time, the therapist felt that any efforts to change the course of the group would fail; perhaps this feeling derived from the diligent manner in which restrictive solutions were maintained. The actual interventions were spontaneous. The therapist was not aware until afterward that one of the patients had just made a comment which indicated that he might be ready for "real life." The style of the intervention was influenced by experience with this group. This group tended to operate on solutions marked by obsessive intellectualization. To introduce an interpretation, especially one documented with evidence from the manifest content, would have constituted an invitation to utilize intellectual argument as another restrictive solution.

Third Illustration: Blocking a Group Solution by Withholding Cooperation

An inpatient group (described in Chapter 2) developed the group focal conflict: "rageful, destructive feelings toward one patient" versus "fear of guilty feelings." The group tried to get the therapist to make a ruling, without mentioning names, against the patient who had aroused the group's anger. In other words, the patients were urging the solution "get the therapist to express and implement angry feelings." Such a solution would allow them to express their angry feelings vicariously. By avoiding direct responsibility for their anger, they would protect themselves from guilt. In this instance, the therapist prevented this solution from becoming established by refusing to introduce condemnations and by insisting that the patients discuss more explicitly what they were concerned about. Because the solution required the active collaboration of the therapist in order to be successful, the therapist was in a powerful position to influence the group. By merely withholding his cooperation, he could prevent the solution from becoming established.

Fourth Illustration: Diminishing the Sense of Safety in the Group

During an early session of an inpatient group, the focal conflict developed: "wish to be helped through revealing themselves" versus "fear of dangerous consequences." During the period in which this focal conflict was emerging, one of the patients mentioned that he had seen a phonograph record which was a sampler of several types of musical compositions. Others questioned him about the record and its cost, and there was some speculation about whether the record was worth its price or was merely a worthless hodgepodge. The therapist suggested that the discussion about the sampler was a veiled reference to the group and that the patients might be wondering whether the group would prove worth while—worth the price they might have to pay. The patient who had first mentioned the sampler record remarked that it had been a good thing he had not been talking about the city dump. Apart from this, there was no overt response to the therapist's comment, although the patients changed the subject.

This intervention was directed toward the whole group and consisted of an interpretation which attempted to relate symbolic material to a hypothesized group focal conflict. More precisely, the interpretation referred to the disturbing and reactive motives: the implicit wish that the group be worth while and the fear that it might not be worth its cost in anxiety and pain. Very probably, the interpretation was accurate, but it was unsuccessful in terms of the therapist's goal. In this case, the therapist was trying to speed the development of the group by getting the patients to discuss more directly their feelings about the group. Instead of achieving this, the interpretation led the patients to be more cautious than before. The interpretation was premature, and the error was primarily one of timing. The comment was introduced when the patients were expressing their feelings in disguised, symbolic terms; in itself, this is an indication that more direct expressions were regarded as impossible and dangerous. Because of its timing, the interpretation acquired a punitive flavor. The patient who made the comment about the city dump felt that he was being accused of something and that he was in danger of being caught expressing critical feelings about the group. Apparently the therapist communicated to this patient, and probably to others, that their most casual conversations would be interpreted in ways which exposed feelings that they did not regard as theirs and that they wished to disown. Thus, the comment actually intensified the patients' reactive fears.

A better choice would have been to say nothing at all, on the assumption that it was necessary for the patients to develop a solution to the issue that confronted them before an interpretation could be utilized. Or the therapist might have interpreted the manifest material in terms closer to the symbolic language of the patients. He might have said something like, "It's hard to know whether something that is made of so many miscellaneous things can be valuable." Such a comment is an interpretation, but instead of pointing specifically to the implications of the manifest material to the current situation, the interpretation abstracts the issue from the symbolism in which it was originally presented without making explicit its relevance to the group situation. Such a comment is likely to be more readily accepted by the patients, and, by observing the patients' reactions, the therapist has more information with which to make a judgment about how to proceed.

Fifth Illustration: A Spontaneous Response Which Increased Safety

> During one of the early sessions of an outpatient group, the patients pressed the therapist to tell them whether they were proceeding satisfactorily. The therapist avoided a direct response, pointing out to the patients their need for approval and the lack of evidence for any feelings of disapproval on the part of the therapist. The conversation became desultory. There were a few hints that patients had formed opinions about one another, but no one was willing to state these opinions openly. The patients again pressed the therapist to give an opinion about their progress, and the therapist again was evasive. The patients began to talk about the coming holidays. Several said it might be impossible for them to attend the group sessions regularly, and a consensus that the group might disband for a two-week period seemed to be developing. The therapist said, "I will be here, and I hope that everyone will come who is able to." After a silence, one of the women remarked that she had been forming opinions about others in the group, had been afraid to express them until now, but suddenly no longer felt frightened. The discussion developed along these lines, and the matter of interrupting the sessions was not brought up again.

Two types of interventions occurred in this episode. The first involved evasive responses to the patients' efforts to get the therapist to express approval of them. This appeal for approval occurred in the context of a group focal conflict which included a wish to express positive and negative feelings about one another and a reactive motive involving fears about the consequences of such disclosures. The patients pressed for a group solution ("guarantee the approval of the therapist") which could only become established if the therapist cooperated by offering explicit approval. The therapist attempted to interpret the situation, but only succeeded in communicating evasiveness. In effect, the therapist refused to cooperate in the group solution. In the interaction which followed, the patients communicated to the therapist "without your approval, we cannot cope with the situation and will have to break up the group" or, perhaps, "if you won't come through for us, we will break up the group." In response to considerable pressure from the group, the therapist reversed his direction, indicating interest in the group and approval of the patients. The effect was dramatic: fears were alleviated, and the patients could suddenly give the disturbing motive greater expression. After the session, the therapist reported that he had felt uncomfortable and anxious. He had not planned the response and had not formulated the group situation in the way in which we have just summarized it. In retrospect, the evasive intervention was an error; the spontaneous intervention proved useful. During this episode, the therapist was cognitively out of touch with the group processes. The later intervention was an emotional response to the group forces. In this case, the unplanned emotional response had a positive effect on the group.

Sixth Illustration: Inadvertent Failure to Encourage Safety

The first illustration in Chapter 3 can be re-examined from the point of view of the therapists' impact on the conditions of safety in the group. In this inpatient schizophrenic group, the patients were beset with reactive fears of being attacked, harmed, and made sicker through contact with other sick patients. This reactive motive operated in conjunction with a disturbing motive which involved a wish to be helped through revealing personal problems. In the course of the session, the patients made a number of comments which contained the seeds of potentially successful solutions. Various patients suggested that they could rely on time to alleviate their fears, that they all had problems in common, that they might tackle their problems bit by bit, that a hospital is an appropriate place to display sick or uncontrolled behavior. Most of these solutions had a restrictive character, yet, if one of them could have been established, it would have contributed a sense of safety which was lacking thus far. The therapists could have helped the patients to adopt one of these possibilities by supporting a particular solution or by pointing out that, although they were frightened, they were also figuring out ways to cope with their fright. Instead, some of the therapists' interventions focused exclusively on reactive fears, while others emphasized reactive fears over other aspects of the group focal conflict. For example, the therapist said, "The living pattern in the hospital is both strange and terrifying," "It's a hell of a grind to get somewhere, and what guarantee do you have that you'll stay better?" "There's a lot of frightening stuff here. Should we expose ourselves?" and "In spite of what common sense tells you, these fears are real and painful." As these interventions accumulated, they kept the patients' fears in the forefront and thus contributed to a high level of anxiety in the group. By omitting any reference to the patients' coping efforts, the therapists failed to support the institution of group solutions. On both counts, the therapists prevented a sense of safety from developing, and so a high level of anxiety was maintained in the group. In this instance, the therapeutic errors may have stemmed from the therapists' failure to be aware of the coping efforts which did emerge, and this in turn may be related to the impact of the patients' primitive fears on the therapists. In other words, if the therapists shared in the patients' fears and also experienced them as overwhelming, they might overlook indications that the group had the capacity to deal with those fears.

Seventh Illustration: Sacrificing Safety to Protect a Patient[4]

In an inpatient schizophrenic group, the first session was dominated by reactive fears about the harm that might come to the patients as a consequence of being in a therapy group. The first comment expressed terror and mistrust about having been placed in a psychiatric ward. One of the patients began to talk about his fears of being persecuted by the police. The others encouraged him, and this became the predominant topic of the session. This pattern constituted the group solution "get one person to expose his fears." It protected all the patients except one from exposing themselves to the presumed dangers and at the same time permitted a displaced, safe exploration of fears by talking about the paranoid ideas of one person. At the next session, the patients again tried to focus the discussion on the same patient. This time, instead of cooperating, he appeared frightened and insistently suggested that they change the subject. The therapist intervened by asking why everyone felt that he had to discuss the problems of one patient. In response, the patients stopped pressuring the paranoid patient.

This intervention referred to the group solution. It interrupted acting on the solution and invited the patients to consider the necessity for maintaining the solution. By so doing, the therapist communicated disapproval of the solution which the patients were attempting to institute. To interfere with this solution re-exposed the patients to the anxiety associated with the group focal conflict and reduced the sense of safety in the group. This move was necessary in order to offer protection to one patient, who, by virtue of being forced into a special role in the group solution, was experiencing increasing anxiety. Had this intervention not been made, the anxiety of the patient might have built up to an intolerable degree, leading him to display a catastrophic reaction or to deal with his feelings by fleeing from the group.

Eighth Illustration: Support of a Group Solution Harmful to One Patient

For several sessions, an outpatient group had been operating on a turn-taking solution. The solutions were directed toward dealing with the group focal conflict "angry, competitive feelings toward one another" versus "fears of losing control over anger and becoming destructive."

> At the beginning of a session, Harry, who had been absent several times, talked about a problem with a professional colleague, complaining about his inability to handle his colleague and soliciting the group's help. The others asked him questions and made suggestions. The therapist joined in, pointing out to Harry that he behaved in a helpless manner with his colleague and in the group, where he presented himself as in need of help. He pointed out that this was understandable in the light of Harry's history, but inappropriate in the group. Some of the patients agreed, pointing out Harry's immature behavior. Harry reacted defensively and stopped talking; the conversation shifted to the problems of another patient.

This intervention was introduced when the patients had been operating for some time on the restrictive solution of turn-taking. By focusing on one patient at a time and carefully (though implicitly) providing each with an equal share, the patients succeeded in suppressing their angry, competitive feelings and, thus, in relieving anxieties about losing control over anger and becoming destructive. The therapist's interventions, although formally interpretations directed toward an individual patient, supported the current restrictive group solution by joining the turn-taking. That is, the therapist also acted as if it were Harry's turn.

In discussing his behavior afterward, the therapist reported that during the session he had been intent on helping Harry and had seen an opportunity to point out a relationship between Harry's current behavior and his history. In retrospect, however, the therapist perceived the hostile nature of his interpretations and realized that he had been angry at the patients for persisting in the turn-taking behavior. His interpretations to Harry were a well-rationalized and displaced attack. Harry's absences made him a logical target, for the therapist may have felt that Harry was spoiling the group, just as he felt the turn-taking solution was spoiling the group. In this example, interpretations directed toward a single individual failed to help the patient, had unintended deleterious effects on both the patient and the group (the therapist lent his support to a restrictive group solution), and were rooted in the therapist's unrecognized reactions to the prevailing group forces.

Ninth Illustration: Capitalizing on a Current Group Focal Conflict

> In an outpatient adolescent group, the conversation turned to how the patients felt about confiding in their roommates and having their roommates confide in them. Virgil told of having met, on a brief vacation, a boy with whom he developed a confidential relationship. He had not seen the boy since, but they wrote frequently. Others suggested that Virgil had felt free because the boy was a stranger to him. Phil mentioned a friend to whom he used to confide. Now that he sees less of his friend, he feels embarrassed when he meets him, as if the friend had some power over him. May said that, although her roommates always told her a lot about themselves, she keeps things to herself. She thought they would not be interested and would not want to trouble themselves about her concerns. Laverne commented that she thought she just liked secrets and that this is the reason she does not tell others more about herself. Virgil said that his roommate was overly curious. One evening when Virgil left their room without saying where he was going, his roommate came out to look for him. Virgil said that he felt as if his roommate was checking up on him; he felt angry and took pleasure in not letting his roommate know where he had been. The therapist commented that all the patients seemed reluctant about telling others about themselves, perhaps in the group as well as outside it. He added that people seemed to feel this way for different reasons: May because it might be a burden on others, Phil because it might give others power over him, and Laverne because she likes to have secrets. A discussion about whether they felt the same way about one another as they did about roommates followed.

In this episode, the therapist was operating on the hypothesis that the group focal conflict involved a wish to reveal oneself to the other group members versus fears of damaging consequences. The therapist's intervention includes several elements: it refers briefly to the group focal conflict in general terms and then proceeds to identify the specific ways in which three patients experience the reactive fears. At the same time, the intervention includes the suggestion that the concerns about confiding in others are experienced in the current group situation. Such an intervention utilizes the shared group concern in order to clarify specific characteristics of individual patients. The comment refers to the manner in which several individuals are participating in the current group focal conflict. Because the group context has been kept in mind, the comments about individuals refer to currently meaningful affect, and the intervention does not pursue any individual at the cost of diverting the patients from their current shared concerns.

In this episode, one patient offered material that might appear to call for a direct interpretation. Virgil told about his feeling that his roommate was unduly curious about him and was checking up on him. Earlier, Virgil had told the group that his problem was primarily one of escaping from an overattachment to his mother. He felt that his mother was jealous of his friends, wanted him with her at all times, and scrutinized his activities so closely that he had little feeling of personal freedom. It is reasonable to suppose that Virgil's reactions to his roommate were based, in part, on these earlier experiences. It might have been of considerable therapeutic value for Virgil to recognize the distortions which might be involved in his perceptions of his roommate's behavior and their roots in his family experiences. The therapist chose not to pursue this line of enquiry. Assuming, for the purposes of illustration, that the therapist recognized this opportunity, one might consider the probable consequences of taking the matter up with Virgil at this time. The group focal conflict during this episode involved the wish to reveal oneself versus fears of damaging consequences. Of course, the patients *were* revealing themselves and were testing in a very tentative way whether damaging consequences would occur in the group. Virgil implicitly told the group that he feared that, if he permitted himself to get close to others, he would lose his freedom. At this point, Virgil might have experienced an individual interpretation as an invasion. The others, too, might consider any extended concentration on Virgil or any one of them as a confirmation of their fears—he who reveals himself will be exposed to pursuit. This episode occurred during the formative phase of the group (third session). At this point, an initial group culture had not been established, and the patients still perceived the group as a potentially dangerous place. In other words, the patients had not yet constructed a set of successful solutions which would provide a sense of safety. Under such conditions, Virgil might well be unable to hear or use such an interpretation. Here we want to emphasize that, although a patient has presented personal information which aids the therapist's understanding of him, this does not mean that it is appropriate for the therapist to use his understanding immediately. This does not, of course, differ from the considerations of timing which face the therapist in individual treatment. However, the group therapist must take into account both the current group processes and the history of the group as it is expressed in its culture. It may be noted that, although in this illustration the therapist referred to the group and to the individual, the dual reference is immaterial. The significant aspect of the intervention is its appropriateness to the current state of the individual in relation to the group processes.

In these illustrations, we have focused on single interventions and their impact on the group and on individual patients. This oversimplifies and omits the cumulative effects of the therapist's interventions. The same type of intervention introduced repeatedly has more than a merely additive effect. For example, a therapist who persistently makes premature interpretations of the group's underlying concerns will generate wariness and mistrust. A therapist who repeatedly displays to the group a readiness to protect individuals from anxiety may generate dependency. A therapist who repeatedly points out to the patients their shared fears without pointing out associated capacities for developing solutions may intensify anxiety. These repetitive patterns are an aspect of therapeutic style and have a significant impact on the character of the group.

Notes

[1] The therapist's goal and the patients' goal differ and stem from differing positions in the group. In establishing a group solution, the patients move toward reducing anxiety and toward permitting as much gratification of the associated disturbing motive as possible. They are oriented toward gratification as well as toward protection. In contrast, the therapist has no stake in the patients' gratification. He is primarily interested in seeing the establishment of predominantly enabling solutions insofar as this is commensurate with appropriate levels of anxiety. Therefore, there will be times when the same group conditions will satisfy the patients' goal and the therapist's goal. On the other hand, many occasions must arise when the characteristics of the milieu are satisfying to the patients because a satisfactory solution is in effect, yet unsatisfying to the therapist because the solution is restrictive.

[2] The intervention is also important for Bill, for it attempts to protect him by preventing him from launching into another uncontrolled psychotic monologue. (It is likely that it was this factor which elicited the intervention.) Though directed toward Larry, the comment has little to do with him. His previous comment was a vehicle for accomplishing other goals.

[3] To this point, illustrations have reported content in summarized form but have avoided interpretive summaries which utilized theoretical language. In the illustrations which follow, we depart from this practice in order to present the background for the therapist's comments concisely. It should be understood that an interpretive summary in which reference is made to a group focal conflict's having developed or a

group solution's having been modified refers to a complex sequence of events which may have extended over considerable time. Similarly, when the effect of the therapist's intervention is summarized in theoretical terms, it should be understood that the effect is not necessarily an immediate one, but may refer to an extended process which the intervention set in motion.

[4] This was the group whose fourth session was described in Chapter 3 and discussed in this chapter.

Perspective

12

Other Theories

In an effort to understand the unique quality of the small group as a setting for psychotherapy, we have emphasized group-level processes as the context of the individual experience. How each patient participates in, contributes to, and reacts to the group forces was seen as crucial to the character of his therapeutic experience. The therapist's role has been viewed in terms of his position with reference to the group forces and the manner in which he may influence and utilize them for the benefit of each patient. In this chapter, we shall contrast our efforts with the theory-building efforts of others and discuss some of the issues and special problems encountered in attempts to conceptualize the therapy group.

An emphasis on group-level processes is one point of departure in the theoretical literature of group therapy. Efforts at theory-building which begin with the individual patient or with personal interaction also appear. Varying points of departure are associated with differing views of what the group is like, what the therapeutic process is like, and what the role of the therapist ought to be. Slavson, Locke, Wolf and Schwartz, and many others have presented theories which focus on the individual patient.[1] Such conceptualizations of group therapy are adapted from models of the psychoanalytic process in the two-person therapy situation. Scheidlinger has presented a systematic discussion of the relevance of Freud's thinking to the group therapeutic situation.[2] Other investigators have focused primarily on interpersonal relationships in the group. Berne has suggested that behavior in the group can be conceptualized in terms of interpersonal "games" and "pastimes."[3] Leary has emphasized the "interpersonal reflex" and reciprocal patterns in the group.[4] In some of his work, Frank has described certain typical roles or behavioral patterns in the therapy group.[5]

Distinct from either of these is a point of departure which emphasizes group characteristics. Bion, Foulkes, and Ezriel each have presented theories which attempt to identify characteristics of the group as a whole, discuss how these characteristics emerge from the patients' interaction, and examine their implications for the patient's therapeutic experience and the therapist's role.[6] Bach has utilized constructs developed in small, non-therapeutic groups to explore therapy groups.[7] Frank has identified certain characteristics—cohesion, conflict, standards—of the group as a whole and has spelled out their implications for the therapeutic experience of the individual.[8] Redl has extended Freud's views about group formation and has defined the ways in which various group members may be utilized as the "central person" around whom the group forms. He has also introduced provocative ideas about contagion in groups and such uniquely group phenomena as the "guilt-and-fear-assuaging effect of the initiatory act."[9]

Both Scheidlinger and Ackerman have suggested requirements for a comprehensive theory of group therapy. Scheidlinger stresses two sets of related factors: "(a) Individual personalities with their genetic and dynamic properties, their motivational and defensive–adaptive patterns, some conscious and some unconscious; (b) Group dynamic elements such as climate, goals, structure, or code which emerge as the product of the interaction within the group. Such interaction can occur on conscious as well as unconscious levels."[10] Ackerman suggests that three factors are involved: "1. The psychodynamics of group behavior, including both the processes of group formation and the processes of group change. 2. The dynamic processes of emotional integration of an individual into a group. 3. The internal organization of individual personality."[11] Ackerman has gone on to develop theory, particularly in the area of relating individual personality and group behavior by the use of social role concepts.[12]

In identifying three primary emphases—the group, the interpersonal, and the individual—we do not wish to imply more similarity than actually exists. Although it is possible to make these broad distinctions, significant variations exist within each category. In fact, no two theories are directly comparable. Not only does the point of departure differ, but each theoretical position utilizes a special language to define central concepts. In some cases, it is possible to translate the language of one theory to that of another; in other instances, differences in language seem to reflect basic differences in conceptualization. Theories also differ in emphasis and comprehensiveness. Certain aspects of the group or the group therapeutic process which are emphasized by one theorist may be omitted by another. Certain issues are made explicit by some and remain implicit in the work of others. Imprecisions and generalities also make comparisons difficult. In attempting to contrast various theories, then, one is continually confronted with the need to translate concepts and with the danger of making forced comparisons.

Any attempt to compare theory must begin with some point of departure of its own, and thus is selective from the start. We have chosen to organize our discussion around a number of considerations which we consider important in understanding the therapy group and the group therapeutic process. Thus, the discussion will not present a comprehensive view of all theoretical approaches to group therapy, nor do we plan to systematically review any single theory. Rather, we shall discuss a series of critical considerations in theory development, attempting to clarify major trends in theoretical thought and place our own work in the context of theory development generally. Various theorists have directed their efforts toward understanding and conceptualizing the following issues:

1. The group situation is constantly shifting, yet the continuous movement which can be observed does not occur haphazardly. Instead, a certain underlying orderliness can be identified. In attempting to understand both the fluidity and the orderliness, theorists have used concepts of equilibrium and development and have struggled with problems of imposing discrete units on a continuous process.

2. The group situation is characterized by intense affect. Theorists have tried to specify the character of this affect and to understand its implications for the therapeutic experience.

3. The group situation is marked by a capacity for problem-solving. Theorists have tried to describe and account for the group's coping capacity and, especially, to understand its relation to the emotional aspects of the group situation.

4. Characteristics of the group as a system emerge out of the interaction of the patients. Theorists have used such concepts as free association, the character of the formative processes, and social role to describe this process.

5. The individual must undergo certain experiences in order for therapeutic change to occur; these are facilitated by the group situation. By participating in the group situation, the patient may achieve some personality reorganization which allows him to function more appropriately, effectively, and satisfactorily. Theorists have attempted to understand the nature of the experiences associated with therapeutic change and the manner in which the group situation facilitates them.

6. The therapist plays a crucial role in influencing the therapeutic experience of each patient. Considerable effort has been directed toward understanding the therapist's role in the therapy group and, particularly, toward clarifying the ways in which he can use the special characteristics of the group to promote growth in each patient.

The Group in Flux

A major task for theorists has been to describe the fluid yet orderly character of the group process. It is recognized that, although the group situation is in constant flux, this movement is lawful rather than random. Over extended periods, certain regularities which involve repetitive cycles and progressive shifts in the group's over-all character can be identified.

Equilibrium models have been used to encompass the related ideas that the group can be described at any given moment in terms of forces in balance, that a change in one element of the system effects a change in the whole, and that change over time can be understood in terms of shifts in equilibrium. This model is central to the formulations of Lewin and of Bales and appears in certain portions of the theories of Bion and Ezriel. In our own theory, the equilibrium model is used to describe the state of the group at any given moment and the manner in which the group moves. We conceptualize the group situation in terms of opposing forces—a disturbing motive and a reactive motive—and a third element—the group solution—which represents the group's efforts to cope with the forces in conflict. These three elements exist in equilibrium with one another; a change in one effects a change in the others. At any moment, the group can be described in terms of these elements and their relation to one another. Whatever happens in the group at the next moment will affect the equilibrium, perhaps by intensifying or changing the character of the disturbing or reactive motive or perhaps by introducing a new solutional feature. The group proceeds by successive shifts in the balance and character of the opposing forces and the associated solution. The notion of balance and change is basic to our view of group movement. We use an equilibrium model to account for the manner in which the group moves toward and away from preoccupation with a single theme and shifts from one theme to another.

Lewin perceives the group existing in a state of quasi-stationary equilibrium.[13] The forces in Lewin's equilibrium model are referred to as the "driving" and "restraining" forces. The driving forces push the group in one direction; the restraining forces exert a counterpressure. The quasi-stationary equilibrium represents the resulting state of the group—the level at which the driving and restraining forces are in balance. A change in one of the restraining or driving forces changes the character of the total equilibrium, and the movement of the group can be understood as successive shifts in equilibrium. Lewin's system is a general one, not directed specifically or exclusively to the psychotherapeutic group. Since its formulation, this conceptual framework has been applied to a variety of small problem-solving groups as well as to larger social systems. Certain of the formal properties of focal-conflict theory are comparable to Lewin's formulations. The disturbing motive, like the driving force, is directed toward some particular condition. The reactive motive opposes the disturbing motive in the same manner that the restraining forces oppose the driving forces. The concept of group solution is similar to yet different from Lewin's concept of quasi-stationary equilibrium. Both concepts refer to the current group situation. However, for Lewin, the quasi-stationary equilibrium is the passive product of opposing forces. In focal-conflict theory, the solution exerts a force of its own and has a dynamic function for the group. It is conceived of as a coping device which is generated to deal with opposing forces. Thus the solution is functional for the group, whereas the quasi-stationary equilibrium is not.

In Bales's view of the problem-solving group, movement occurs by action and reaction, disturbance and re-establishment of equilibrium. The group proceeds by ". . . a repetitive series of cycles, each of which consists of: (1) an initial disturbance of the system (precipitated by the introduction of a new idea, or opinion, or suggestion into the group) followed by (2) a 'dwindling series of feedbacks' and corrections as the disturbance is terminated, equilibrated, or assimilated by other parts or members of the system."[14] The group, confronted with a specific task, devotes itself sequentially to problems of orientation, evaluation, and control. A logical unit, for Bales, is the period during which the group is dealing with a particular problem. This generally coincides with the period in which equilibrium is upset and then restored.

Talland and Psathas have applied Bales's theories and procedures to therapy groups.[15] As they point out, the therapy group differs from the problem-solving group in that no explicit public goal exists and the patients are not committed to following a single theme to a conclusion. Unit, in Bales's sense, does not exist in the therapy group. In applying Bales's views to therapy groups, they accept the single session as a unit, although they acknowledge that this is an arbitrary choice. Using this unit, however, they have shown therapy groups to display some of the same rhythms and processes as do problem-solving groups. For example, Psathas has demonstrated that the same phase pattern is found in therapy groups as in problem-solving groups when a number of group therapy sessions are combined, though not necessarily when each is considered separately. He has also found that the balance of action and reaction occurs only when the total system—patients and therapist—is taken into account. It is difficult to make direct comparisons between this work and our own. Bales's unit is defined in terms of the group's public goal and ours in terms of the covert shared need to achieve some solution to the group focal conflict. Bales concentrates on task-oriented and personal-oriented behaviors in the context of group problem-solving; we concentrate on affective aspects of the interaction.

An equilibrium model is implicit in the theories of Bion and Ezriel. Bion describes the group as continually shifting from operation on one "basic assumption culture" to another.[16] In describing the mechanism whereby this shift occurs, an equilibrium model is implied. Bion sees the group functioning in one of three basic-assumption cultures—dependency, pairing, and fight–flight. During the period in which one of these prevails, the others exist in a latent state. When a dependency culture is predominant, the group functions as if it needs to find someone or something on which it could rely for direction. In a fight-flight culture, the group operates as if it needs to escape through aggressive, hostile activities or through avoidance. The third basic-assumption culture, pairing, refers to periods when the members act as if they need to establish intimate, sexually-oriented pair relationships. Basic-assumption culture refers to the non-rational, unorganized, unconscious, affect-laden aspects of the group's functioning. Bion uses "work group" to refer to the rational, orderly, cognitive aspects of the group's functioning. He hypothesizes that work and emotional aspects coexist in the group and that the work function is at times interfered with and at times supported by the emotional functions. Bion assumes that the course of the group can be understood as the emergence, development, and subsidence of successive basic assumption cultures. Each basic-assumption culture involves certain inherent satisfactions and threats which exist in a varying balance. When the threat associated with the current basic-assumption culture builds up sufficiently, the group shifts into behavior characteristic of one of the other cultures.

The concept of equilibrium is implicit in Ezriel's thinking when he suggests that the group situation can be conceptualized in terms of the "required relationship," the "avoided relationship," and the "calamity." These three "object relations" exist in a dynamic relationship. Ezriel defines this relationship as follows:

> The three kinds of object relations are thus: first, one which the patient tries to establish with the analyst and which I call the *required* relationship, since he requires it in order to avoid the second, which I accordingly call the *avoided* relationship; this he feels he has to avoid in external reality because he is convinced that if he gave in to his secret desire of entering into it this would inevitably lead to the third relationship, a *calamity*.[17]

Ezriel describes a situation in which the patients in a therapy group try to idealize the therapist (the required relationship) in order to prevent themselves from attacking him (the avoided relationship), behavior which they fear would lead to their harming the therapist or his harming them (the calamity). Ezriel's conceptualization of group-level phenomena overlaps significantly with our views. His concept of the required relationship is comparable to our concept of group solution, for both refer to an overt state of affairs which deals functionally with an underlying conflict. Ezriel's concept of the avoided relationship is related to the concept of disturbing motive, in that both refer to behavior which the patients are afraid to put into operation because of their possible consequences. In Ezriel's terms, the frightening consequences are referred to as the "calamity"; in focal-conflict terms, they are referred to as the "reactive motive." However, some of the characteristics attributed to these terms differ. Ezriel's required relationship, comparable to a restrictive solution, is primarily defensive. The required relationship (restrictive solution) deals with the calamity (reactive motive) by giving up the desires in the avoided relationship (disturbing motive). Focal-conflict theory also includes enabling solutions which allow some gratification of the disturbing motive while alleviating fears. Thus, one difference between our view and Ezriel's is that the group solution (comparable to the required relationship) has a defensive-enabling function rather than a primarily defensive one. Another difference, which is perhaps one of emphasis, is that Ezriel perceives all three elements in his system as involving object relations. We agree that all aspects of the focal conflict involve object relations and that they are an essential feature of the disturbing and reactive motives. However, in solutions, object relations may or may not be of central importance.

Any consideration of long-term movement in the group requires some way of differentiating successive periods in the group's life. Not all theorists have directed themselves specifically to this issue, but some concept of unitization is implied by everyone who examines the group over an extended time span. Bales has defined units in equilibrium terms. The introduction of a problem disturbs the equilibrium of the group, and its solution restores the equilibrium. Such units are more appropriate to problem-solving groups than to therapy groups. We, like Bion and Ezriel, have defined the primary unit in terms of the group's affective characteristics. Ezriel implies that an appropriate unit is the period during which a common group tension prevails in the group. He sees such a period as terminated by the therapist, who interprets the character of the common group tension and thereby permits the group to move toward a more direct examination of the issue. Bion's unit is the basic-assumption culture. He has pointed out that the period during which a group is dominated by one of the basic-assumption cultures may vary greatly in duration. Several basic-assumption cultures may operate successively in a single group session or a single basic-assumption culture may dominate a group for months. In focal-conflict theory, two types of units are implied. The basic unit is the group focal conflict—a single focal conflict terminated by the establishment of a successful solution. A broader unit is the group theme, a sequence of related focal conflicts linked by the same or closely related disturbing motives. What is common to all three views—Bion's, Ezriel's, and our own—is that the unit is based on the affective characteristics of the group. This differentiates these views from the one presented by Winder and Hersko, for example, who utilize the concept of theme but identify theme in content terms.[18] Powdermaker and Frank use the term "theme" to refer to periods several sessions in duration in which the same issue is explored in the group.[19] Here it is difficult to determine from the descriptions provided whether they are referring to content themes or to covert affective issues.

Apart from sharing a concern with the covert emotional aspects of the group situation, important differences exist between our view and those of Bion and Ezriel. As units, Ezriel's common group tension and our group focal conflict have much in common. But Ezriel has no concept that corresponds to our idea of theme, which seems more closely related to Bion's concept of the basic-assumption culture. The basic-assumption culture is a more inclusive concept than the group focal conflict; it includes more diverse elements and often extends over longer periods than does a particular group focal conflict.

We have suggested that, during the time that a group is dominated by a particular theme, a certain development can be observed. Powdermaker and Frank, in studying sequences of sessions devoted to the same theme, have noted that a progression may occur toward more direct exploration of the issue. This compares with our observations about movement into a group theme. In our view, the movement into the theme occurs through the establishment of enabling solutions which allow more direct expression of the disturbing motive. As this more direct exploration proceeds, new concerns or more anxiety-provoking aspects of the old concerns inevitably emerge. The existing solutions are no longer adequate to bind anxiety, and the group attempts to establish more adequate, often restrictive, solutions. Movement away from direct exploration follows. Bion's descriptions of the way in which the group moves into and out of the basic-assumption cultures is similar to this view. Bion accounts for shifts in terms of certain inherent anxieties associated with each of the basic-assumption cultures. As the group persists in operating on a particular basic assumption, anxieties inherent in the culture become intensified and eventually force a shift into one of the other basic-assumption cultures. In describing this process as it occurs with reference to the dependency culture, Bion says:

> The basic assumption in this group culture seems to be that an external object exists whose function it is to provide security for the immature organism. This means that one person is always felt to be in a position to supply the needs of the group, and the rest in a position in which their needs are supplied. When the group enters into this culture, and establishes it as an alternative to whichever one of the other two cultures it has been experiencing, much the same sort of relief is in evidence as I have already described in the change from the fight-flight group to the group met to pair. As the culture becomes established, individuals again begin to show their discomfort. One quite frequent phenomenon is the emergence of feelings of guilt about greed. . . . But the group designed to perpetuate the state of dependence means for the individual that he is being greedy in demanding more than his fair term of parental care. There is, therefore, a quite sharp clash in

> this group between the basic assumption and the needs of the individual as an adult.[20]

In examining movement over extended periods, Bion thinks in terms of recurring basic-assumption cultures—one culture maintains itself for a time, then gives way to another, and so on. Although Bion's description appears similar to our concept of recurring themes, these two views differ in that we see themes recurring under progressively shifting cultural conditions. The culture of the group makes a crucial difference in the manner in which recurrent themes are expressed.

Much theoretical thinking about the long-term movement of the group has been based on the identification of successive developmental phases. Bach perceives the group as moving from an initial interpersonal testing phase to a relatively stable clinical work phase.[21] He identifies seven developmental phases: (1) initial situation testing, (2) leader dependence, (3) familial regressive, (4) associative compeering, (5) fantasy and play, (6) in-group consciousness, and (7) the work group. Bach points out that this is a theoretical model and that one does not expect to see so orderly a developmental sequence in any actual group. Martin and Hill identify six phases in group development which include (1) individual unshared behavior in the imposed structure, (2) reactivation of fixated interpersonal stereotypes, (3) exploration of interpersonal potential within the group, (4) an awareness of interrelationships, subgrouping, and power structures, (5) responsiveness to group dynamic and group process problems, (6) the group as an integrative–creative social instrument.[22] Geller postulates four stages in early development: (1) the stage of uncertainty, marked by diffuse anxiety on the part of the group members, avoidance of involvement with the group situation or the group leader; (2) the stage of over-aggression, characterized by hostile, aggressive content and a compulsive, poorly controlled interaction; (3) the stage of regression, "in which individual members can exhibit deeper features of personality dynamics"; and (4) the stage of adaptation, in which the group "functions efficiently and with satisfaction for its participants."[23]

These views bear little resemblance to our own, nor do they resemble one another. Various investigators have based their theories of development on the observation of therapy groups in various settings and have focused on different levels of the group. Although we refer to some of the same phenomena, we do not locate them in specific phases of group growth. For example, Geller mentions member satisfaction as an aspect of his ultimate phase. We see feelings of satisfaction varying throughout the life of the group, depending, generally, on whether the patients have been able to establish a successful solution to the current focal conflict and, more specifically, on whether a patient is currently successful in operating on an anxiety-reducing personal solution. If Martin and Hill's final phase—the group as an effective integrative-creative social instrument—refers to the capacity of the patients to work together in problem-solving, we see such a capacity present from the beginning and brought to bear on successive focal conflicts throughout the life of the group. Similarly, dependence on the leader, listed by Bach as the third of seven phases, may occur at various times during the life of the group, either as an aspect of a group solution or an aspect of a disturbing motive in which the leader is the object of dependency wishes.

We have identified only two major phases: an initial, relatively brief formative phase and a more extended established phase. In contrast, the developmental schemes just described have conceptualized the group in terms of more highly differentiated phases. Views of development which emphasize phasing have to contend with the fact that phases are never clear-cut, that mixed and transitional phases occur, and that behavior assumed to be primarily characteristic of one phase also appears in others. Consequently, any definite statement about phases must be heavily qualified.

Coffey has suggested a developmental task approach to the problem of group movement.[24] He thinks of any group as being confronted with certain basic issues. These include (1) the relation of the individual to the group (preserving individuality yet accomplishing the group's work), (2) the problem of authority (coming to terms with the relationship with the leader), (3) the problem of conflict (dealing with differences within the group), and (4) the problem of consensus (the development of emotional support). Coffey suggests no particular sequence. The implication is that the group deals repeatedly with these issues. But he does suggest that group maturity can be understood in terms of the extent to which the group has mastered them. The aspect of Coffey's point of view which is congenial to focal-conflict theory is the concept of the group being confronted with the necessity for dealing with issues, emotional tasks, and conflictful feelings.

Two questions associated with considerations about the development of a group are "When is a group a group?" and "When can a group be regarded as mature?" Freud differentiated a true group from a collection of individuals on the basis of the presence or absence of libidinal ties.[25] He postulated primary libidinal ties between each member and the leader and secondary libidinal ties among members by virtue of their mutual identification with the leader. Redl further developed this view of groups, pointing out that the types of libidinal ties which Freud described constitute only one of the possible routes to group formation.[26] Redl introduced the term "central person" to refer to the member around whom the group forms. He described ten types of central person who could function prominently in the formative process. For example, the members might choose one person to be the object of their aggressive drives. Through the common feelings directed toward this central person, the remaining members develop "group emotions" about one another. Another example is the central person as seducer. Redl describes a group situation in which a strong increase in the intensity of unacceptable drives occurs, but the members are prevented from expressing them by strong superego controls. The seducer is the first person to express the unacceptable drive in behavior. He renders a service to the ego of the potential group members by committing the "initiatory act." The other members can then express the same unacceptable impulse openly without experiencing anxiety and guilt. Common to both Freud and Redl is the view that shared group emotions develop through a special relation with a particular person in the group. Both emphasize the function which this person fills for the group. Both put the relationship with the central person in terms of libidinal ties. In Freud's thinking, the central person is the leader. In Redl's view, the central person may be the leader but may also be some other person in the group.

In Redl's view as well as Freud's, the point at which group emotions develop around a central person is the point at which a collection of individuals becomes a group. We have suggested that, under the special conditions of the therapy group, shared affect emerges immediately—not necessarily around a central person but by virtue of exposure to common stresses. If the presence of shared affect is the primary criterion for the existence of a group, then we would say, with Bion and Ezriel, that the group exists from the beginning. If the existence of libidinal ties is the primary criterion, then we would say that the first *directed* affect marks the moment of group formation. If one emphasizes a third kind of group emotion—the development of commitment to the group—then we would say that the group becomes a group at the time when a minimum culture is established. It is at this point, when satisfactory solutions to the initial focal conflicts have been established, that the patients and the therapist can experience some feeling that the group is functioning and will continue to function.

Bach, Martin and Hill, and Geller all define a phase which they regard as the ultimate mature stage of the therapy group. Coffey, speaking of non-therapeutic groups, suggests that a mature group is one which has adequately dealt with four basic tasks or issues. In contrast, focal-conflict theory does not define a stage of maturity or of ultimate development for the therapy group. Although it is true that we distinguish between a formative phase and an established phase, the latter is seen as involving much internal development and never reaching a stage of final maturity. We adopt this view not because we feel that groups are incapable of achieving a mature stage of development, but because the character of a therapy group precludes the achievement of this stage. The therapy group is always pushing toward dealing with new aspects of conflicts, feelings, and relationships. These are inevitably associated with anxiety and inevitably require the establishment of group solutions. Certain of the solutions which the group establishes, even late in its development, may have a regressive character in that they are more typical of earlier periods in the group's life. The therapy group is always in a state of becoming and, because of its unique task, will dissolve before it reaches a mature state of being.

Affective Characteristics

Most group therapists attribute an intense, primitive quality to the affective components of the group.[27] Patients may experience profound fears of destroying or being destroyed, swallowed up, or overwhelmed. They may direct potent feelings of love, hate, or need toward one another or toward the therapist. The very language which is used to describe affect in groups underlines this point. Bion may speak of the patients in the fight–flight culture as seeking a leader who can define an enemy. Ezriel mentions shared fears of doing irreparable harm to the therapist.[28] We have described focal conflicts in which the patients experience the wish to possess the therapist exclusively or the fear of losing a sense of self through enforced contact with one another.

The shared affect which develops in the therapy group is a crucial feature of focal-conflict theory. The state of the group at any time is understood in terms of impulses and fears in which each patient shares and to which each patient reacts. Ezriel speaks of the common group tension—the covert affect which is shared by all the members of the group. Bion defines three basic states with reference to group affect—fight-flight, pairing, and dependency—and points out that a wide range of affect, influenced by the prevailing emotional culture, may occur in each.

Theorists who have been influenced by Kleinian concepts have suggested that the affect which emerges under group conditions is an expression of group-induced regression.[29] In Bion's view, regression occurs in response to the individual's failure to cope with the emotional life of the group:

> I hope to show that in his contact with the complexities of life in a group the adult resorts, in what may be a massive regression, to mechanisms described by Melanie Klein . . . as typical of the earliest phases of mental life. The adult must establish contact with the emotional life of the group in which he lives; this task would appear to be as formidable to the adult as the relationship with the breast appears to be with the infant, and the failure to meet the demands of this task is revealed in his regression.[30]

Although all group therapists recognize that patients may experience intense affect in the group, a distinction can be made between those who see this experience as inextricably associated with group forces and those who do not. In the latter view, the affect occurs not so much on a group basis as on an interpersonal basis. The patients establish one-to-one or multiple-person "family" relationships among themselves. Sometimes the patient has feelings about the group as a whole, but these are conceptualized as an extension of interpersonal feelings, since the group is regarded as a kind of person-surrogate. In contrast, Bion, Ezriel, Foulkes, we, and possibly Redl believe that the patient experiences affect by virtue of his participation in a matrix of group forces.

Coping or Problem-Solving

"Problem-solving" is a term which ordinarily refers to activity directed toward achieving a solution to a publicly defined task. It usually involves making a decision, formulating a plan, or carrying out some work. "Coping" is a term ordinarily applied to dealing with emotional issues in the group—problems which are sometimes referred to as "group-maintenance" or "interpersonal" problems. Such theories as that of Bales, which deal primarily with task groups, are likely to emphasize the group's problem-solving capacities, although it is recognized that a task group must simultaneously cope with emotional issues. Theories which deal primarily with therapy groups are likely to emphasize the group's coping capacities, for the group is more likely to be called upon to deal with emotional issues than with an overt, publicly defined task.

Several theorists point both to the potent affect in the therapy group and to the group's coping capacity. Two theories—Bion's and our own—are directed specifically to this point. Although both theories recognize and emphasize the group's coping capacity, rather different concepts have been invoked to account for it. Bion makes a primary distinction between the basic-assumption cultures (the affective, nonrational aspects of the group) and the work group (the rational, problem-solving capacities of the group). He assumes that the group is engaged in a continual struggle to make the work group triumph over the basic-assumption cultures. He perceives these two as simultaneous aspects of the group which exist in a varying relationship: "Work-group activity is obstructed, diverted, and on occasion assisted" by the basic assumption cultures.[31] With reference to the work group, Bion says:

> I attribute great force and influence to the work group, which through its concern with reality is compelled to employ the methods of science in no matter how rudimentary a form. I think one of the striking things about a group is that, despite the influence of the basic assumptions, it is the W group that triumphs in the long run.[32]

Thus Bion locates the coping capacity of the group in the work group, defines it as the rational, "scientific" aspect of the group, and differentiates it from the emotional, "instinctual" aspects of the group.

Focal-conflict theory, too, recognizes the coping capacity of the group but locates it in a way which does not require so sharp a distinction between cognitive and emotional aspects of the group. In focal-conflict theory, the coping capacity of the group lies in its members' ability to achieve solutions to successive focal conflicts. The solution has a defensive–enabling function with reference to the underlying focal conflict. By various devices, the patients establish procedures which alleviate shared fears and allow some gratification of impulses.

These first three issues refer to the group as a system. One of the hazards of building theory about the group as a system is the tendency to make implicit analogies between individual personality and the group as a whole. It is difficult to avoid expressions like "the group wants . . . ," "the group is . . . ," and so forth. Anthropomorphizing the group—treating the group as if it were a single mind—has been justifiably criticized by many writers. They fear that treating the group as a system, if carried to an extreme, could lead to misleading analogies between the individual and the group or, worse, to the total disregard of the individual. In our conceptual system, the possibility of anthropomorphizing occurs with all three aspects of the focal conflict. In referring to the disturbing motive, one might say, "The group wants. . . ." In referring to the reactive motive, one might say, "The group fears. . . ." In referring to a group solution, one might say, "The group is suppressing, is denying, is testing out, is rationalizing, is displacing." Some connotations of such phrases are inappropriate and misleading, although others appropriately describe the phenomena being considered.

Sometimes the group has such an impact on the therapist that he feels as if the patients are acting as a single force. This is most striking when he is the target of the patients' shared feelings. For example, the therapist may feel an insistent pressure to provide answers. The assumption that he knows but will not tell is so pervasive that it seems to fill the room. If the therapist says, at such a point, "The group wants me to tell it what to do," he is describing the impact of the current group situation on him. If, by a multitude of indications, the therapist detects heightened anxiety in the group situation, he may summarize this by saying to himself, "The group is anxious." There are times when the group's impact on the therapist (or on any of the patients) has an emotional quality which leads him to experience the situation as if some single, overpowering affect were being expressed. This quality leads him to experience the group as if it were a single entity and perhaps think and speak of the group in anthropomorphic terms.

However, the impact on the individual must be differentiated from the group phenomena. When a therapist says to himself "The group is afraid of being punished," he is referring to a complex, differentiated phenomenon. Earlier, we described a group situation in which the reactive motive was "fear of punishment from therapists" (see Chapter 4, first illustration). The sequence of events included the patients' sitting along a wall in what they jokingly referred to as a "line-up," tense silences, and talk about schoolrooms in which pupils who did not know what to say waited for the teacher to pounce on someone. The patients participated in quite different ways. Some were silent, some participated in the joking, and others shared in building the schoolroom fantasy. Each contributed verbally to the over-all communication of fear of punishment, displayed relevant non-verbal behavior, or merely failed to challenge or shift the topic. Perhaps some did not fear punishment; certainly, not everyone experienced it in the same way. Yet these discrete behaviors contributed to an over-all state of affairs which could be correctly referred to as a prevailing fear of punishment.

The emotional impact generated in the group at such a time is very like the impact generated by a fear-ridden, demanding patient in individual therapy. But the phenomenon which generates this impact is quite different in the two situations. In individual therapy, it is a single patient who communicates the predominant feeling. In the group, a number of patients contribute to the prevailing group affect. From the point of view of impact, it is quite appropriate to say, "The group is afraid of being punished." This meaning of the phrase is appropriate. But from the point of view of the phenomenon involved, it is not appropriate to say, "The group is afraid of being punished," because it is not the group as ego, but the interacting patients who generate the situation. Any connotation which portrays the group as actor, or as undifferentiated mass is inappropriate.

Perhaps this point requires special clarification with respect to group solutions, since, in describing group solutions, we have sometimes used terms which are ordinarily applied to the individual: intellectualization, distancing, denial, displacement, acting out, and projection. Although the same words are used, the phenomena are different, for in the group, solutions require collaboration or social interaction to become effective. Sometimes the solution involves general reinforcement of some individual mechanism (e.g., denial); sometimes it involves elaborate role differentiation (e.g., scapegoating). The group solution serves the same function for its members that the defense mechanism serves for the individual. Both are protection against confrontation with feared impulses. But they refer to two distinct systems and are based on two distinct processes.

The Generation of Group Characteristics

Some theorists who have studied group-level characteristics of psychotherapy groups have also developed theories about the way in which group-level phenomena generate from the behavior of the individual patients. The central question facing the investigator has been how to relate a series of individual acts—the observable data of the group—to highly abstract concepts about group-level phenomena. Many theorists have assumed that a particular form of free association occurs in the therapy group. The patients' successive contributions are seen to be linked and relevant to underlying shared concerns. Foulkes, Bion, Ezriel, and we postulate such a process. Foulkes has said:

> I instructed the patients who had had previous psychoanalysis to associate freely in the same way as in the individual situation. As expected, the associations which patients were able to produce were modified by the group situation. I then waited and observed developments over a number of years, eliciting the process to which I later gave the name of "free-floating discussion." Only at a much later date consequent on my studies in analytic groups did it become clear to me that the conversation of *any* group could be considered in its unconscious aspects as the equivalent of free association. . . .

> In a casually thrown together social group, such as is seen in a railway carriage, or on conducted motor tours, though there is nobody to interpret, the ongoing conversation approximates to "free group association," the unconscious meaning readily shows itself to my own observation in such contexts.[33]

Foulkes implies that, in the therapy group, the manifest content relates to latent meanings in a way similar to the manner in which manifest dream content relates to latent meanings. He sees these free associations blending to form an integrated whole. He says:

> Looked at in this way it becomes easier to understand our claim that the group associates, responds and reacts as a whole. The group as it were avails itself now of one speaker, now of another, but it is always the transpersonal network which is sensitized and gives utterance, or responds. In this sense we can postulate the existence of a group "mind" in the same way that we postulate an individual "mind." Whereas it is difficult for us to abstract from the concept of an individual in a physical, bodily way, it should not be so difficult to do so in the mental field, and to perceive that the matrix of response is indeed an interconnected whole.[34]

Foulkes's use of the term "group mind" is unfortunate since it has frequently been misunderstood. We believe that his general point is comparable to our own position that the manifest material of the group interaction, to which many individuals contribute, can be conceptualized as being linked together associatively in such a way that a common underlying theme may be identified and that the underlying theme can be regarded as a property of the group as a whole. Ezriel makes this point in language which is less likely to be misunderstood:

> The *manifest* content of discussions in groups may embrace practically any topic. They might talk about astronomy, philosophy, politics, or even psychology; but it is one of the essential assumptions for psychoanalytic work with groups that, whatever the manifest content may be, there always develops rapidly an *underlying* common group problem, a *common group tension* of which the group is not aware but which determines its behaviour. This common group tension seems to represent what I should like to call the "common denominator" of the dominant unconscious phantasies of all members.[35]

Diverse manifest behaviors, in Bion's view, gain coherence if one assumes that the patients are operating on a common basic assumption. Silence, as well as overt participation, is seen as part of this process, for Bion has indicated that he regards material from only a few patients as sufficient evidence that a common concern prevails for the group as a whole.

Perhaps the term "free association" is unfortunate because of the connotations that accrue from its use in individual therapy. There, the successive associations of the patient are understood to refer to some covert concern. Free association is utilized as a therapeutic device. The patient is encouraged to verbalize whatever comes to his mind. In the individual analytic session, the patient associates to his own and the analyst's comments. In the group situation, various patients' successive comments are understood to refer to a shared underlying concern. The therapist may not specifically instruct the patients to say whatever comes to their minds, but for long periods he refrains from structuring or interrupting the flow of the conversation in order to permit the underlying concerns to become apparent. Each patient reacts to the others' contributions as well as to his own. Thus, in the group, the patient does not free associate in the same sense that he does in the individual analytic situation. As we use the term, free association in groups is an explanatory concept which accounts for the manner in which diverse individual comments generate a shared group theme. Free association as described by Ezriel, Foulkes, Bion, and us is different from free association in individual psychoanalysis, and both are different from another kind of associative process encouraged by some group therapists. For example, Wolf and Schwartz may ask the patients to associate to dream material introduced by one patient.[36] In this case, the patients' associations, although free in one sense, are channeled toward a specific task.

Not all theorists who have utilized concepts referring to group-level phenomena have focused their attention on the generation of such phenomena from successive individual acts. Nor is such theorizing necessary to a system which deals with properties of the group as a whole. For example, Frank has discussed cohesion as a property of the therapy group but has not considered the manner in which cohesion is generated. Rather, he has been concerned primarily with its effects on the patients. Truax has also studied the effects, but not the generation, of certain group characteristics.

On the whole, social psychologists who have studied non-therapeutic groups have not turned their attention to this issue. They have tended to primarily focus on the effects of group properties on problem-solving or on the members' feelings of satisfaction or achievement. An exception is the work of Bales, who has assessed the quality of individual contributions in problem-solving groups and, through an additive process, identified characteristics of the group as a whole. Free association is not a relevant concept in Bales's work, although he does see successive comments as involving action and reaction. Rather, he assumes that information about the group as a whole can be achieved through adding up the individual acts. This additive method and procedure seem appropriate to Bales's goals, since he is interested in assessing the problem-solving characteristics of the group and the manner in which it moves toward accomplishing a public task. He is not concerned, as are the group therapists whom we have mentioned, with conceptualizing group processes in terms of covert affective issues. The use of free association to explain the relationship between individual acts and group-level phenomena makes additive procedures inappropriate, for successive units of behavior cannot be regarded as equivalent. The same is true in a clinical interview, in which a single revelation or slip of the tongue gives meaning to the whole and some comments are more important than others in providing clues about the meaning of the material.

Although free association is a useful explanatory concept, in itself it does not explain why a certain patient introduces a particular association at a particular point in a group session. To account for this, one must define the relation of individual personality, behavior, and interpersonal context. An understanding of such relationships would also account for the uniqueness of each patient's behavior in the group situation. Ezriel, Bion, and Ackerman, as well as we, have devoted attention to this problem. Bion utilizes the term "valency" to account for the individual's participation in the group. By this, he means "the capacity for spontaneous instinctive co-operation in the basic assumptions."[37] Bion uses this term not only to account for the individual's behavior, but also to account for the readiness of the patient to participate in unconscious collaboration to support a specific group culture. He suggests that the patient's valency may be high or low, but never absent. We take him to mean that every patient is capable of participating in the group affect to some extent, but that individuals vary in their capacity for participating in the three basic-assumption cultures. Ezriel's explanation includes motivational elements. He says, "Each [patient] brings to the group meeting some unconscious relationships with 'phantasy objects,' which may be dominant in his mind at the moment and which unconsciously he wishes to act out by manipulating the other members of the group into certain positions like pawns in a private game of chess."[38] Ackerman utilizes the concept of social role as the mediating concept between individual personality and the group processes. He suggests that the patient displays adaptive aspects of his personality through the role he assumes in the interpersonal setting. He says, "The role of the individual in the group represents a particular form of integration of his emotional tendencies in a specific situation. The adaptive expressions of the person are limited and shaped in two ways: by the relative fixed organization of the individual personality, and by the requirements of the given situation as this individual interprets them."[39]

Our own view is related, in some measure, to those of Ezriel and Ackerman. We have described the patient as motivated to establish a viable group situation. Thus the patient's goal is to participate in a way which will generate conditions of maximum reward and comfort for himself, given the possibilities of the interpersonal setting. The character of the interpersonal setting is important in two ways: first, from the patient's point of view, the group situation is anxiety-provoking in varying degrees at different times; second, the success of the devices the individual employs in the group is limited by the group culture. These views share the assumption that the patient's behavior in the group is a product of his own personality and needs, elicited and shaped by the interpersonal situation.

Up to this point, we have examined issues which have been considered only by those theorists who regard group forces as crucial. The therapists who regard group forces as irrelevant or incidental to the process of therapy have not, of course, been concerned with these aspects of the group situation. However, everyone who has written about the therapy group has considered, explicitly or implicitly, issues relating to the character of the therapeutic process and the role of the therapist. These are related matters: choices or assumptions made in one area limit or channel the choices made in the other. No matter what kind of therapeutic setting the therapist employs—a two-person situation, a small group, or a social milieu—he makes certain assumptions about what experiences will be useful to the patient. Once this is decided, he will direct his efforts toward maximizing the likelihood that such experiences will occur.

The Therapeutic Process

Corsini and Rosenberg have described the problems of attempting to compare theories about the mechanism of therapeutic change in the therapy group.[40] No two theorists describe exactly the same process or emphasize the same mechanisms. For example, Slavson suggests the following as requirements for therapeutic change: the establishment of transference relationships, catharsis, insight and/or ego-strengthening, reality-testing, and sublimation.[41] Frank emphasizes the corrective emotional experience and suggests that this experience is facilitated by support, stimulation, and reality-testing. Ezriel perceives reality-testing as the essence of the psychotherapeutic process. Ackerman suggests the following as processes which provide the bases for therapeutic change:

> (1) The development of an emotional relationship with a dynamic "give and take" between patient and therapist. (2) Through this relationship, provision of emotional support for the patient. (3) Reality testing: modification of concept of self, and patterns of relations to others in the direction of more realistic perception. (4) Release of pent-up emotion. (5) Expression of conflict, both conscious and unconscious. (6) Change in patterns of resistance and defense against anxiety. (7) Diminution of guilt and anxiety. (8) Growth of new insight, and emergence of new and healthier patterns of adaptation.[42]

Confronted with this diversity, Corsini and Rosenberg attempt to categorize therapeutic mechanisms discussed by various authors and reduce them to a concise list. They identified nine factors or mechanisms thought to be involved in the therapeutic experience: acceptance, altruism, universalization, intellectualization, reality-testing, transference, interaction, spectator therapy, and ventilation.

In our discussions of the therapeutic process, we distinguish between the patient's therapeutic experience and the therapeutic conditions which facilitate such an experience. We have suggested that the crucial therapeutic experience for the individual involves the discovery that feared consequences do not occur: the patient finds that the habitual solution—a maladaptive interpersonal pattern—which he has implicitly regarded as essential to his existence can be safely relinquished, or the patient finds that the impulses which he has disguised, suppressed, or ignored can be recognized and sometimes expressed without exposing himself to damaging consequences. Ezriel presents a similar position:

> . . . reality testing . . . is the essence of the therapeutic process in psycho-analysis. The interpretation enables the patient to test his unconsciously determined fears in the external reality of the analytic situation when the avoided relationship materializes through being made explicit by the analyst (in group therapy it is sometimes made explicit by another patient). The patient is thus helped to assess the true effects of the avoided relationship and, when he compares them with the unconsciously expected calamity and realizes that the latter has not taken place, his need for the required relationship is removed and he becomes capable of giving less disguised expression in external reality to his hitherto avoided behaviour pattern; and, although the interpretation may have contained no reference to his current life outside the analytic situation or to his past, he can then link up the experience

> gained in the session with his contemporary and past life—especially with his infantile past as shown by the patients' reports of childhood memories sometimes coming to their minds after such interpretations.[43]

Ezriel sees the testing of unconsciously determined fears as the essence of the patient's therapeutic experience. Such reality-testing enables the patient to differentiate the true from the fantasied consequences of recognizing or exposing feared impulses. Frank and Ascher also emphasize the vital role of an experience which is counter to the patient's expectations. They describe a patient as follows:

> Mr. Jones instead of hiding his feelings under an affable exterior was able for the first time to express them openly and to his astonishment found them acceptable to the others, instead of leading to their rejection of them . . . the patients discovered that some resolution of the situation other than the usual or expected one was possible. This was followed by a change of behavior accompanied by increased insight. . . . These examples then would seem to represent genuine corrective emotional experiences in that they disrupted habitual patterns of thought and action and gave new ones a chance to form.[44]

Although these positions differ in language and detail, all emphasize the crucial role of experiences in which the patient finds that the calamity he expects as a result of what he did, said, or didn't do or say does not occur. The positions differ as to the centrality of this experience in the therapeutic process and the role of other mechanisms and conditions—particularly those of transference and insight.

Transference experiences and insight into one's own transference reactions are widely regarded as critical to therapeutic change. However, comparisons are difficult because the concept of transference has accumulated various meanings. Sometimes it refers to positive or negative feelings toward the therapist, sometimes more strictly to the reproduction of past relationships. Freud defined transferences as "new editions or facsimiles of the tendencies and phantasies which are aroused and made conscious during the progress of the analysis; but they have this peculiarity which is characteristic of their species, that they replace some earlier person by the person of the physician. To put it another way: a whole series of psychological experiences are revived, not as belonging to the past but as applying to the person of the physician at the present moment."[45] Freud suggests that some transference manifestations are direct representations of past experience, involving only a shift in object, and others undergo certain transformations which make their reference to the past less direct, though equivalent psychologically. Transference, as it occurs in the two-person therapeutic situation, is understood to involve the distortion of reality. The therapist, a relatively neutral figure, is experienced as if he possessed various specific characteristics. Thus the concept of transference includes the idea of feelings and reactions which are now inappropriately directed toward the therapist but which were appropriate to past figures.

It has been widely recognized that transference must have a different character in the group than it does in the two-person therapeutic situation, both because more people are present and because these people are more "real" in the sense of providing more information about themselves and responding more spontaneously. Yet, the meaning of this difference for the character of transference in group therapy is by no means clearly understood. Very often, transference as it occurs in individual psychoanalysis is taken as the model, and transference in the group is defined in analogous terms, with only such modifications as are forced on the theorist by the change in therapeutic environment. Thus, the transference relationship with the therapist is seen as primary and all other relationships as secondary, substituting for or diluting the primary relationship. Or, multiple transference relationships are recognized, but defined in one-to-one terms. Efforts to understand transference in therapy groups have led to various attempts at definition. Slavson suggests three types of transference: libidinal, sibling, and identification transferences.[46] A distinction is often made between "transference" and "mirror" reactions; the latter term refers to experiences in which the individual perceives some aspect of himself in another and is thus provided with a special means of self-observation and objectification. Hulse has suggested that the primary transference feelings are directed to the therapist but that those which are not accepted by the therapist are turned toward other group members, "who as co-therapists become secondarily the objects of the patient's transferential needs."[47] He seems to be approaching a definition of transference which goes beyond merely perceiving multiple one-to-one transference relationships in the group. He suggests that the transference phenomena which are specific to the therapy group might be called the "group neurosis" in analogy to the "transference neurosis" of individual therapy.

Ezriel makes the concept of transference the cornerstone of his theory. He says that the patient

> . . . tries to find relief through his establishing a certain kind of relationship between himself and his analyst in the "here and now" situation of the analytic session. This attempt is considered as one particular in-

> stance of a more general tendency, as one of many unconscious endeavours which the patient makes to establish such a relationship between himself and his environment in general. The "transference situation" is therefore not something peculiar to treatment, but occurs whenever one individual meets another.[48]

When the patients are brought together in the group, the resulting common group tension is a product of all the individual transference tendencies. "The *unconscious common group tension* may therefore be described as the total of the various unconsciously determined pushes and pulls exerted by the members of the group upon one another and upon the therapist, in leading to a certain *structuring* of the group."[49]

Focal-conflict theory does not utilize the term or concept of transference. This omission does not mean that phenomena subsumed under this concept are not included in our theoretical system, nor does it mean that we are simply using other terms to refer to the same phenomena. Rather, focal-conflict theory is so organized that certain features of the phenomenon referred to by the term "transference" are included in the theory but that it would be misleading to utilize the term. To clarify this point, it is necessary to differentiate various aspects of transference as the term is commonly defined. The term assumes that the patient develops, over time, a transference relationship with the therapist or the patients in the group, that distortion of reality takes place in that the expectations and reactions centering around the transference object are inappropriate, and that a simulation of personal history occurs in which the current experience reproduces past relationships. In focal-conflict terms, the patient and his experience can be summarized as follows: the patient who enters the group can be described in terms of nuclear conflicts—unresolved issues to which the patient remains vulnerable. The individual repeatedly experiences focal conflicts which are derived forms of these core conflicts. The focal conflicts are rooted in the associated nuclear conflicts but are colored by the characteristics of the current interpersonal setting. In the therapy group, too, the patient re-experiences nuclear conflicts in a derived form. Throughout life, the individual has constructed habitual solutions to cope with these recurring focal conflicts. When he experiences crucial conflicts in the group, he will attempt to put relevant personal solutions into operation. These habitual solutions may be rooted in early experiences, or they may have been adopted relatively recently. Although this view bears a resemblance to one aspect of the concept of transference—the simulation of personal history—the emphasis is not historical. Rather, the emphasis is on the experience of the conflict itself. The experience may simulate the historical experience in form and in object, or it may not. In our view, it is immaterial whether and to what degree simulation occurs. What is crucial is that the patient experiences this conflict and attempts to utilize habitual maladaptive solutions.

The implication that transference develops over time has no analogue in focal-conflict theory. We assume that the patient experiences personal focal conflicts immediately and recurrently throughout his period in the group and that this occurs through his participation in the group focal conflicts which emerge. He does not experience all relevant personal conflicts simultaneously; such experiences are elicited and subside over a period of time. Along with this, the patient attempts to put habitual personal solutions into operation. Thus, the concept of the development of a transference relationship does not apply. A further departure is the fact that we do not consider the distortion of reality a critical feature. At times, the patient's experience may involve distortion of reality—he may read feelings, reactions, and characteristics which do not exist into other people in the group. At other times, he may accurately assess the personalities or reactions of the other group members. From a focal-conflict point of view, possible distortions are not so important as the fact that the patient experiences crucial conflicts in the group and attempts to institute habitual personal solutions. In this sense, the patient is not distorting the events in his environment, but accurately responding to them.

Finally, the concept of transference implies an object relationship. Either the patient experiences transference feelings toward one other group member or he is involved in a network of relationships in which, again, the feelings are directed toward specific people. In the therapy group, the experiencing of critical personal conflicts may occur without the affect's being so highly focused. Pervasive affect develops in the group, and the patients generally share in certain impulses and fears. Each patient will experience the shared affect in a unique way, and each patient may single out specific people as objects of his impulses or fears. But the primary feature is the shared affect experienced under group conditions rather than the object relationship itself.

Insight as an experience leading to change is regarded as central by many theorists. Others relegate the concept of insight to a secondary position or accord it a restricted, specialized function. Papanek points to occasions when constructive change occurs without any apparent insight.

> Rather, a slow change of perceptual organization and concept formation takes place in the patient, but at no point does he give an

> indication that he comprehends the dynamics of his behavior. This kind of perceptual reorganization, which no doubt occurs through the experience of therapy, is similar to the non-insightful learning which takes place before the patient enters therapy.[50]

We regard the sequence of events labeled the therapeutic experience as the core of therapy, often occurring prior to the development of insight. Frank takes a similar position, pointing out that the corrective emotional experience can be followed by a change of behavior accompanied by increased insight or awareness. Ezriel places a greater emphasis on the role of insight: he suggests that it is interpretation and the subsequent cognitive recognition which enable the patient to test his fears in the therapeutic situation. All these views perceive insight as having some role in the therapeutic experience. For Ezriel, insight appears to be crucial and is prior to the reality-testing experience. In our view and in Frank's theory, insight is less crucial.

In our view, the therapeutic experience, sometimes supported by insight, is of central importance. Other mechanisms seem secondary. For example, catharsis is a mechanism which, according to Corsini and Rosenberg, was mentioned frequently in articles about group therapy as a critical aspect of the therapeutic experience. We do not see the expression of affect as a sufficient condition for a productive therapeutic experience. Rather, the ventilation of feelings or impulses can be conceptualized as an aspect of the therapeutic experience. Occurring alone, catharsis or ventilation is likely to provide only minimal, temporary relief rather than stable changes in behavior. Universalization, also mentioned by Corsini and Rosenberg, is the recognition that one's problems, impulses, and fears are shared by others. This is understood to provide comfort or reassurance. But, although it may operate in this way, there are also times when it is not comforting or reassuring to the patient to perceive that certain feared impulses are universal and, hence, apparently inescapable. The observation of one's own characteristics in others occurs in "mirror reactions," a process described by Frank. The patient sees some aspect of himself or his ego ideal in others and is thus provided with a special means of self-observation and objectification. We perceive the opportunity to observe others as a special source of information which the group setting makes available to the patient. Often—and this begins to involve what is sometimes called "spectator therapy"—the patient has an opportunity to observe that others express feelings that he does not dare to express or that others display differing attitudes about certain issues or feelings. But the therapeutic benefits which may derive from such mechanisms, in and of themselves, are minimal. In general, we view such mechanisms as catharsis or ventilation, universalization, and spectator therapy as aspects of the therapeutic experience or special sources of information for the patient.

Our discussion so far has emphasized the experience which the individual must undergo in order for therapeutic benefit to occur. We have said little, directly, about the conditions for therapy—events in the therapeutic enviroment which facilitate a productive therapeutic experience. We believe that this is an important distinction in differentiating group therapy from individual therapy and in clarifying relations among various theories. The therapeutic experience and insight are commonly assumed to be central features of individual therapy as well as of group therapy. What is distinct are the conditions under which these experiences are achieved. The route is different, though the result for the patient may be the same. Ackerman has presented a similar view, suggesting that, although the therapeutic experience may be the same whatever the therapeutic environment, the manner in which the interpersonal environment affects the patient may differ considerably in the group and the two-person therapeutic setting. He says, "It is unlikely that therapeutic change in an individual setting, as in psychoanalysis, and therapeutic change in a group, are dependent on unique psychological influences; rather, the basic processes of therapeutic change are the same, but are differently integrated and balanced in accordance with the differences of social structuring in the two situations."[51] Ezriel makes it clear that he feels that what is required for the patient—reality-testing and insight into the required, avoided, and catastrophic object relations—is the same in individual analysis and in the group. But he makes it equally clear that he regards the group setting as something distinct from the individual setting. In contrasting his own view to that of other group therapists, Ezriel says:

> According to this other conception, the "group" is seen essentially as a collection of individuals who come for treatment with their individual problems, which they unfold in the presence of others . . . but which are dealt with by the therapist on an individual basis. . . . Many therapists would, however, consider at least that benefit may be derived from the presence of other patients whose frank remarks may, for example, encourage an unusually inhibited patient to speak more freely about himself, or make him realize that his problem is not unique, the group thus acting as a powerful reassuring (or in other cases pressure-exerting) agent. Some would go considerably further in their recognition that the group is "more than just a collection of individuals"; but when interpreting they would still try to deal separately with segments of the total group behaviour, i.e., to treat the material produced by

patients in a group session as if it were contributed by isolated individuals in a two-person relationship with the therapist.

> However, I think that such an approach does not do justice to the underlying dynamics of the group, and that a remark by a patient in a group can only be understood and effectively interpreted *in its context,* i.e., in conjunction with the remarks of all the other members of the group in that session.[52]

Foulkes does not deal with this distinction explicitly. He describes the neurotic process and the goal of therapy in orthodox, intrapersonal terms. But he also points out that the patient becomes involved in differing ways in the group situation and in individual analysis and that, therefore, it is necessary to conceptualize the situation in differing terms.

In trying to contrast individual and group therapy, these authors distinguish between, on the one hand, the neurotic process, the goal of therapy, and the experience of the individual, which are the same no matter what the therapeutic vehicle and, on the other hand, the focus of therapy, the route to therapy, and the conditions for therapy, which are specific to the particular therapeutic setting. We make a primary distinction between the therapeutic experience, which is always the same and transcends the specifics of the therapeutic setting, and the therapeutic conditions, which are specific to the setting.

Over-all, our views and the views of Ezriel, Foulkes, and Bion, although differing in important ways, are similar in that the group processes are seen to encompass and intersect the individual's concerns in such a way that the individual's therapeutic experience cannot be understood except as it occurs in and through the group processes. This way of looking at the group therapeutic situation is very different from the views of such group therapists as Slavson, Alexander and Wolf, and Locke, who are inclined to disregard or de-emphasize group forces in their theories. For such therapists, the group functions primarily to stimulate one-to-one or "family" transferences or as an arena in which interpersonal behavior can be observed and interpreted. Other aspects of the group are viewed as intrusive and deleterious to the therapeutic process. This position is understandable if one assumes not only that the therapeutic experience is the same in the group as in individual therapy, but that the therapeutic conditions must also correspond as closely as possible. In our view, such a position represents an inappropriate analogy from the individual therapeutic situation and does not take into account the unique features of the group which, if capitalized on, can crucially contribute to the individual's therapeutic experience.

The theorist who begins from a position that the group therapeutic setting has unique properties is confronted with the task of defining the manner in which participation in the group can benefit the patient. Foulkes has made the comment that, if one treats the group, the individual will take care of himself. This comment has been widely misunderstood to mean that Foulkes is interested only in treating the group and that his goal is to make the group, rather than the patient, a healthy and mature organism. Actually, Foulkes has indicated that what he means by this statement is that the individuals who comprise the group and the group itself are so interdependent that change in one is concomitant with change in the other. He has referred to the group as the "matrix" within which individual change occurs. The individual as a participant in the dynamics of the group cannot fail to be acted upon by the group situation. It is in this sense that he feels that attention to the group as a whole is coincidental with attention to the individual. He says, "Any change, any modification in the group goes together with a change in the individual and vice versa. It follows that if we treat the group, we treat at the same time the individuals composing it, even if we do not apply ourselves to them in particular."[53] He points out that the patients in the group become involved in an effort to function as a group. In order to do this, they have to learn about interferences or resistances that are located in the transference neurosis, so that they can correct them. Thus it is inevitable that each patient becomes involved in activity that is relevant to his pathology. Foulkes says:

> He [the patient] thus becomes engaged in work which concerns the essential character of his disturbance, contains the area of ultimate pathogenic conflict. Whose liberation? His or theirs? His *and* theirs is the answer, they are the same thing. This is true *currently* and *ultimately* and herein lies the potentially therapeutic character of the group.[54]

In other words, Foulkes sees the group task as inevitably encompassing the therapeutic task. It is in this context that his comment—that, if one treats the group, the individual takes care of himself—must be understood.

Bion also points out that the individual is so inextricably involved in the group that dealing with the group includes crucial therapeutic operations relevant to each patient:

> . . . we are not concerned to give individual treatment in public, but to draw attention to the actual experiences of the group, and in this instance the way in which the group and the individual deal with the individual. . . . If [the therapist] has the strength of mind to avoid this pitfall [e.g., to do individual therapy in the group] he will observe that the exasperation, at first sight so reasonable of the patient whose pressing, personal difficulty is being ignored, is dictated, not so much by the frustration of a legitimate aim, as by the exposure of difficulties the patient has *not* come to discuss, and in particular his characteristics as a group member, the characteristics of group membership, basic assumptions and the rest of it. Thus a woman who starts off with a personal difficulty which she feels the psychiatrist could relieve, if he would respond by analyzing her associations, finds, that if the psychiatrist does not do this, that a totally unexpected situation has developed, and it will be surprising if the psychiatrist is not then able to demonstrate difficulties of the group, which will include difficulties of the patient in question which the patient might think quite important, but which turn out in the end not to be so. This of course is quite common in psycho-analysis—the topics discussed are not the ones the patient came to discuss. Nevertheless it is important to realize that the psycho-analyst can easily make a blunder in a group that he would never make in a psycho-analysis, by treating the group as if the procedure were psycho-analysis in public. The psychiatrist should be suspicious if he feels that he is dealing with the problem which the patient or the group thinks he should deal with. This point is critical; if the psychiatrist can manage boldly to use the group instead of spending his time more or less unconsciously apologizing for its presence, he will find that the immediate difficulties produced are more than neutralized by the advantages of a proper use of his medium.[55]

These views are similar, in part, to our own, for we, too, assume that the meaningful affective experience for each patient lies in the manner in which he participates in, contributes to, and reacts to the group forces. More specifically, we believe that each patient, by virtue of sharing in the affect involved in the group focal conflict, experiences crucial personal conflicts and is led to attempt to institute habitual personal solutions. When this occurs and when certain other conditions in the group are optimal, the individual has the opportunity to undergo a therapeutic experience, to be exposed to information relevant to his own situation, and to utilize this information for the generation of insight. The crucial feature of our theory which is not central in other theories is the emphasis on optimal group conditions. We identify certain group conditions which we regard as crucial in determining whether the individual's experience will be profitable. The core concept is group culture and, particularly, the restrictive or enabling character of the group solutions which comprise the culture. This becomes crucial, for under certain group cultural conditions the patient is either forced to insulate himself against the group experience or permitted to retain maladaptive interpersonal patterns. In either case, therapeutic change cannot occur, for the patient remains insulated from meaningful emotional experiences and insulated from perceiving the relevance of group events to his own concerns. In contrast, certain other group cultural conditions provide the patient with the sense of safety which leads to a readiness to involve himself emotionally in the therapeutic situation and a receptiveness to relevant information.

In our view, the group culture is comprised of the successful group solutions which are constructed to deal with successive group focal conflicts. As such, the elements of the culture—the group solutions—are functional for the group. A solution copes with the associated group focal conflict by establishing some procedure, some interpersonal pattern, or some view of the group situation or members which alleviates reactive fears and may also allow some gratification of the disturbing impulse. Thus the group culture is seen to emerge lawfully out of the interaction of the group and to be associated integrally with shared concerns. The culture is subject to continual modification, and this modification also occurs lawfully, concomitant with certain shifts in the associated conflicts. The character of the culture varies, at times emphasizing restrictive solutions which deny, suppress, disguise, or inhibit the underlying shared issues. At other times, the group culture emphasizes enabling solutions, which allow more direct expression and exploration of underlying concerns. The kind of culture under which the group is operating is important for the patient in a number of ways. If predominantly restrictive solutions persist, certain affective issues, crucial for the patient, may be effectively outlawed from the group situation. Or he may be permitted to retain and play out habitual maladaptive patterns. Under certain solutions, the information offered him in the form of interpretations and feedback may be irrelevant, inaccurate, or unusable. As this suggests, the concept of group culture is central to our theory, and we have developed several ancillary concepts regarding its development, modification, character, and meaning for the patient. Various group therapists have emphasized one or another aspect of what we call group culture. Although the term is not in general use, one sees many references to such terms as "acceptance," "climate," "supportive atmosphere," and "permissiveness." It is taken for granted that a maximally effective therapy group will operate within very broad boundaries, so that the patients will feel free to reveal themselves and express their feelings directly. Papanek and Truax have emphasized group conditions associated with therapeutic gain—in our terms, enabling solutions. Slavson and Wolf and Schwartz have emphasized potentially destructive aspects of the group—in our terms, restrictive solutions. Frank has pointed to both aspects. Papanek, in discussing the fact that therapeutic change often occurs without evidence that insight has taken place, suggests that the group can be viewed as a therapeutic milieu rendered so by the operation of certain social norms:

> A prerequisite [for therapeutic change] is that in the subculture of the therapy group certain social norms are promoted by the therapist and shared by the patients. Thus the group becomes therapeutic if its structure is democratic, with equal rights for all patients and with responsible leadership by the therapist. In such a setting freedom of expression and openness of communication, as well as mutual helpfulness and respect for each other, are encouraged.[56]

Papanek goes on to say that she feels that open communication and mutual helpfulness ". . . are underneath all interaction in the group and account more for therapeutic change than any interpretations and insight."[57]

Truax identified a number of characteristics of the group atmosphere and tested their relationship to the extent of intrapersonal exploration in the group.[58] He demonstrated that intrapersonal exploration in the group was associated with such characteristics as the concreteness of the group discussion, empathy among the patients, a cooperative group spirit, sociability, group cohesion, and the ego involvement of the members in the discussion.

Frank has suggested that cohesiveness is a crucial group characteristic which may support the therapeutic process in a number of ways. He says, "A cohesive group with proper standards protects and enhances the self-esteem of its members, fortifies their ability to consolidate and maintain beneficial changes in behavior or attitudes, helps them to resolve conflicts, and facilitates constructive release of feelings."[59] From our point of view, the most crucial aspect of this comment is Frank's reference to proper standards rather than his reference to cohesiveness as such. As he points out later, "The cohesiveness of a group might conceivably impede therapy if its standards were such as to strengthen members' resistance."[60] The importance of the character of the group standard is underlined in Frank's comment:

> The therapeutic relevance of group cohesiveness lies chiefly in the fact that the more a group's members are attracted to it, the more they are influenced by its standards. If these approve diversity of outlook, nondefensive expressions of feelings and honest attempts at self-exam-

> inations; if they reward maintenance of communication no matter how angry patients get at each other; and if they put a premium not on mutual liking but on mutual respect—then the more cohesive the group is, the more likely it is to induce therapeutic change in its members.[61]

Slavson has emphasized cohesiveness as a destructive force in the group. In our view, cohesiveness may function constructively or destructively. For example, potentially destructive effects occur when the patients establish a restrictive solution that only friendly feelings exist in the group. This kind of cohesiveness functions to protect the patients from confrontation with underlying feelings of hostility, envy, or competitiveness, which are regarded as dangerous. At other times, cohesiveness may be built into enabling solutions, as, for example, when mutual acceptance becomes established as a group solution, reduces certain fears, and allows patients to express themselves more freely. Wolf and Schwartz have expressed concern about the potentially damaging effects of group standards and of pressures toward conformity in therapy groups.[62] Here too, the situation seems to us to be a complex one. Group solutions are maintained through the collaboration of all the patients. Pressures on certain patients to conform to group solutions are especially likely to occur when the patient stands in a deviant relation to the group. In general, it is an error to assume that group standards (in our terms, solutions) have an inevitably negative effect. For, as we have pointed out, group solutions have differing characters, and their effects are also varied. As Cartwright and Zander have suggested, "Groups may sometimes agree that they will not allow pressures for uniformity to develop in certain areas of the group's life in order for example, that . . . freedom of thought will be respected."[63] Both Kotkov and Redl have discussed group resistances.[64] This term refers to the observation that collaborative efforts in which the patients collectively defend against some aspect of the therapeutic experience occur in groups. In focal-conflict terms, such group resistances would be referred to as restrictive solutions.

In general, then, we believe, with Bion, Foulkes, and Ezriel, that the individual's experience and the group forces are inextricably associated and that one cannot understand the therapeutic process in the group without taking these group forces into account. We differ in that we believe it necessary to elaborate the ways in which the group forces may impinge upon the patient and their positive or negative implications for his therapeutic experience.

The Therapist's Role

All theories of group therapy consider the question of how the therapist contributes to the therapeutic experience. However, positions differ as to how crucial a role the therapist plays in the total therapeutic process and as to the specific manner in which the therapist should conduct himself in order to facilitate maximum therapeutic benefit. The view one adopts about the therapist's role is, of course, related to one's assumptions about the character of the therapeutic process. For those authors whose theories of group psychotherapy are closely analogous to theories of psychotherapy in a two-person relationship, views of the therapist's role have been drawn from theories about his role in individual therapy.[65] Such theorists recognize, of course, that a multi-person setting involves unique opportunities as well as unique constraints. The role of the therapist has been adapted accordingly. However, these adaptations seem to us to be tactical modifications rather than departures in theory. For example, Wolf and Schwartz sometimes encourage alternate focusing on specific patients within the group. A patient may bring in a dream, and other patients are encouraged to comment about it; the patients may engage in a practice of "going around" in which reactions are offered to each patient in turn. The therapist's role is analogous to his role in a two-person situation. Emphasis is placed on offering interpretations directly to the patients, encouraging patients to offer interpretations and reaction to one another, and dealing with individual resistance and transference reactions. The therapist is likely to be seen as the major source of support and therapeutic benefit.

This position about the therapist's role may be contrasted with one which stresses group processes as crucial to the therapeutic enterprise. Among theorists holding the latter view are those who regard group conditions as the context for the therapeutic experience and those who perceive the group process as identical with the therapeutic experience. Many therapists who emphasize the value of such group conditions as an atmosphere of acceptance and freedom also feel that the therapist plays a central role in establishing such conditions. Papanek says that the group's norms are "promoted" by the therapist; Hill has suggested that the therapist sets the climate by his own style of behavior; Dreikurs says, "There can be no doubt that the group leader is responsible for the type of relationship which exists in the group."[66] Generally, it is assumed that the patients will model themselves after the therapist or that the therapist will train the patients to operate in certain ways by offering or withholding approval. The first mechanism seems to involve identification, and the second emphasizes the therapist's teaching function.

Our own position on the manner in which the therapist influences the group condition begins from another premise. We assume that standards develop from the interaction of the patients themselves. The standards of the group are solutions to shared conflicts. Often, the therapist has no role—except non-interference—in the establishment of a group solution. When he does have a role, it is in influencing the processes whereby solutions are established, maintained, or modified in response to emerging or shifting group forces. It is this rule which we regard as the primary one.

Ezriel, Foulkes, and Bion, though differing among themselves, have all gone beyond the position that the group merely provides the conditions for therapy. The individual experience and the group processes are seen as inseparable aspects of the therapeutic experience. The individual derives benefit from the group in and through his participation in the group processes. The therapist's role is defined in terms of this view.

Ezriel has been most explicit about the therapeutic tactics which he regards as appropriate and those which he regards as pointless. He emphasizes interpretations of the here-and-now experience which are simultaneously group-centered and individual-centered. He says that such interpretations

> . . . are group-centred in that they first point out the unconscious common group tension and resultant structuring of the group; and they are individual-centred in that they also pin-point the common contributions of individual group members to this group tension. Only such interpretations, I think, can reflect correctly the dynamically significant unconscious factors underlying the individual's behaviour in the group, and can therefore be effective for that individual.[67]

Ezriel points out that in an approach centered on the common group tension, it is necessary to deal with here-and-now group tensions as they emerge, since the members have no common past as well as no common contemporary life outside the group. He goes on to suggest that, for the same reason, interpretations which are not directed to the here-and-now situation are certain to be segmented, individually focused interpretations. By focusing his interpretations on the common group tension, Ezriel feels that he capitalizes on the group emotional situation and, at the same time, identifies the unique character of each individual's participation. In later articles, Ezriel emphasizes even more strongly his conviction that the only effective interpretation is one which focuses on the here-and-now situation. He suggests that the maximally effective interpretation is one which identifies the three aspects of the current emotional situation in their relationships with one another: the required relationship, the avoided relationship, and the catastrophe. It is his feeling that an interpretation should be made only when it is possible for the therapist to identify these three aspects of the current emotional situation and to indicate the relationship among them. Ezriel regards this as the only kind of intervention which makes it possible for the patients to experience or recognize the common group tension in direct terms. He sees other interventions as merely feeding the associational process. Ezriel also points out that material introduced in a group therapeutic setting might be dealt with quite differently from the same material introduced in a two-person therapeutic setting, since the transference implications are likely to be quite different in the two cases.

Foulkes refers to the group therapist as the "conductor" who deals with the group by indirect methods, functioning like a catalyst. The emphasis is on interventions which deal with group forces rather than directly with individuals. Bion suggests that interpretations on an individual basis—interpretations which do not take group forces into account—are inappropriate. Although he recognizes that phenomena observed in individual psychoanalysis can also be observed in the group, he feels that focusing on the individual level makes inadequate use of the special characteristics of the group. He says:

> . . . I used to be beguiled into giving individual interpretations as in psycho-analysis. In doing this I was doing what patients often do—trying to get to individual treatment. True, I was trying to get to it as a doctor, but in fact this can be stated in terms of an attempt to get rid of the "badness" of the group and for the doctor, the "badness" of the group is its apparent unsuitability as a therapeutic instrument—which is, as we have already seen, the complaint also of the patient . . . . The failure, at the moment when the analyst gives into his impulse to make individual interpretations, lies in being influenced by baD [basic assumption dependency] instead of interpreting it, for, as soon as I start to give supposedly psycho-analytic interpretations to an individual, I reinforce the assumption that the group consists of patients dependent on the doctor, which is the baD.[68]

These theories emphasize interpretations of the group process and the individual's role within this process. This is seen as the essence of the therapist's role. Our own theoretical position is both similar to and distinct from these views. We emphasize the patient's participation in and reaction to the group focal conflict in ways which are analogous to Bion's views of the patient's relation to the basic-assumption culture and to Ezriel's views of the patient's relation to the common group tension. We assume that the nature of the group forces and the concomitant experiences which the patient undergoes are crucial to the therapeutic process. We assume that the emotional experience in the immediate group situation is critical. But we also assume that the character of the group culture has a crucial impact on the nature of the individual's experience. Consistent with this view, a crucial task for the group therapist is to influence the group situation toward a maximally beneficial group culture. Subsumed under this is alertness to the role which patients play in particular restrictive group solutions, a patient's success or failure in maintaining habitual personal solutions in the group, and the relevance and usability of the information which is made available to the patient through interpretations and feedback. Depending on his assessment of the group situation, the therapist will introduce interventions of various types: he may interpret group-level characteristics, he may point out the manner in which certain patients are participating in the group forces, he may direct interpretations to individuals, he may ask a question, or he may introduce a personal reaction of his own. Certain of his interventions may be directed to influencing the character of the group culture. Certain others may be directed to exploiting the group situation for the specific benefit of certain patients. In either case, it is understood that any intervention must take the group forces into account and that any intervention will have simultaneous importance for the individual and the group. This position can be differentiated from Ezriel's in that we do not place exclusive emphasis on the interpretation of shared concerns. It is similar to the views of Ezriel, Foulkes, and Bion in that simultaneous attention to group and individual forces is stressed—the individual is always viewed and dealt with in the context of the immediate group situation.

The core theoretical issues which have been reviewed in this chapter have this in common: further progress in their clarification depends on the careful examination of the events which actually take place during the course of therapy groups. For example, the markedly divergent views about group development can be compared and a reasonable choice made among them only by the systematic examination of the development of a number of groups utilizing public, reproducible methods. In order to clarify the manner in which the individual's acts relate to group-level characteristics, investigations must examine the sequential characteristics of the interaction and the manner in which these elements are integrated into a whole. A convincing demonstration of the way the group influences the patient's experience requires an examination of this experience as it evolves throughout the life of the group. The central question for the group therapist is and will continue to be what characteristics of the therapeutic setting and what events in the setting allow the patients to undergo significant personal change.

It is our opinion that major advances in knowledge will require the development of increasingly more sophisticated, precise, and reproducible methods for studying groups and that these must include new methods for studying the processes which occur within the therapeutic setting as well as the selection and adaptation of methods already available from social psychological research. As we suggested in Chapter 2, we believe that the traditional procedures of social psychology are inadequate for studying therapy groups because they are unsuited to the examination of variables which are of crucial interest to the investigator of therapy. At the present stage of knowledge, we have accepted the necessity for a basically clinical approach—one which recognizes that the elements of the therapeutic situation are diverse and unequivalent, that multiple facets and levels of the situation must be grasped simultaneously, and that a single element in the situation may provide the key for understanding the whole. Such an approach is particularly relevant when the question one is investigating involves sequential events or covert or affective aspects of the group situation. It is with reference to such questions that the more easily controlled additive procedures are inadequate. In adopting a clinical approach, however, one is confronted with the necessity for clarifying procedures so that independent analyzers of clinical data are likely to arrive at similar formulations of the same data and to use the same words to refer to the same phenomena. We have already described our approach to this methodological goal. Our procedures are not entirely satisfactory. They are cumbersome and time-consuming, and the levels of the agreement which can be achieved among independent analyzers is inadequate for many problems. Yet it is in this direction that we believe that further methodological efforts will prove most rewarding.

As we suggested in our introductory chapter, in the history of small group research, it was the development of appropriate methodology which led to the rapid accumulation of pertinent information about group properties and the relationships among them. A parallel point can be made with reference to research and theory development about group therapy. New investigatory procedures and new combinations of procedures can be expected to coincide with the further development of knowledge about group therapy.

Notes

[1] S. R. Slavson, *Analytic Group Psychotherapy With Children, Adolescents and Adults* (New York: Columbia University Press, 1959); *idem,* "Are There 'Group Dynamics' in Therapy Groups?"; *idem,* "Sources of Counter-Transference and Group-Induced Anxiety," *International Journal of Group Psychotherapy,* III (1953), 373–388; Norman Locke, *Group Psychoanalysis: Theory and Technique;* A. Wolf and E. K. Schwartz, *Psychoanalysis in Groups.*

[2] Saul Scheidlinger, *Psychoanalysis and Group Behavior* (New York: W. W. Norton and Company, 1952).

[3] Eric Berne, *Transactional Analysis in Psychotherapy* (New York: Grove Press, Inc., 1961).

[4] Timothy Leary, *Interpersonal Diagnosis of Personality.*

[5] J. D. Frank, Eduard Ascher, *et al.,* "Behavioral Patterns in Early Meetings of Therapeutic Groups"; J. D. Frank, J. B. Margolin, *et al.,* "Two Behavior Patterns in Therapeutic Groups and Their Apparent Motivation."

[6] W. R. Bion, *Experiences in Groups, and Other Papers; idem,* "Group Dynamics: A Re-View"; Henry Ezriel, "A Psychoanalytic Approach to Group Treatment"; *idem,* "A Psychoanalytic Approach to the Treatment of Patients in Groups"; *idem,* "Experimentation Within the Psycho-Analytic Session"; *idem,* "Reply to Mr. Spilsbury"; *idem,* "The Role of Transference in Psycho-Analytic and Other Approaches to Group Treatment"; S. H. Foulkes, "Group Analytic Dynamics with

Specific Reference to Psychoanalytic Concepts"; *idem*, "Group Process and the Individual in the Therapeutic Group"; *idem*, "Psychotherapy 1961"; *idem*, "The Application of Group Concepts to the Treatment of the Individual in the Group"; *idem*, *Introduction to Group-Analytic Psychotherapy;* S. H. Foulkes and E. J. Anthony, *Group Psychotherapy: The Psychoanalytic Approach.*

7 George Bach, *Intensive Group Psychotherapy.*

8 J. D. Frank, "Some Aspects of Cohesiveness and Conflict in Psychiatric Out-Patient Groups"; *idem*, "Some Values of Conflict in Therapeutic Groups"; *idem*, "Some Determinants, Manifestations, and Effects of Cohesiveness in Therapy Groups."

9 F. Redl, "Group Emotion and Leadership," *Psychiatry*, 5 (1942), 573–596; *idem*, "The Phenomenon of Contagion and 'Shock Effect' in Group Therapy," in K. R. Eissler, *Searchlights on Delinquency* (New York: International Universities Press, Inc.), pp. 315–322; *idem*, "Resistance in Therapy Groups," *Human Relations*, I (1948), 307–314.

10 Saul Scheidlinger, "Group Process in Group Psychotherapy," I and II, *American Journal of Psychotherapy*, 14 (1960), 353.

11 Nathan W. Ackerman, "Psychoanalysis and Group Psychotherapy," *Group Psychotherapy: Journal of Sociopsychopathology and Sociatry*, III (1950), 204–215.

12 Nathan W. Ackerman, "Interaction Processes in a Group and the Role of the Leader," *Psychoanalysis and the Social Sciences*, IV (1955), 111–120; *idem*, "Psychoanalysis and Group Psychotherapy"; *idem*, "Some Structural Problems in the Relations of Psychoanalysis and Group Psychotherapy," *International Journal of Group Psychotherapy*, IV (1954), 131–145; *idem*, "Symptom, Defense and Growth in Group Process," *International Journal of Group Psychotherapy*, II (1961), 131–142.

13 Kurt Lewin, "Frontiers in Group Dynamics: Concept, Method, and Reality in Social Science: Social Equilibria and Social Change."

14 R. F. Bales, "The Equilibrium Problem in Small Groups," in T. Parsons, R. F. Bales, and E. A. Shils, *Working Papers in the Theory of Action* Glencoe, Ill.: Free Press, 1953), p. 117.

15 G. A. Talland, "Task and Interaction Process: Some Characteristics of Therapeutic Group Discussion," *Journal of Abnormal and Social Psychology*, 50 (1955), 105–109; G. Psathas, "Phase Movement and Equilibrium Tendencies in Interaction Process in Psychotherapy Groups," *Sociometry*, 23 (1960), 177–194.

16 The concept of "culture" appears both in Bion's theory and in focal-conflict theory but refers to somewhat different phenomena. When Bion says that the group is operating on a basic-assumption culture of dependency he means that the patients are acting as if they are helpless and need support from some outside source. In their efforts to establish such a culture, the patients may seek a certain relationship with the

leader or seek security by relying on their own history or procedures. These specifics would, in our terms, correspond to certain solutions and, therefore, to particular elements of the group culture.

[17] Henry Ezriel, "Experimentation Within the Psycho-Analytic Session," p. 39.

[18] A. E. Winder and M. Hersko, "A Thematic Analysis of an Outpatient Psychotherapy Group," *International Journal of Group Psychotherapy,* 8 (1958) 293–300.

[19] Florence Powdermaker and J. D. Frank, *Group Psychotherapy.*

[20] W. R. Bion, *Experiences in Groups, and Other Papers,* p. 74.

[21] George Bach, *Intensive Group Psychotherapy.*

[22] E. A. Martin, Jr., and W. F. Hill, "Toward a Theory of Group Development," *International Journal of Group Psychotherapy,* VII (1957), 20–30.

[23] Joseph J. Geller, "Parataxic Distortions in the Initial Stages of Group Relationships," *International Journal of Group Psychotherapy,* 12 (1962), 27–34.

[24] Hubert S. Coffey, "The Significance of Group Life in Personal Change" (Mimeographed manuscript, Department of Psychology, University of California, Berkeley, 1962), pp. 1–7.

[25] S. Freud, *Group Psychology and the Analysis of the Ego* (New York: Bantam Books, 1960).

[26] F. Redl, "Group Emotion and Leadership."

[27] Theorists studying non-therapeutic groups also refer to emotional elements in a situation, but the affect to which they refer has a less primitive and intense quality. This difference may exist in part because of differences in the group studied—therapy groups as compared with problem-solving groups. Although profound affect is not alien to problem-solving groups, solutions which suppress or disguise much of the affect are likely to become established rapidly. Then too, the intellectual climate within which the two sets of theorists operate differs. For group therapists, the influence of psychoanalytic thought, with its emphasis on primitive impulses, makes the notion of primitive, potent affect a familiar one.

[28] Ezriel is referring to the patient's experience in the two-person analytic situation. However, he makes it clear that he believes that the same conceptualization can be applied to patients in a group.

[29] Theories which emphasize powerful shared affect and group-level forces have been developed for the most part in England, whereas in the United States, there has been relative neglect of the role of group forces. When recognized, they are often regarded as potentially destructive. Perhaps one factor is that English theorists are exposed to a Kleinian climate, whereas the United States is dominated by neo-Freudian thought. A Kleinian orientation regards primitive affect of a "psychotic" quality crucial material for therapy. In contrast, therapists

who work within a Freudian or neo-Freudian framework operate from within a tradition which regards group forces as potent but inherently damaging to the individual.

[30] W. R. Bion, *Experiences in Groups, and Other Papers,* pp. 141–142.

[31] *Ibid.,* p. 146.

[32] *Ibid.,* p. 135.

[33] S. H. Foulkes, "Group Analytic Dynamics with Specific Reference to Psychoanalytic Concepts," p. 50.

[34] *Ibid.,* p. 51.

[35] Henry Ezriel, "A Psychoanalytic Approach to the Treatment of Patients in Groups," p. 776.

[36] A. Wolf and E. K. Schwartz, *Psychoanalysis in Groups.*

[37] W. R. Bion, *Experiences in Groups, and Other Papers,* p. 116.

[38] Henry Ezriel, "A Psychoanalytic Approach to Group Treatment," p. 62.

[39] Nathan W. Ackerman, "Psychoanalysis and Group Psychotherapy," p. 208.

[40] Raymond J. Corsini and Bina Rosenberg, "Mechanisms of Group Psychotherapy: Processes and Dynamics," *Journal of Abnormal and Social Psychology,* 51 (1955), 406–411.

[41] S. R. Slavson, "Are There 'Group Dynamics' in Therapy Groups?"

[42] Nathan W. Ackerman, "Psychoanalysis and Group Psychotherapy," p. 211.

[43] Henry Ezriel, "The Role of Transference in Psycho-Analytic and Other Approaches to Group Treatment," pp. 111–112.

[44] J. D. Frank and Eduard Ascher, "Corrective Emotional Experiences in Group Therapy," p. 130.

[45] S. Freud, "Fragment of an Analysis of a Case of Hysteria," *Collected Papers* (London: The Hogarth Press, 1953), III, 139.

[46] S. R. Slavson, *Analytic Group Psychotherapy With Children, Adolescents and Adults.*

[47] Wilfred C. Hulse, "Multiple Transference or Group Neurosis?" *Acta Psychotherapeutica,* 9 (1961), 348–357.

[48] Henry Ezriel, "A Psychoanalytic Approach to the Treatment of Patients in Groups," p. 775.

[49] *Idem,* "The Role of Transference in Psycho-Analytic and Other Approaches to Group Treatment," p. 115.

[50] Helene Papanek, "Psychotherapy Without Insight: Group Therapy as Milieu Therapy," *Journal of Individual Psychology,* XVII (1961), 185.

[51] Nathan W. Ackerman, "Some Structural Problems in the Relations of Psychoanalysis and Group Psychotherapy," p. 143.

[52] Henry Ezriel, "The Role of Transference in Psycho-Analytic and Other Approaches to Group Treatment," p. 113.

[53] S. H. Foulkes, "The Application of Group Concepts to the Treatment of the Individual in the Group," p. 4.

[54] *Ibid.,* p. 3.

[55] W. R. Bion, *Experiences in Groups, and Other Papers,* pp. 80–81.

[56] Helene Papanek, "Psychotherapy Without Insight: Group Therapy as Milieu Therapy," p. 187.

[57] *Loc. cit.*

[58] Charles Truax, "The Process of Group Psychotherapy: Relationships Between Hypothesized Therapeutic Conditions and Intrapersonal Exploration," *Psychological Monographs,* 511 (1961), 1–35.

[59] J. D. Frank, "Some Determinants, Manifestations, and Effects of Cohesiveness in Therapy Groups," pp. 60–61.

[60] *Ibid.,* p. 61.

[61] *Ibid.,* p. 63.

[62] A. Wolf and E. K. Schwartz, *Psychoanalysis in Groups.*

[63] D. Cartwright and A. Zander (eds.), *Group Dynamics: Research and Theory* (1st ed.; Evanston, Ill.: Row, Peterson, and Co., 1953), p. 141.

[64] Benjamin Kotkov, "Common Forms of Resistance in Group Psychotherapy," *Psychoanalysis and the Psychoanalytic Review,* 44 (1957), 88–96; F. Redl, "Resistance in Therapy Groups."

[65] We believe that this view is the one which generally prevails, although many variations could be identified. Locke and Wolf and Schwartz have presented extended discussions which are based on this premise. See Norman Locke, *Group Psychoanalysis: Theory and Technique* and A. Wolf and E. K. Schwartz, *Psychoanalysis in Groups.*

[66] Helene Papanek, "Psychotherapy Without Insight: Group Therapy as Milieu Therapy"; Rudolph Dreikurs, "The Unique Social Climate Experienced in Group Psychotherapy," *Group Psychotherapy: Journal of Sociopsychopathology and Sociatry,* 4 (1951), 292–299; William F. Hill, "Therapeutic Mechanisms," *Collected Papers in Group Psychotherapy.*

[67] Henry Ezriel, "The Role of Transference in Psycho-Analytic and Other Approaches to Group Treatment," p. 115.

[68] W. R. Bion, *Experiences in Groups, and Other Papers,* p. 115.

13

The Threat and Promise of the Group

Many group therapists perceive the group and the individual as antithetical. What is good for the group is bad for the individual and vice versa. This view may prevail because of a recognition of the powerful and seemingly mysterious quality of the group forces. The implication is that, when group forces are unleashed, the individual becomes their victim. He is in danger of losing control, of committing uncharacteristic acts, of being forced to do things which he does not want to do or which are damaging to him. In psychoanalytic terminology, loss of a sense of identity, loss of ego control, and the emergence of primitive id-impulses are feared.

If one is to avoid perceiving the group as a mystery or a monster, it is necessary to understand the group characteristics which lead people to see it in this way. In focal-conflict terms, concerns about the destructive potential of the group reflect a recognition of the potent character of the group affect and the compelling character of the group solutions. At the same time, they reflect an inadequate appreciation of the coping capacities (problem-solving potential) of the group.

The threat which the group poses to individuality and to rational thinking was emphasized by Freud. Thus, Freud quotes LeBon:

> ". . . in a group the individual is brought under conditions which allow him to throw off the repressions of his unconscious instinctual impulses. The apparently new characteristics which he then displays are in fact the manifestations of this unconscious, in which all that is evil in the human mind is contained as a predisposition. . . .
>
> "We see, then, that the disappearance of the conscious personality, the predominance of the unconscious personality, the turning by means of suggestion and contagion of feelings and ideas in an identical direction, the tendency to immediately transform the suggested ideas into acts; these, we see, are the principal characteristics of the individual forming part of the group. He is no longer himself, but has become an automaton who has ceased to be guided by his will."[1]

Although LeBon was referring primarily to crowds and mobs, Freud recognized the relevance of his comments to small groups. Many others have referred to the potent character of the affect which may characterize a group. Bion speaks of the clash between the work group and the basic-assumption groups.

> When I spoke of the group that wished to see the session as a seminar, I said that one reason for this was an unconscious fear that unless the group were pegged to a mature structure the obtrusion of the kinds of group I have described would be facilitated and the ostensible aims of the individuals in joining the group thwarted instead of forwarded by coming together as a group.[2]

In a later discussion of the same point, he says that the group makes an effort ". . . to keep its behavior pegged to a sophisticated level." The patients expect the therapist to provide an agenda and rules of procedure. When the therapist fails to do this

> . . . the group sets out to make good my omissions, and the intensity with which it does this shows that more is at stake than a passion for efficiency. The phenomena against which the group is guarding itself are none other than the group manifestations I described in the last article—the "flight or fight group"; the "pairing group"; and the "dependent group." It is as if the group were aware how easily and spontaneously it structures itself in a manner suitable for acting on these basic assumptions unless steps are taken to prevent it; just as a group of students may use the idea of a seminar or lecture on which to found a sophisticated structure, so the patient group has a basis for structure ready to hand in the commonly accepted convention of neurotic disability as an illness and of the therapists as "doctors."[3]

In Bion's view, the group's members always unconsciously fear that, if the group departs from a cognitive, "sophisticated" structure, the non-rational, "instinctual" basic-assumption groups will emerge.

Slavson has pointed to the anxiety-inducing character of groups. He says:

> All groups evoke anxiety in all people. No person can be in a group without feeling anxious, even though the group may be one to which he is accustomed. The degree of anxiety is diminished with acquaintance and length of membership in it. However, no person feels as comfortable in a group as he does with one individual. An individual is seldom as threatening as a group, where anxiety is always present.[4]

In groups certain phenomena can be observed which contribute to the concern that participation in a group may subvert individuality. These include contagion, what Redl calls "magical exculpation through the initiatory act," splitting, projection, scapegoating, unanimity and its potent impact, and pressures toward conformity. Some of these phenomena can occur only in a group setting; others are assumed to be more malignant and harder to control under conditions of face-to-face interaction in a group.

Contagion is a phenomenon in which such strong affects as panic, depression, or silliness spread through the group, seemingly forcing all the members to participate in the affect whether they want to or not. Redl suggests that contagion occurs under the following conditions:

> 1. *Existence of an acute conflict area* within the imitators: strong impulse urge toward fulfillment of vehement need on the one hand; on the other sufficient pressure from ego or super-ego forces to keep it down. 2. *High degree of lability of this "personality balance"* in the area concerned: impulses strong enough to press for release, controls only just strong enough to prevent that release. If they were somewhat stronger, no contagion would occur, if impulses were stronger or controls just a little weaker they would not have to wait for somebody else's initiatory act. 3. Existence of a *similar type of strong urge* toward impulse expression along the same line in the initiator. His urge must lie in the same direction of those in his imitator . . . for *open acting out* in favor of impulse satisfaction by means of an initiator, with equally open display of an *entire lack of fear or guilt.*[5]

In focal-conflict theory, the phenomenon of contagion is a special case of the process whereby shared affect emerges in the group. There are times when shared feeling emerges so rapidly that one is hardly aware of the associative links. In fact, these appear to be short-circuited, often because one is seeing more-or-less simultaneous reactions to some event which operates like a trigger. It is as if the affect were simultaneously ignited. This trigger may be a precipitating event—something within the group, such as the announcement of an impending interruption, or something outside the group, such as a suicide on the ward or a dramatic threat to international peace. Such events call forth specific fears or specific impulses. Sometimes the trigger may be a single comment. Its effect in setting off contagion must be understood in terms of its timing in relation to the balance of group forces at that moment. In an adolescent group, the comment "that's another phallic symbol" triggered a period of silliness in which each patient topped the other in a confused melee of references to clarinets, flutes, and so on. To the therapists, contagion seemed rampant. This comment operated like a trigger because it was introduced when rather profound worries about sex were being made explicit and anxiety was intense. The comment provided the group with a new solution—"make fun of sexual interests"—and, because of its potential anxiety-reducing function, it was immediately taken up by the others. Here, the solution permits the release of previously inhibited impulses under anxiety-free conditions.

Redl has pointed to the universal tendency among children and adults, primitive and sophisticated peoples, to accept the assumption that whoever does something first is the real culprit and that those who follow in the same behavior are blameless. Redl suggests that in a group an individual may perform a service for the group by assuming the guilt of all the others through initiating some act. In our terms, this occurs through group solutions which involve projection. Affect is located in one member of the group. Such a solution requires the collaboration of all of the members of the group: one person must play the role of the person on whom the affect is projected, thus allowing all the others to feel absolved from responsibility for or possession of such feelings. Under such conditions, behavior which the individual would otherwise regard as unacceptable may find free expression. It is this phenomenon which leads people to comment that, under the impact of a group, individuals may lose their judgment. This is not precisely the case; rather, in the context of the group, the individual has available to him this mechanism for coping with unacceptable impulses. Or, we would say, in the group setting, solutions may emerge in which the patients are protected from anxiety by maintaining the shared assumption that an unacceptable impulse belongs to only one member. A related group solution is that of scapegoating. In this device one patient—the scapegoat—functions as the repository of unacceptable impulses and is then attacked as a way of attacking or destroying the impulse that he now personifies. Another form of scapegoating involves displacement. Those feelings which are expected to elicit dangerous consequences were they directed toward their real target are directed toward a scapegoat.

It is sometimes assumed that affect or opinions which are unanimous are, therefore, valid. If everyone in the group feels that the therapist is failing to communicate or that a patient is interfering with the group's progress, this unanimity in itself lends "consensual validation" to the feeling, and it is as if the therapist *is* failing and the patient *is* interfering. This assumption—the majority must be right—prevails in the general culture. If one hypothesizes a group situation in which rationality prevails and everyone has access to all the facts or several people have access to several facts, majority rule might carry consensual validation. Pockets of ignorance and prejudices are canceled. But in the therapy group the situation differs. If the therapist feels that everyone in the group thinks he knows the answer but is holding back, he may be correctly assessing a shared feeling, but the consensus may or may not be correct. Consensual validation is by no means automatically involved. The sense of consensual validity is probably one more indication of the potency of the group affect.

Pressures toward conformity are ordinarily understood to consist of pressures which the majority of a group exerts to make a minority conform to some standard. In a therapy group, a solution is the product of collaboration. As such, it ordinarily is a compromise which can be accepted by all. Under such circumstances, one cannot properly speak of pressures toward conformity, although an individual might find himself accepting a solution or standard which is not entirely congenial to him. Strong pressures toward conformity arise in a therapy group when the patients move toward establishing a solution which one person finds intolerable. This patient may protest against or challenge the solution in some way, thus becoming a deviant. When this occurs, the others will try to deal with the situation by putting pressure on the deviant to accept the solution, for the failure of the deviant to accept the group solution threatens the group's very existence, raising the potential for gross and unmanageable anxiety in the other patients. The deviant patient is likely to resist these pressures, because for him it is just as intolerable to accept the group solution as it is for the others to abandon it. This resistance to pressure contradicts the findings of some social psychological investigators who have found that people respond readily to pressures from group members to conform. In both the therapy group and the social psychological experiment, the individual experiences discomfort because of the pressures placed on him to conform. But the relationship between the deviant individual and the group standard is different in the two situations. In laboratory experiments, one cannot be certain of the meaning which the standard—usually an imposed one—has for the individual. If the standard has no relevance to the individual, he does not mind conforming to it. In therapy groups, the instances of deviation which we have observed always occur when conformity to the group standard could not be achieved without causing the individual intolerable anxiety. Under such conditions, the individual tenaciously resists any of the group's efforts to get him to conform. It is this difference which accounts for both the general tendency to conform that has been observed in laboratory studies and the resistance to pressure noted in therapy groups.

In part, viewing the group as a potentially destructive force is related to a person's view of the group's capacities for coping with the affect which may emerge. For, if one perceives the group and the patients as helpless in the face of primitive affect, he is likely to stress the group's destructive potential. On the other hand, if one perceives resources for dealing with the affect which emerges and the conflicts which arise, he is less likely to perceive the group affect as inevitably destructive. Ackerman has pointed out that, although groups are likely to be regarded as deleterious, encouraging irrational behaviors and in general being responsible for social ills, this is a curious phenomenon since "the group, in fact, is the repository of civilized values, the source of control of destructive impulses, the matrix of reality testing, the ultimate basis of security and esteem for the individual."[6] Ackerman goes on to say that the confusion lies in "our inability to distinguish clearly between healthy and unhealthy group formation."[7]

Concerns about the group's threat to individuality are felt more strongly in therapy groups, mobs, and large, "impersonal" organizations than in small, face-to-face, task-oriented groups. We believe that the crucial difference between these groups is the character of the group solution and the manner in which the individual has participated in the generation of these group solutions. As this implies, we assume that the same basic processes occur in all groups. All groups are characterized by a potential for powerful affect, by covert affective levels about which the manifest behavior provides clues, and by capacities for coping or problem-solving. All groups have forces which are generated by the interaction of the members and, in turn, have an impact on the members. But various groups can be distinguished by their solutions. The kind of solution, in turn, is very much influenced by the size of the group, the opportunity for forming subgroups, the goal structure of the group, and the prior expectations of the members.

In small, task-oriented groups the members are usually informed about the official purposes of the group before or when they join it.

The official purpose or goal usually implies certain procedures and certain assumptions about the character of the group. Under these conditions, solutions or standards involving the suppression of, denial of, or inattention to affective aspects of the situation are established quickly. Affect is either suppressed, or channels are provided for its expression. The small group is marked by restrictive solutions which in this case are appropriate, for the most part, to the goals of the group. This is not to suggest that affective forces are not present or that one never sees their manifestations or effects. But, for the most part, the kinds of solution which become established are those which alleviate anxiety by suppressing impulses. Under such conditions, fears about loss of individuality and of control over impulses are not so likely to arise.

The situation differs greatly in a mob. A collection of individuals becomes a mob under the impact of some precipitating event; previously it has been an audience, a congregation, or a collection of bystanders. The event, whether it be a fire in a theatre or the appearance of a teenagers' idol, elicits strong affect. Before the appearance of the precipitating event, there has been no interaction to generate solutions capable of coping with such strong affect. With no control in the form of solutions available, the affect reaches a peak of intensity very quickly. Individual members experience an overwhelming sense of anxiety, loss of control, and a sense of being overwhelmed by the group's emotional forces. A mob is comparable to one form of contagion in a small group, that in which a precipitating event finds the group unprepared so that there is no solution capable of coping with the affect elicited by the event.

The situation differs in a large organization, where pressures toward conformity are often felt to be particularly strong. Organizations are highly structured in terms of solutions, but the individual who is bound by the solutions may have had little to do with making them except by passive acquiescence. Although passive collaboration also occurs in small, face-to-face groups, in a larger organization it may occur not because the individual really acquiesces in the solution but because there has been no way for him to influence it. Under such circumstances, the individual feels helpless, and the organization is seen as a powerful, conformity-inducing entity. In the organization, the individual may feel helpless or apathetic, but he is not likely to experience panic or the threat of overwhelming anxiety, as he might in a therapy group or in a mob. Certain solutions are possible in an organization which are not possible in a small group or in a mob. Most notably, there may be solutions in which certain functions are assumed by subgroups. In a dormitory, for example, a rebellious subgroup may coexist with a decorous, well-behaved majority. Such a subgroup may play a role in a group solution for the larger group. For example, the members of the subgroup may express feelings that are forbidden to the group as a whole or may be a scapegoat for the larger group. Because the group is not required to cope with all group focal conflicts in a face-to-face setting, many events that could provoke anxiety are circumvented.

Certain characteristics of the therapy group make it likely that the individual's affective experience will be more intense and primitive than that which is likely to occur in an organization or a small problem-solving group and more manageable than that which is likely to occur in a mob. The situation is more manageable because successful solutions emerge from the patients' interaction and because the therapist helps the patients maintain less than overwhelming degrees of anxiety. But the situation carries more intense affect and a higher level of anxiety than a small task group or an organization because certain solutions are not available in the therapy group. For example, the requirement that all issues be worked out in the face-to-face setting maximizes the likelihood of an intense experience. Extra-group solutions come to be regarded as out of bounds. Therapy groups are deliberately left unstructured, again maximizing the affective experience. The therapist does not ordinarily offer an agenda, define a goal, or suggest a procedure. There is no external task to provide direction and control. This is all part of the therapist's strategy. He wants to encourage emotional interaction and discourage restrictive solutions. Under these conditions, strong group affect is certain to come to the fore, bringing with it all the anxieties which the patients and the therapist may share about the power and the destructive potential of the group. The same conditions, however, also provide a setting in which meaningful affective experiences occur and where individual patients may find opportunities for personal growth and change.

Notes

[1] S. Freud, *Group Psychology and the Analysis of the Ego,* pp. 9, 11.

[2] W. R. Bion, *Experiences in Groups, and Other Papers,* p. 75.

[3] *Ibid.,* pp. 77–78.

[4] S. R. Slavson, "Sources of Counter-Transference and Group-Induced Anxiety," p. 386.

[5] F. Redl, "The Phenomenon of Contagion and 'Shock Effect' in Group Therapy," pp. 320–321.

[6] Nathan W. Ackerman, "Interaction Processes in a Group and the Role of the Leader," p. 112.

[7] *Loc. cit.*

Bibliography

ACKERMAN, NATHAN W. "Interaction Processes in a Group and the Role of the Leader," *Psychoanalysis and the Social Sciences,* IV (1955), 111–120.

———. "Psychoanalysis and Group Psychotherapy," *Group Psychotherapy: Journal of Sociopsychopathology and Sociatry,* III (1950), 204–215.

———. "Some Structural Problems in the Relations of Psychoanalysis and Group Psychotherapy," *International Journal of Group Psychotherapy,* IV (1954), 131–145.

———. "Symptom, Defense and Growth in Group Process," *International Journal of Group Psychotherapy,* II (1961), 131–142.

ASCH, SOLOMON E. "Effects of Group Pressure Upon the Modification and Distortion of Judgments," in *Groups, Leadership and Men,* ed. H. GUETZKOW. New York: Carnegie Press, 1951.

BACH, GEORGE. *Intensive Group Psychotherapy.* New York: Ronald Press, 1954.

BALES, ROBERT F. "The Equilibrium Problem in Small Groups," in *Working Papers in the Theory of Action,* ed. T. PARSONS, R. F. BALES, and E. A. SHILS. Glencoe, Ill.: Free Press, 1953.

———. *Interaction Process Analysis: A Method for the Study of Small Groups.* Reading, Mass.: Addison-Wesley, 1950.

BERNE, ERIC. *Transactional Analysis in Psychotherapy.* New York: Grove Press, 1961.

BION, W. R. *Experiences in Groups, and Other Papers.* London and New York: Tavistock Publications and Basic Books, 1961.

———. "Group Dynamics: A Re-View," *International Journal of Psychoanalysis,* 33 (1952), 235–247.

CARTWRIGHT, D., and A. ZANDER (eds.). *Group Dynamics: Research and Theory.* Evanston, Ill.: Row, Peterson, and Co., 1953.

COFFEY, HUBERT S. "The Significance of Group Life in Personal Change," Unpublished manuscript, Department of Psychology, University of California, Berkeley, 1962.

CORSINI, RAYMOND J., and BINA ROSENBERG. "Mechanisms of Group Psychotherapy: Processes and Dynamics," *Journal of Abnormal and Social Psychology,* 51, No. 3 (1955), 406–411.

DREIKURS, RUDOLPH. "The Unique Social Climate Experienced In Group Psychotherapy," *Group Psychotherapy: Journal of Sociopsychopathology and Sociatry,* 4 (1951), 292–299.

DURKIN, HELEN. "Toward a Common Basis for Group Dynamics: Group and Therapeutic Processes in Group Psychotherapy," *International Journal of Group Psychotherapy,* 7 (1957), 115–130.

EZRIEL, HENRY. "A Psychoanalytic Approach to Group Treatment," *British Journal of Medical Psychology,* 23 (1950), 59–74.

———. "A Psychoanalytic Approach to the Treatment of Patients in Groups," *Journal of Mental Science,* XCVI (1950), 774–779.

———. "Experimentation Within the Psycho-Analytic Session," *The British Journal for the Philosophy of Science,* VII (1956), 29–48.

———. "Reply to Mr. Spilsbury," *British Journal for the Philosophy of Science,* VII, No. 28 (1957), 342–347.

———. "The Role of Transference in Psycho-Analytic and Other Approaches to Group Treatment," *Acta Psychotherapeutica,* 7 (1959), 101–116.

FOULKES, S. H. "The Application of Group Concepts to the Treatment of the Individual in the Group," *Topical Problems of Psychotherapy,* Vol. 2, 1–15.

———. "Group Analytic Dynamics with Specific Reference to Psychoanalytic Concepts," *International Journal of Group Psychotherapy,* 7 (1957), 40–52.

———. "Group Process and the Individual in the Therapeutic Group," *British Journal of Medical Psychology,* 34 (1961), 23–31.

———. *Introduction to Group-Analytic Psychotherapy,* New York: Grune and Stratton, 1949.

———. "Psychotherapy 1961," *British Journal of Medical Psychology,* 34 (1961), 91–102.

FOULKES, S. H., and E. J. ANTHONY. *Group Psychotherapy: the Psychoanalytic Approach.* Baltimore, Maryland: Penguin Books, 1957.

FRANK, JEROME D. "Some Aspects of Cohesiveness and Conflict in Psychiatric Out-Patient Groups," *Johns Hopkins Hospital Bulletin,* 101 (1957), 224–231.

———. "Some Determinants, Manifestations, and Effects of Cohesiveness in Therapy Groups," *International Journal of Group Psychotherapy,* 7 (1957), 53–63.

———. "Some Values of Conflict in Therapeutic Groups," *Group Psychotherapy,* 8 (1955), 142–151.

FRANK, JEROME D., and EDUARD ASCHER. "Corrective Emotional Experiences in Group Therapy," *American Journal of Psychiatry,* 108 (1951), 126–131.

FRANK, JEROME D., *et al.* "Behavioral Patterns in Early Meetings of Therapeutic Groups," *American Journal of Psychiatry,* 108 (1952), 771–778.

FRANK, JEROME D., JOSEPH B. MARGOLIN, HELEN NASH, ANTHONY R. STONE, EDITH J. VARON, and EDUARD ASCHER. "Two Behavior Patterns in Therapeutic Groups and Their Apparent Motivation," *Human Relations,* 3 (1952), 289–317.

FRENCH, THOMAS M., *The Integration of Behavior,* Vols. I, II. Chicago: University of Chicago Press, 1952.

FREUD, SIGMUND. "Fragment of an Analysis of a Case of Hysteria," (1905), in SIGMUND FREUD, *Collected Papers,* Vol. III. London: The Hogarth Press, 1953.

———. *Group Psychology and the Analysis of the Ego.* New York: Bantam Books, 1960.

GELLER, JOSEPH J. "Parataxic Distortions in the Initial Stages of Group Relationships," *International Journal of Group Psychotherapy,* 12, No. 1 (1962), 27–34.

HILL, WILLIAM F. "Therapeutic Mechanisms," in WILLIAM F. HILL, *Collected Papers in Group Psychotherapy.*

HULSE, WILFRED C. "Multiple Transference or Group Neurosis?" *Acta Psychotherapeutica,* 9 (1961), 348–357.

KOTKOV, BENJAMIN. "Common Forms of Resistance in Group Psychotherapy," *Psychoanalysis and the Psychoanalytic Review,* 44 (1957), 88–96.

LEARY, TIMOTHY. *Interpersonal Diagnosis of Personality.* New York: The Ronald Press, 1957.

LEWIN, KURT. *Field Theory in Social Science.* New York: Harper, 1951.

———. "Frontiers in Group Dynamics: Concept, Method, and Reality in Social Science: Social Equilibria and Social Change," *Human Relations,* I (1947), 5–41.

LOCKE, NORMAN. *Group Psychoanalysis: Theory and Technique.* New York: New York University Press, 1961.

LOESER, LEWIS H., and THEA BRY. "The Position of the Group Therapist in Transference and Countertransference: An Experimental Study," *International Journal of Group Psychotherapy,* III (1953), 389–406.

MARTIN, E. A., JR., and WILLIAM F. HILL. "Toward a Theory of Group Development," *International Journal of Group Psychotherapy,* VII (1957), 20–30.

PAPANEK, HELENE. "Psychotherapy Without Insight: Group Therapy as Milieu Therapy," *Journal of Individual Psychology,* XVII (1961), 184–192.

POWDERMAKER, FLORENCE, and J. D. FRANK. *Group Psychotherapy.* Cambridge: Harvard University Press, 1953.

PSATHAS, G. "Phase Movement and Equilibrium Tendencies in Interaction Process in Psychotherapy Groups," *Sociometry,* 23 (1960), 177–194.

REDL, FRITZ. "Group Emotion and Leadership," *Psychiatry,* 5 (1942), 573–596.

———. "Resistance in Therapy Groups," *Human Relations,* I (1948), 307–314.

———. "The Phenomenon of Contagion and 'Shock Effect' in Group Therapy," in K. R. Eissler, *Searchlights on Delinquency.*

ROSS, W. DONALD, and ARIK BRISSENDEN. "Some Observations on the Emotional Position of the Group Psychotherapist," *The Psychiatric Quarterly* (1961), 1–7.

SCHEIDLINGER, SAUL. "Group Process in Group Psychotherapy," I and II, *American Journal of Psychotherapy,* 14 (1960), 104–120, and 346–363.

———. *Psychoanalysis and Group Behavior.* New York: W. W. Norton and Company, 1952.

SLAVSON, S. R. *Analytic Group Psychotherapy with Children, Adolescents and Adults.* New York: Columbia University Press, 1950.

———. "Are There 'Group Dynamics' in Therapy Groups?" *International Journal of Group Psychotherapy,* VII, No. 2 (1957), 131–154.

———. "Sources of Counter-Transference and Group-Induced Anxiety," *International Journal of Group Psychotherapy,* III (1953), 373–388.

STOCK, DOROTHY. "Interpersonal Concerns During the Early Sessions of Therapy Groups," *International Journal of Group Psychotherapy,* 12 (1962), 14–26.

STOCK, DOROTHY, and MORTON A. LIEBERMAN. "Methodological Issues in the Assessment of Total Group Phenomena in Group Therapy," *International Journal of Group Psychotherapy,* 12, No. 3 (1962), 312–325.

STOCK, DOROTHY, and ROY M. WHITMAN. "Patients' and Therapist's Apperceptions of an Episode in Group Therapy," *Human Relations,* 10, No. 4 (1957), 367–383.

STOCK, DOROTHY, ROY M. WHITMAN, and MORTON A. LIEBERMAN. "The Deviant Member in Therapy Groups," *Human Relations,* Vol. 11, No. 4 (1958), 341–372.

TALLAND, G. A. "Task and Interaction Process: Some Characteristics of Therapeutic Group Discussion," *Journal of Abnormal and Social Psychology,* 50 (1955), 105–109.

TRUAX, CHARLES. "The Process of Group Psychotherapy: Relationships Between Hypothesized Therapeutic Conditions and Intrapersonal Exploration," *Psychological Monographs,* 511 (1961), 1–35.

VARON, EDITH J. "Recurrent Phenomena in Group Psychotherapy," *International Journal of Group Psychotherapy,* 3 (1953), 49–58.

WHITMAN, ROY M., MORTON A. LIEBERMAN, and DOROTHY STOCK. "Individual and Group Focal Conflicts," *International Journal of Group Psychotherapy,* 10 (1960), 259–286.

WHITMAN, ROY M., and DOROTHY STOCK. "The Group Focal Conflict," *Psychiatry, Journal for the Study of Interpersonal Processes,* 21, No. 3 (1958), 269–276.

WINDER, ALVIN E., and MARVIN HERSKO. "A Thematic Analysis of an Outpatient Psychotherapy Group," *International Journal of Group Psychotherapy,* 8 (1958), 293–300.

WOLF, ALVIN, and EMANUEL K. SCHWARTZ. *Psychoanalysis in Groups.* New York: Grune and Stratton, 1962.

Index

ACKERMAN, NATHAN W., 242, 260–262, 268, 290
Affective characteristics, 253–254
Anxiety level, management of, 185
ASCH, SOLOMON E., 4
ASCHER, EDUARD, 162, 184, 263

b

BACH, GEORGE, 5, 242, 250–251
BALES, ROBERT F., 244–246, 259–260
Basic-assumption culture, 246
BERNE, ERIC, 242
BION, W. R., 5, 242, 244, 246–250, 253–255, 257–260, 269–271, 274, 277, 286

c

CARTWRIGHT, D., 274
Catharsis, 261, 267
Closing sessions, 132
COFFEY, HUBERT S., 251
Cohesiveness, 273–274
Common group tension, 17–18, 276–277
Composition of group
  influence on early sessions, 119–120
  policy about, 204–207
Confidentiality, 209–210
Conformity, 289–290
Consensual validation, 289
Contagion, 287–288
Continuity
  between sessions, 90–91
  impact of external events, 131–132
Coping capacity of group, 254–257, 290
Corrective emotional experience, 261
CORSINI, RAYMOND J., 261–262, 267
Counter-transference, 199

d

Development of group, 116–138
  characteristics of, 116–117
  established phase, 117

Development of group (*Cont.*):
formative phase, 117
other theories, 249–251
Deviant patient
illustrations, 50–57, 99–101
reactions to, 111–112, 171
resistance to pressure, 289–290
Displacement, 122–123, 172
Disturbing motive
compared with Ezriel's "avoided relationship," 247
definition, 19
in relation to group themes, 63–64
typical of early sessions, 121–122
DREIKURS, RUDOLPH, 275
DURKIN, HELEN, 5

e

Enabling solutions
definition, 23
effect on therapy experience, 164
Equilibrium
character of, 59–60
at close of a session, 90–91
contribution of individual patients, 60–62
illustrations, 42–50, 50–57
other theories, 244–248
within single session, 41–62
Established phase of group. *See also* Development of group
compared with formative phase, 128–130, 133–137
solutions characteristic of, 132–133
External events, impact of, 91, 131–132
EZRIEL, HENRY, 5, 17–18, 146, 160, 242, 244, 246–249, 253–254, 257–258, 260–265, 267–269, 274, 276–277

f

Feedback, 173–174
Formative phase, 117–127
compared with established phase, 128–130, 133–137
compared with other theories, 251–252
impact on individual, 147–149
influence of
character of situation, 119
group composition, 119–120
patients' expectations, 117–118
termination of, 127
FOULKES, S. H., 162, 184, 242, 254, 257–258, 269–270, 274, 277
FRANK, JEROME D., 5, 162, 184, 242, 248, 259, 261–263, 267, 273–274
Free association, 257–259
FRENCH, THOMAS, 143–144, 159
FREUD, SIGMUND, 242, 251–252, 263, 285–286

g

GELLER, JOSEPH J., 250–251
Generalization of personal change, 180–182
Group culture
appropriate culture as goal of therapist, 216–217
compared with other theories, 272–274
definition of, 95–98
formation of, 125
modification of, 98, 101–112
persistence of, 99–101
Group dynamics. *See* Group processes
Group focal conflict. *See also* Common group tension
compared with individual focal conflict, 159–160
definition of, 19
illustrations, 20–22, 24–33
patients' awareness of, 22
patients' rationalization of, 123
procedure for assessing, 35–38
as unit of group life, 24
Group processes
attitudes of theorists toward, 4–6
constructive potential of, 290
destructive potential of, 285–290

Group processes (*Cont.*):
eliciting function of, 163
existence of, 3–4
theories which focus on, 242–243, 275
Group theme
definition of, 63–64
illustrations, 64–87
influence of intervals between sessions, 90–91
movement within, 87–89
shifts in, 92–93

h

Hersko, Marvin, 248
Hill, William F., 250–251, 275
Hostility, group theme involving, 64–74

i

Individual focal conflict, 143–144
compared with group focal conflict, 159–160
illustration, 144–145
Individual habitual solutions
attempt to institute in group, 149
success or failure of, 149–150
Individual patient
ability to influence group, 60–62, 155–156
efforts to deal with threat, illustrations, 152–155
excessive anxiety in, 219
expectations about group, 117–119
experience of threat, 147, 151–152
motivation for behavior in group, 149–151
motivation for entering therapy, 146–147
perceptions of group, 157–158
position in group focal conflict, 60–62
sources of new information for, 170–175
state on entering therapy, 145–147, 161–162
theories which focus on, 242–243, 275
therapeutic experience of, 161–184
Individual sessions, 211–213
Initial sessions. *See* Formative phase
Initial structuring of group, 208–209
Insight, 163, 169–170, 261, 266–267
Interaction process analysis, 34
Interpersonal reflex, 34
Interpersonal relationships
theories which focus on, 242–243
Interpretations
increasing anxiety level through, 228
interfering with a restrictive solution through, 225–226
by patients to patients, 171–173
by therapists, 220–221
Interventions
cumulative impact of, 235
multiple effect of, 193
target of, 193
timing of, 221–224

k

Kotkov, Benjamin, 274

l

Leary, Timothy, 242
LeBon, G., 285–286
Lewin, Kurt, 2–4, 244–245
Lieberman, Morton A., 159, 184
Locke, Norman, 241

m

Manifest and covert levels, 15–18
illustration, 24–33
Martin, E. A., 250–251

Maturity of group, 132
compared with other theories, 252–253
Methodological considerations, 33–38
holistic approach, 35
molecular procedures, 34
procedure for assessing group focal conflict, 35–38
reliability, 37–38
Mirror reactions, 267
Mobs. *See* Solutions, in mobs

n

Nuclear conflict, 143–144

o

Organizations. *See* Solutions, in organizations
Outside contacts among patients, 210–211

p

PAPANEK, HELENE, 266–267, 272–273, 275
Patient. *See* Individual patient
POWDERMAKER, FLORENCE, 248
Precipitating event, 21
Problem-solving. *See* Coping capacity of group
Problem-solving groups. *See* Solutions, in problem-solving groups
Projection, 288–289
PSATHAS, G., 246

q

Quasi-stationary equilibrium, 245

r

Rationalization. *See* Group focal conflict, patients' rationalization of
Reactive motive
compared with Ezriel's "calamity," 247
definition, 19
typical of early sessions, 121
Reality-testing, 262–263
REDL, FRITZ, 242, 251–252, 254, 274, 287–288
Restrictive solutions
definition of, 23
effect on therapy experience, 164
ROSENBERG, BINA, 261–262, 267

s

Safety, 165–166. *See also* Therapist, goals of, maintaining safety
Scapegoating, 172–173, 288–289
SCHEIDLINGER, SAUL, 242
SCHWARTZ, EMANUEL K., 5, 241, 273–275
Sexuality, group theme involving, 75–87
Silent patient, 178–179, 185
SLAVSON, S. R., 5–6, 241, 261, 264, 273, 287
Solutions
compared with Ezriel's "required relationship," 247
definition of, 19
enabling solution, definition, 23
as group culture, 95–98
as group goal, 57–58
in mobs, 291
in organizations, 291–292
persistence and modification, 99
in problem-solving groups, 290–291
properties of, 23
relation to intra-theme movement, 87–89
restrictive solution, definition of, 23
as source of safety, 165–166
typical of early sessions, 122, 126
typical of later sessions, 132–133
Solutional conflict
definition of, 22
illustration, 50–57

Spectator therapy, 267
Standards and norms
solutions as, 95–98
other theories, 272–274
STOCK, DOROTHY, 159–160

t

TALLAND, G. A., 246
Theory-building
requirements for a comprehensive theory, 7–8, 242
Therapeutic change. *See also* Therapeutic experience
conditions for, 262
mechanisms of, 261–262
Therapeutic contract, 118
Therapeutic errors, 198–199
illustration, 53, 227–232
Therapeutic experience, 161–184, 262
compared with other theories, 261–274
description of, 163
effect of enabling solutions on, 164
effect of restrictive solutions on, 164
Therapeutic failure
group conditions associated with, 176–180, 185
Therapist, 189–201
compared with other theories, 274–278
as deviant, 196–197
focusing on individual versus group, 190–193
goals of
establishing an appropriate culture, 216–217, 225–227
maintaining safety, 217–219, 227–232
using group events to benefit individual, 219–221, 233–235
influence on group, 195–198, 200
perspective of, 193–194
policies about
group composition, 204–207
initial structuring, 208–209
outside contacts among patients, 210–211
individual sessions, 211–213
revealing own feelings, 226–227
position regarding group focal conflict, 193
power of, 195–198
pressures on, 199–201
as source of solution, 124
targets of intervention, 193. *See also* Interventions
using interpretations, 225–226. *See also* Interpretations
withholding cooperation, 227
Transference, 146, 261
compared with individual therapy, 264
compared with other theories, 263–266
TRUAX, CHARLES, 272–273
Turn-taking, 124, 172

u

Universalization, 261, 267

v

Valency, 260
Viability
definition of, 148–149
ways of rendering group viable, 149, 151
Vulnerability, 204, 215

w

WHITMAN, ROY M., 159–160, 184
WINDER, ALVIN E., 248
WOLF, ALVIN, 5, 241, 273-275

z

ZANDER, A., 274